When Is a Kiva?

When Is a Kiva?

And Other Questions About Southwestern Archaeology

Watson Smith

Edited by Raymond H. Thompson

THE UNIVERSITY OF ARIZONA PRESS   TUCSON

The University of Arizona Press
Copyright © 1990
The Arizona Board of Regents
All Rights Reserved

This book was set in Caledonia.
⊗ This book is printed on acid-free, archival quality paper.
Manufactured in the United States of America.

94 93 92 91 90   5 4 3 2 1

Library of Congress Cataloging-in-Publication Data

Smith, Watson, 1897-
   When is a Kiva? : and other questions about Southwestern
archaeology / Watson Smith : Raymond H. Thompson, editor.
        p.   cm.
   Includes bibliographical references.
   ISBN 0-8165-1155-1 (alk. paper)
   1. Pueblo Indians—Architecture.   2. Hopi Indians—Architecture.
3. Kivas—Southwest, New.   4. Pueblo Indians—Antiquities.   5. Hopi
Indians—Antiquities.   6. Southwest, New—Antiquities.
I. Thompson, Raymond H. (Raymond Harris).   II. Title.
E99.P9S62   1990
979'.01—dc20   89-29089
                                                                      CIP
British Library Cataloguing in Publication data are available.

Contents

Illustrations

Preface

The main purpose of this volume is to share with a wider readership some of Watson Smith's writings, which until now have been available only in the professional literature of Southwestern archaeology: descriptions and discussions of kivas, mural paintings, and decorated pottery from the region of northern Arizona that is the ancestral homeland of the Hopi Indians. In selecting the material reprinted on these pages, I was guided by a desire to help the reader know, appreciate, and understand Watson Smith himself. I have tried to overcome somewhat the almost complete lack of personal information in his own professional writing by preparing a brief introduction to each selection. I hope that these introductory essays will enable readers to feel that they have some basis for knowing Watson Smith for the modest, witty, complex, inspiring, and delightful Edwardian personality that he is.

Richard B. Woodbury has contributed significantly to that understanding in his excellent biographical essay on Smith. It was originally prepared for another volume and I am indebted to both Woodbury and Andrew L. Christenson, the editor of that work, for agreeing to publish it here instead.

The selections from Smith's writings have not been abridged. Every effort has been made to maintain the mood of the original and to present the thrust of Smith's scholarship and erudition. Footnotes have been included in the text except for a small number of very long lists, which have been included by reference only in order to avoid lengthy interruptions in the text. Smith's cross references to other sections of the monograph from which each selection came are also referenced. Several errata and grammatical slips have been corrected.

Except in titles of books, archaeology is spelled throughout with the digraph (ae), pit house as two words, Zuñi with an ñ, and Navajo with its original Spanish aspirant. All of the illustrative material directly relevant to each text has been included but renumbered by chapter. No effort has been made to reproduce the many illustrations that Smith cross references, but each one is referenced. Every major site mentioned is shown in Figure 1.1.

I am indebted to several people who have encouraged and assisted me in a multitude of ways: Jorge A. Acero, E. Charles Adams, Connie L. Alexander, Jeanne M. Armstrong, Ellen B. Basso, Ronald J. Beckwith, Theodore R. Bundy, Bernard L. Fontana, Carol A. Gifford, Mary E. Graham, Emil W. Haury, Dorothy A. House, Kathleen E. Hubenschmidt, Anne E. Laurie, Stephen H. Lekson, Alexander J. Lindsay, William D. Lipe, Stanley J. Olsen, Nancy J. Parezo, J. Jefferson Reid, Sue C. Ruiz, Claudine G. Scoville, Lucy Cranwell Smith, Emory Sekaquaptewa, Helga G. Teiwes, Molly K. Thompson, R. Gwinn Vivian, Nathalie F. S. Woodbury, and Richard B. Woodbury.

Most of all, however, I am grateful to Watson for his writing skills, his descriptive clarity, his witty asides, his archaeological insights, and for much more. Rather than surprise him in the early years of his tenth decade with an anthology of his work, I decided to ask his assistance in the preparation of this volume. He has been a willing accomplice, an efficient research assistant, an oral history informant, and a helpful critic. More than this, of course, he has been a friend and a colleague, a supporter and a patron, a role model and a source of inspiration throughout the many years that it has been my privilege to know him.

R.H.T.
Tucson, Arizona
1 June 1989

When Is a Kiva?

1. "And Then There Was Watson Smith"

With these six words, John Otis Brew, Director of the Peabody Museum at Harvard University and Director of the museum's Awatovi Expedition, introduced Watson Smith. In the Foreword to Smith's monograph on the kivas at the ruined Hopi town of Awatovi in northern Arizona, Brew (1972: ix) listed forthrightly other members of the Awatovi Expedition, and then casually added those enigmatic words. What kind of an image did Brew intend to evoke with those words? What kind of a person did he want his readers to visualize?

J. O. Brew was a confirmed romanticist, so I am sure that the image that he had in mind was a romantic one. I am equally certain that he did not intend to conjure up a swashbuckling adventurer. It is more likely that he was trying to portray a somewhat more mysterious, serendipitous, and ineffable kind of romantic figure. Like the good raconteur that he was, Brew wanted us to see Watson Smith as somewhat larger-than-life, an extraordinary individual who was almost a legend in his own time. In fact, Brew used most of the rest of his Foreword to record, or rather to advance, the story of Watson Smith that he had adumbrated in forewords to earlier Smith monographs (Brew 1952, 1971).

As any good legend should, the one suggested by Brew derived great credibility from the fact that it was more or less true. His two-paragraph biographical sketch is an essentially correct chronological account of some of the main events in the life of Watson Smith. However, the events chosen and the way they were presented lend an air of romanticism and mystery to the story. Brew clearly identified his intent by concluding his remarks in the language of mythical history: "This is one way in which an archaeologist is made" (Brew 1972: x).

Watson Smith, on the other hand, almost never said anything about himself in his archaeological monographs. For many years it seemed as though Brew's somewhat apocryphal contribution to the legend of W. Smith would be our main source of information on him. Fortunately, a few years ago Smith (1984a, 1984b) produced two autobiographical chronicles full of detail and brimming with authenticity, even though he referred to them as little more than a "picaresque record." They have a wonderful folkloric quality and they provide valuable insight into the man who was the subject of Brew's proposed myth.

Even these autobiographical "musings" do not adequately reveal Watson Smith to us. He writes about himself with a refreshing sense of humility and a frustrating amount of modesty that contrast sharply with the more Homeric view that some archaeologists have of themselves. His anecdotes are well written, delightfully entertaining, and as factual as what he called the "unreliable crutch of memory" would allow. He willingly shares with us the events and the chronicle of his life, but he is almost self-deprecating about his role in the unfolding of those events: "What I have done with my life is another matter, into whose recesses I choose not to peer" (Smith 1984a: 2).

It is clear that Watson Smith does not see himself as legendary in any way, but fortunately for us, he thoroughly enjoyed recording his participation in and contribution to the fascinating story of the Southwest in American culture history. With typical modesty, he prefaced his *One Man's Archaeology* with the hope that he had been able "to contribute a modicum to the greening of a legend that is dear to many persons" (Smith 1984a: 2).

In the following essay, Richard Woodbury has tried to present an objective account of Watson Smith in which he balances Brew's larger-than-life approach with Smith's self-effacing attitude. The real Watson Smith is an urbane, humorous, scholarly, whimsical, literate, witty, learned, down-to-earth, and thought-provoking individual. The selections presented in this volume are intended to assist the reader in appreciating both Watson Smith and his role in the legendary history of the region, as well as his contribution to Southwestern archaeology. The appraisal of his life and work that Woodbury has prepared can only provide the context for that appreciation. The appreciation itself must come from the reading of the essays by Smith that make up the rest of this volume. There is no better way to introduce our subject and his work than to repeat Brew's six provocative words: "And then there was Watson Smith."

R. H. T.

Watson Smith and Southwestern Archaeology

RICHARD B. WOODBURY

For many years the canyon and mesa country of northern Arizona and adjacent New Mexico has attracted visitors and tourists, looters and collectors, and above all archaeologists and ethnologists (Fig. 1.1). The attractions are many: the romance of the rugged beauty and splendid isolation of what seems to be the last remnant of a rapidly disappearing western frontier; the superb preservation of a full range of archaeological materials; the spectacular cliff dwellings in huge rock shelters; the well-fired and elaborately decorated pottery; the modern Hopi and Zuñi pueblos that continue the Anasazi tradition to the present day; and the Navajo herders and farmers who gave archaeology the word Anasazi for the ancient occupants of this region.

When American archaeology was in its infancy, this land of contrasts was one of the first to be explored and studied, but for many years following these pioneering efforts it received little serious attention. By happy coincidence, the revival of interest in the Western Pueblo region in the 1930s happened at the same time that Watson Smith was beginning his archaeological career. As a result of a series of serendipitous events, Smith participated in several of the important archaeological projects that produced the basic information on which our knowledge of the prehistory of this part of the Southwest is based. The history of research in this region for the past 50 years is, in many ways, a chronicle of Watson Smith's archaeological career.

Smith's route to archaeology was long and circuitous—not unusual in the 1930s and 1940s—but a few details will suggest the path that led him, finally, to his archaeological career. He writes of his earliest years: "I was born in Cincinnati, Ohio, on August 21, 1897, into

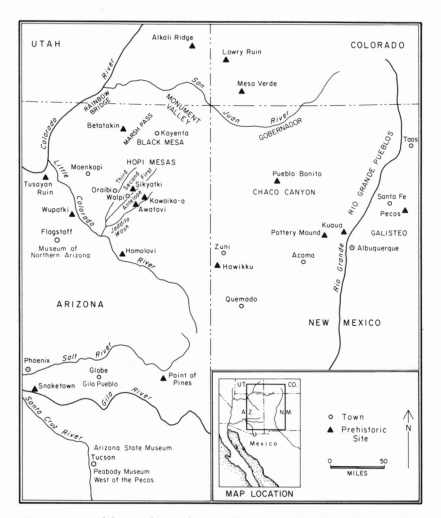

Fig. 1.1. Map of the Southwest showing the major archaeological sites and modern pueblo villages mentioned in the text.

moderately well-to-do family circumstances, and I lived my childhood happily enough in that city, without notable experiences beyond those permitted by the parameters of the time and the place. . . . Nothing in my earlier years suggested that in my later ones I would find myself at the bottom of an archaeological hole in the ground" (Smith 1984a: 3). His childhood exposures to archaeology brought no dreams of participation in future explorations. "About 1907 . . . my mother took me by trolley car to observe the exhumation of skeletons by R. E. Merton of the Peabody Museum [Harvard] at the Madisonville site, which was only a few miles from home" (Smith 1984a: 8). Smith also saw the site of Fort Ancient and its local museum, as the family "used to go there occasionally for picnics" (Smith 1984a: 8).

Watson Smith entered Brown University in 1915 and, after a brief period of duty in World War I, graduated in 1919. Following several short and unglamorous jobs in industry, he decided to go to Harvard Law School, "motivated largely by the fact that several of my close friends from college had begun the study of the law and were finding it rewarding" (Smith 1984a: 6). After graduation in 1924 he worked in a law firm in Providence, Rhode Island, but in 1930 the death of his parents required him to return to Cincinnati, where he was mainly occupied until 1933 in settling their estates.

At about this time, he writes, "I entertained a semi-romantic illusion of what an archaeologist was, with a trowel in one hand, a skull in the other, and a pipe in his mouth. . . . I was more interested in the Past, in history and geology, than in the Present, and hardly at all in the Future" (Smith 1984a: 7). A long-time friend, Carl W. Blegen, an archaeologist and professor of classics at the University of Cincinnati, was excavating Homer's Troy, and in 1930 had invited Watson Smith to accompany him in the field. The death of Smith's parents prevented this, but, as he says, the possibility did "crystallize in my mind the desire to catch archaeology on the hoof wherever I might" (Smith 1984a: 7).

In 1933, through mutual friends, he made the acquaintance of Paul S. Martin of the Field Museum and arranged to join him that summer at the excavation of the Lowry Ruin in southwestern Colorado (Martin 1936). Martin correctly recognized Lowry's Chaco-like features, but it was not until later that others could identify Lowry as an extreme northerly member of the ruins collectively known today as Chaco Outliers. These sites reflect a vast social, economic, political, and religious phenomenon in which Lowry Ruin, from about the 1080s to 1120s, played an important part (Powers, Gillespie, and Lekson 1983: 4, 252, 268).

Thus, through chance, good fortune, and his growing interest in archaeology, Smith found himself a "laborer and a learner," in fieldwork of major importance, and in an "association [that] turned out to be the beginning of a whole new life" (Smith 1984a: 13). This was his first experience of the Southwest and of field archaeology, and he found it immensely satisfying. He recalls the splendid panorama with the La Salle Mountains to the northwest and Mesa Verde 30 miles to the southeast (Smith 1984a: 20):

> I had never known so vast and so seemingly empty a
> world. . . . The combined vision of its natural grandeur, to-
> gether with the imagined lives of the Ancient Ones and the
> very immediacy of the struggling [Colorado] homesteaders,
> created for me almost a spiritual climate that has endured.
> And to me, archaeology has ever since meant the Southwest,
> and the Southwest has meant the San Juan country.

Watson Smith gained more than archaeological experience that summer, however, as he met and came to know James A. ("Al") Lancaster and his wife Alice, who were to be lifelong friends (Fig. 1.2). Al had worked for Paul Martin in earlier years and was J. O. Brew's assistant director at Alkali Ridge. Another new and permanent friend was Robert Burgh. While working as a summer ranger at Mesa Verde, Burgh had met Martin through Earl Morris, and had been hired as cartographer and surveyor at Lowry Ruin. On weekend visits Smith saw Mesa Verde and Brew's excavations at Alkali Ridge, and also much of the vast country of the Four Corners and beyond, including Flagstaff, to which he would return later, and where he now met Lyndon L. Hargrave. Like others before and since, he was captured by the incredible landscape and its wonderful people. Also, he was enlarging the group of archaeologists with whom, in the years ahead, he would be working on many of the problems of Southwestern archaeology.

In the spring of 1934, while in Berkeley, Smith met Max Radin, dean of the Law School at the University of California and brother of the anthropologist Paul Radin. Smith returned for the winter of 1934–35 to take courses under Max Radin's direction. These studies, a combination of law, anthropology, and history, only indirectly led him further toward his career in archaeology, but many years later influenced him to collaborate with the ethnologist, John M. Roberts, in a study of Zuñi law (Smith and Roberts 1954). By the autumn of 1934, Smith was hooked on Southwestern archaeology: "I had begun to think seriously of devoting myself permanently to archaeology, although the means to do it in a practical sense were not apparent. . . . I would have loved to dig in the dirt of Colorado for the rest of my life, but how do you do that?" (Smith 1984a: 45).

Fig. 1.2. Al Lancaster and Watson Smith at the University of Arizona Snaketown excavation, 1965. Photo by Helga Teiwes, Arizona State Museum, University of Arizona.

KAYENTA

Watson Smith took another important step toward an archaeological career in the spring of 1935, persuading Ansel Hall, whom he had met in Berkeley, to let him join the Rainbow Bridge–Monument Valley Expedition (RBMVE), which Hall had created and of which he was the guiding spirit. Hall advertised for paying participants, added a few trained experts, and promised experience in archaeology and a wide spectrum of natural sciences. The expedition did important pioneering archaeology in the Kayenta area and helped start the careers of several future archaeologists. Smith joined the expedition in its third year (Fig. 1.3), along with George W. Brainerd, Edward T. Hall, and John B. Rinaldo, all of whom became professional archaeologists. Others who worked with the RBMVE and would become archaeologists or social anthropologists were Charles A. Amsden, Ralph L. Beals, John B. Bennett, Donald Collier, Omer Stewart, and Richard S. MacNeish. Smith took part in a detailed site survey in lower Tsegi Canyon, and then with a small student crew dug a Pueblo II site on northern Black Mesa, which became the type site

Fig. 1.3. Watson Smith and Roy R. Crawford trenching a refuse dump at
a site near Marsh Pass, Rainbow Bridge—Monument Valley Expedition,
1935. Crawford, who was primarily involved with the pack mules that were
used to supply subsidiary camps, occasionally took part in the excavations.
Photo by Clifford Bond, courtesy of Museum of Northern Arizona.

for this period in the region (Colton 1939: 56). The genesis, history, and accomplishments of the Rainbow Bridge–Monument Valley Expedition are admirably told in Crotty (1983) and Christenson (1987).

For Watson Smith an important result of the summer, beyond providing him with new archaeological experience and adding to his growing circle of professional friends, was talking with Lyndon Hargrave, of the Museum of Northern Arizona, who was director of archaeology for RBMVE in 1933–34. Hargrave invited him to come to Flagstaff in the fall and assist in the preparation of the "Handbook of Northern Arizona Pottery Wares." So, in September Smith moved into the Monte Vista Hotel and became a member of the Museum of Northern Arizona Staff. The "Handbook" was prepared under the direction of Harold S. Colton, and reflected both his archaeological interests and his background in zoological taxonomy. Smith is not listed as a co-author but is thanked in the foreword "for his valuable criticism of the text and for his aid in preparing the glossary" (Colton and Hargrave 1937: ix). He worked closely with Hargrave, who wrote the actual pottery type descriptions, and soon realized that Hargrave had two weaknesses, "a tendency toward classificational dogmatism" and "an inadequate ability to write precisely." Smith tactfully introduced "a degree of consistency and stylistic improvement" that, he felt, contributed to the value of the "Handbook." He has said: "It is, in any case, a deep satisfaction to have had a part in the creation of a product that was unique in its time, and that has materially influenced ceramic taxonomy and description in the Southwest for almost fifty years" (Smith 1984a: 63–64). This was Smith's first major step into archaeological publication, and it is apparent that his expertise and insights were rapidly developing to the professional level, even at this "early" stage in his archaeological career.

Watson Smith recalls with enthusiasm his life in Flagstaff, then a relatively small town (population about 5000, and Route 66 not yet paved), and his involvement with the Museum and its small staff. He added Harold and Mary-Russell Colton to his growing circle of close archaeological friends, as well as Katharine Bartlett, Major Lionel Brady, and John C. McGregor. In the spring of 1936 he was requested by Colton to visit Gila Pueblo and study its northern Arizona sherd collections. Gila Pueblo, in Globe, Arizona, was founded in 1928 by Harold and Winifred McCurdy Gladwin, enthusiastic and highly capable newcomers to archaeology. It was already a major archaeological research center, making substantial contributions to

Southwestern archaeology. However, Colton and Gladwin disagreed profoundly on many archaeological matters. Perhaps for this reason Smith felt himself an observer rather than a participant in sessions where Gladwin tried out his ideas on other archaeologists, including A. V. Kidder, Charles Amsden, Paul Martin, George Woodbury, and the geologist Ernst Antevs.

Smith spent the early summers of 1936 and 1937 with the RBMVE, in the latter year occasionally sharing small outlying field camps with Ralph Beals, who had become field director of the Expedition. That winter Beals asked Smith and Brainerd to join him at the University of California, Los Angeles, to help prepare a report on the archaeological work, a report that was not published until much later, because of the interruption of World War II (Beals, Brainerd, and Smith 1945). It was, and remains today, an important contribution to Southwestern archaeology. It includes Brainerd's pioneering use of statistical techniques for ceramic analysis, with evaluation of the effects of sorting and sampling errors, the degree of sherd fragmentation, the personal factor, and the sample size, and techniques for "Formation of Chronological Sequence." The report is also notable for the meticulous description, with ample illustration, of the several pottery types discussed (probably mostly Smith's work). In this respect it is a worthy successor to A. V. Kidder's monumental reporting a decade earlier of the pottery of Pecos, New Mexico (Kidder 1931, Kidder and Shepard 1936). The relationship of recent erosion and deposition to human occupation of Tsegi Canyon was carefully examined in an appendix by John T. Hack, a student of Kirk Bryan, who had pioneered such studies in the 1920s with Neil M. Judd in Chaco Canyon. Although the sites dug were unspectacular, they yielded, through this careful study and reporting, major new understanding of the archaeology of the Kayenta area.

AWATOVI

Early in his stay in Flagstaff Smith had again met Jo Brew, with results that neither could have imagined. For Smith, it set the focus of his archaeological career for the next four decades. For Brew it added an invaluable new member to his research staff, one who would outlast all the others in studying and reporting on the results of the fieldwork. For Harvard's Peabody Museum, Brew had begun a major program of excavation in northeastern Arizona at the prehistoric and historic Hopi town of Awatovi, as well as other nearby sites. Because

Fig. 1.4. Jo Brew and Watson Smith examining sherds at the field laboratory for the University of Arizona Snaketown excavation, 1965. Photo by Helga Teiwes, Arizona State Museum, University of Arizona.

Smith still had commitments to the RBMVE, he spent the first part of the summers of 1936 and 1937 there, and the latter part at Awatovi. Then Brew (Fig. 1.4) asked him to join the expedition for the full 1938 field season, which he did, with work continuing far into the fall. He writes that he "was naturally pleased at the prospect, but what it was to do for me in its fulfillment, I could not have dimly foreseen. Perhaps I do not, even now, in retrospect, fully comprehend it, because it became and remains a continuing and living experience" (Smith 1984a: 98).

When Smith had first arrived at Awatovi in 1936, a kiva in the process of excavation had just revealed extensive painting on its walls. As everyone else was already occupied with other tasks, he was given the job of exposing and recording these painted walls, although, of course, he had no more experience than anyone else in such work. "That rather meager and unpromising beginning turned out to be one of the bonanzas of the whole [Awatovi] expedition. . . . [I] continued [the kiva murals work], devoting almost all of my four years to it" (Smith 1984a: 179–180).

Smith has described in detail the processes by which he and his assistants cleaned and copied the murals with scale drawings and photography, salvaged some of the originals, and produced restored reproductions (Chapter 2, this volume), and he has discussed the complex implications of the murals' iconography for our knowledge of prehistoric Hopi myth and ritual in his magnificent publication, "Kiva Mural Decorations at Awatovi and Kawaik-a, with a Survey of Other Wall Paintings in the Pueblo Southwest" (Smith 1952b; Chapters 6–8, this volume). Murals of comparable extent and complexity have been found at only two other sites in the Southwest, Kuaua and Pottery Mound, both in New Mexico, and in neither case has the final publication (Dutton 1963, Hibben 1975) approached Smith's in scholarly detail and insight. In a review in the *American Anthropologist* Edward P. Dozier (1954) called Smith's report "a fine example of the contribution that archaeology can make toward the understanding of present-day pueblo art and religion. . . an excellent foundation from which significant studies of pueblo art, symbolism and religion can begin." Smith made no claims to being an ethnologist, but was well aware of the continuity between past and present in the Southwest.

Although Smith began work on the Awatovi kiva murals with no special knowledge of the techniques that would be successful, he taught himself by experiment and by inquiry of other archaeologists. He was able to solve the countless problems created by the fragile nature of the medium, the elaborateness and size of many of the murals, and their sheer number, which demanded many months of painstaking work by him and several assistants (Figs. 1.5, 2.1–2.4). When the expedition ended in the fall of 1939, he was asked by Donald Scott, the Director of Harvard's Peabody Museum, to continue research on the murals and prepare a report. Smith moved to Cambridge, rented a small apartment in the Commander Hotel, and continued his work on the murals at the Peabody Museum. He and his assistants, Penrose Davis (now Worman) and Marjorie Vasey, finished most of their work in March 1942, just barely ahead of Smith's induction into the Army Air Corps. In late 1945 he returned from his military interruption and resumed work on the report, completing it in 1949 (Smith 1952b). It is

Fig. 1.5. Watson Smith at Awatovi, 1937. Photo by Hattie Cosgrove, Arizona State Museum, University of Arizona.

a masterpiece of meticulous, thoughtful, and pioneering research, ignoring no promising avenue for comparison and interpretation, but modestly claiming no finality for his interpretations of the esoteric meanings of the paintings.

Smith had become, quite unintentionally, an international authority on the salvaging and recording of mural paintings. Even before the mural research and publication were completed he found himself sought after as a speaker, and addressed audiences across the nation. Copies of the murals were exhibited widely, including at the Museum of Modern Art in New York and the California Academy of Sciences in San Francisco. At the Museum of Northern Arizona a Hopi kiva has been reconstructed with some of the original murals on its walls. The Santa Fe Railroad's Super Chief used adaptations of some of the Awatovi murals to decorate its cars. Smith (1984a: 224) has commented on the impact of the Awatovi murals on his career:

> I have not succumbed to the delusion that I am a kachina, but I have sometimes speculated on how the course of my archaeological life has been conditioned by those murals, and how different it might have been if they still lay quietly in their native earth.

The murals also became the means by which Smith, at long last, went to Greece to take part in archaeological work there. Carl Blegen was now excavating the Bronze Age Palace of Nestor in the western Peloponnesus and asked Smith to assist with the murals that were discovered there in the summer of 1953. Smith accepted with pleasure and found archaeology in Greece as fascinating, in its own very different way, as in Arizona. And he applied to a Classical Greek problem the insights gained from his work on the Awatovi murals (Blegen and Rawson 1966: x; Lang 1969: viii).

However, Watson Smith's archaeological activity was not limited to work deriving from the Awatovi murals, in spite of his continuing deep involvement with them. He spent the summer of 1941 in the field in the Southwest again, with Edward T. ("Ned") Hall, who had been on the Awatovi staff and was now a graduate student at Columbia University doing research for his dissertation. They dug several late Basket Maker (Rosa Phase) pit houses in the Gobernador area of New Mexico (Hall 1944). For Smith the summer was an opportunity to experience another portion of the Southwest, as well as to continue his friendship with Ned Hall and his talented wife, E. Boyd.

Smith's archaeological career was interrupted by service in World War II. His overseas duty included New Zealand, Noumea, Espiritu Santo, and Guadalcanal. It was in New Zealand that he met Lucy M. Cranwell, a widely recognized botanist, who in 1943 became Mrs. Watson Smith. When the Smiths settled in Cambridge in 1945, he became what he calls "a full-time functionary" of the Peabody Museum, meaning that he made himself invaluable in many ways, most of which he is too modest to say much about.

Fig. 1.6. Watson Smith at the 1948 Pecos Conference, Point of Pines, at which he presented the first report on his excavations at Big Hawk Valley, Wupatki National Monument. Photo by Odd Sigurd Halseth, Arizona State Museum, University of Arizona.

In 1948 Dr. Colton, Director of the Museum of Northern Arizona, asked him to be field director for the Museum's excavation of several small Pueblo II or Sinagua sites at Wupatki National Monument (Fig. 1.6). The Smiths, with 15-month old Benjamin, moved to one of the Museum's houses for visiting personnel and also set up a camp at Wupatki, shared with Milton Wetherill as field foreman, several Hopi and Navajo crew members, and Richard Shutler, Eugene Frosio, and George H. Ennis as student assistants. Smith's report on his work, "Excavations in Big Hawk Valley" (Smith 1952a), includes not only his observations on the light that this work shed on the contacts among Kayenta, Sinagua, and Cohonina, but also his thoughtful and unique chapter, "When is a Kiva?" In this seminal essay he analyzes the details of kivas reported from Alkali Ridge and the Kayenta area for clues to the interpretation in the San Francisco Mountain area of structures which might be "kivas," and in so doing provides an excellent model of how to extract "meaning" from refractory data (Chapter 3, this volume).

Smith's contributions to the Awatovi Expedition had not ended with the completion of his report on the kiva murals. In 1954 the Smiths moved to Tucson, leaving Cambridge fifteen years after he had moved there. He has said that he had never intended or desired to stay there indefinitely as an "affiliate of the Peabody Museum." But his conscientiousness now plunged him deeper into the unfinished business of the Awatovi Expedition (Smith 1984a: 322–324):

> It became apparent at about the time of our arrival in Tucson, and I think it must have been in my mind before then, that an enormous backlog of material was hanging over my head awaiting study and reporting. I had become aware, and I remain aware, of the awesome examples of the failure of many archaeologists ever to complete the writing and publishing of their fieldwork. I can well understand this, for I know how much fun it is to go out and dig in the dirt in strange places. . . . but it isn't any fun to go back to a dusty basement and compile charts and columns of figures. . . . It soon began to appear that I was, or soon would be, the only survivor of Awatovi to be in a position to work further upon it. . . . Three main facets of the work were still unplanned. . . a study of the massive quantities of pottery, a report on the architecture of

Fig. 1.7. Bob Burgh and Watson Smith at the Peabody Museum West of the Pecos, Tucson, 1958. Photo by Lowell Lurvey, courtesy of Watson Smith.

the site, and a general summary or review of its archaeology, history, and significance in the context of its immediate surroundings and in the Southwest as a whole. . . . It was upon these elements, then, that my interest was focused in 1954, and with the full and enthusiastic support of Jo Brew, I forthwith bit off what I was not competent to masticate. I was comparatively footloose, not being employed in a teaching capacity, and without any mature thought, I came to the conclusion that "This will be fun! For the rest of my life I can write about Awatovi on and on into happy senility." And after moving to Tucson in 1954, I began to formulate a plan for doing it in that spirit.

To describe briefly what Smith did is not easy. He converted the former guest house behind his Tucson home to an archaeological lab, borrowed specimens and records from the Peabody, and secured the able assistance of his old friend Bob Burgh, who had moved to Tucson for his health (Fig. 1.7). This unique research center came to be known, at Jo Brew's suggestion, as Peabody Museum West of the Pecos, an "official field office of Harvard University" (Smith 1984a: 325). For 15 years it was the scene of active research, mainly on the Awatovi materials. One major result was a detailed study of the pottery of the earlier part of the long occupation of the site, the "Painted Ceramics of the Western Mound at Awatovi" (Smith 1971; Chapters 9, 10, this volume). One reviewer (Gumerman 1973: 249) said of it:

> Never to my knowledge has such a large corpus of broken pots been examined so thoroughly from so many different perspectives and for so many different attributes. . . . In spite of the large amount of detailed description, Smith has not treated the pottery types and design styles solely as isolated segments of a spectrum, but has rather integrated the Awatovi ceramic types into a ceramic school which is more than the typical agglomeration of traditional types.

And the reviewer adds an unusual compliment: "Finally, the monograph is written in an extremely engaging and free flowing style, a difficult accomplishment in a 630-page volume dedicated to describing 32,000 pieces of pottery." It can be noted, however, that this should not surprise those who have read Smith's scholarly reports. He is the master of an elegant style of writing, free of pedantry, and occasionally spiced with humor and esoteric asides, that clearly communicates his observations, speculations, and conclusions. On any topic he considers, he gives long and careful thought and reaches sound and often highly original conclusions.

The innovative views with regard to the study of ceramics that Smith was developing from his studies of the Awatovi pottery had already been set forth in "Schools, Pots, and Potters," in the *American Anthropologist* (Smith 1962; Chapter 10, this volume). The article reflects his dissatisfaction with the traditional typological treatment of Southwestern pottery, which he suggests should be only a beginning and not an end in ceramic analysis. He asks if it is "really necessary or even desirable for the productive study of archaeological objects and their implications to reduce every last one of them to taxonomic precision?" And he quotes W. C. McKern's comment that "the lure of being methodical at all costs is a constant threat to the wholly profitable use of any method. . . . It is convenience and orderliness. . . that is required *of* the classification, not a flawless, natural regimentation of the facts required by the classification" (McKern 1939: 312; emphasis added by Smith).

Smith proposes in this paper that by analogy with the practice in the fine arts of identifying a Florentine School, an Impressionist School, and so on, one could advantageously define a Jeddito School for the black-on-white and polychrome pottery of Awatovi and environs. A School would be a "loose and flexible entity," not a taxonomic device like Colton's Ceramic Group (1953) or the Ceramic System of Wheat, Gifford, and Wasley (1958), nor would it substitute for horizon markers and co-traditions. Smith's suggestions, put forth with his usual elegance, modesty, and wit, have not transformed Southwestern ceramic studies, but have nevertheless provided a healthy bridge between the art historian's study of the products of human activity and the "scientific" analysis of potsherds. His article also shows what a free-roaming and ingenious mind can add to a problem some might have thought was already studied to excess.

Even earlier, Smith's ideas were adumbrated in comments he and Brew contributed in a symposium at the 1953 meeting of the American Anthropological Association. Of a paper by J. B. Wheat on the concept of area co-tradition, they (Brew and Smith 1954: 587) said:

> We must. . . guard rigorously against getting into the difficulty
> with this new terminology that we have just experienced in
> the period of wasted time and fruitless argument over "types,"
> "wares," "branches," and "phases." There seems to persist
> among us the entirely unscientific. . . tendency to postulate

terms and then to squeeze discovered facts into these precon-
ceived and all too often ill-conceived hypothesized patterns.

An important product of the research at Peabody Museum West
of the Pecos was "Prehistoric Kivas of Antelope Mesa, Northeastern
Arizona" (Smith 1972; Chapters 4, 5, this volume), in which Smith reported with meticulous detail, frequent keen insights, and stimulating
inferences on the many kivas excavated at Awatovi, Kawaika-a, and
other nearby sites, information that he had intentionally excluded
from his earlier study of the kiva murals. The more than forty kivas
from these two large sites and a few smaller ones probably make up
the largest group from any part of the Western Anasazi area. Their
careful publication provides an invaluable corpus of data for comparative studies, as other Pueblo III and IV sites are examined and reported.

In 1978 another major monograph was produced at the Peabody
Museum West of the Pecos, "Gray Corrugated Pottery from Awatovi
and other Jeddito Sites in Northeastern Arizona" (Gifford and Smith
1978). This research had started with James Gifford's study of the corrugated pottery, work he began as a graduate student in the 1950s in
collaboration with Smith and Burgh. The work, which was interrupted
by Gifford's broadening interests, particularly in Mesoamerica, was
ended by his death in 1973. Smith, assisted by Gifford's widow, Carol
A. Gifford, brought the manuscript to publishable form, as yet another in the series of "Reports of the Awatovi Expedition."

QUEMADO

Another important segment of Smith's career, Harvard University's Peabody Museum Upper Gila Expedition, took much of his time
from 1947 to 1952, before his move to Tucson and "return" to work on
the Awatovi materials. Donald Scott, the retiring director of the
Peabody Museum, and Brew, his successor, had long considered the
possibility of a field program in west-central New Mexico, a large and
poorly known area, "in which the Anasazi people of the Tularosa area
had come in contact with Mogollon groups coming in from the south
through the Mogollon Mountains and the Gila drainage system"
(Smith 1984a: 275). J. O. Brew and E. B. Danson (1948: 211), in an-
nouncing plans for the research, had described this as the area between the Pueblo and the Hohokam cultures, where "an enigmatic
Mogollon culture is postulated, an intriguing prospect as yet not sup-

ported with a sufficient number of distinct traits to give it acceptable validity as a useful concept in our historical reconstructions."

The plans came to fruition in 1947. The first field season consisted of the start of excavation in Bat Cave by Herbert Dick, in collaboration with the School of American Research, and the beginning of an "Upper Gila" survey by Danson—both graduate students at Harvard who later used these projects for their doctoral dissertations (Dick 1965; Danson 1957).

In 1948 Danson completed his survey and sites were selected for excavation, which began in 1949, with Smith as field director, assisted by Raymond H. Thompson and Charles Robert McGimsey III, also Harvard graduate students. A field camp was built near Quemado, about 40 miles north of Reserve, and perhaps most important of all, Lin Thompson, who had cooked at Awatovi, was persuaded to leave Utah for the summer and provide his famous cuisine for the camp personnel. Excavation was started at a large masonry pueblo, the Horse Camp Mill site, one of the latest sites in the area.

Smith was not in the field during the 1950 season, and McGimsey continued work at Horse Camp Mill, the report of which (together with other sites nearby) was his 1958 Ph.D. dissertation, later revised for publication in collaboration with Smith (McGimsey 1980). The Upper Gila Expedition's 1951 field season was on a reduced scale, McGimsey "mopping up" previous work and Smith directing work at the Williams site, which spanned the pit house to pueblo transition of the 10th to 11th centuries, and lay at the Mogollon-Anasazi frontier (Smith 1973). In his characteristically modest way, he remarks: "The summer was of little significance archaeologically" (Smith 1984a: 283).

No fieldwork was done in 1952, but in 1953 and 1954 Smith was again involved in the field program, when the Cerro Colorado site, a large pit house village, was dug (Bullard 1962). With that, Smith completed his long stint of fieldwork in the Quemado area, which he followed with substantial participation in the publication of its results. One of the frontiers of the Western Anasazi was now known in considerable detail and a large body of new information was brought to bear on the controversy over the validity of the Mogollon culture.

The summer of 1952 found Smith undertaking a quite new and different kind of research, a project that had its roots in his studies at Berkeley in 1934–35 and in his early legal experience. It was a study of Zuñi law, part of the "Rimrock Project," more formally known as the Comparative Study of Values in Five Cultures, conceived by

Clyde Kluckhohn of Harvard University, and directed by him from 1948 until his death in 1960. Two of the participants, also Harvard faculty, Evon Z. Vogt and John M. Roberts, proposed that Smith spend the summer at Zuñi collaborating on a study of Zuñi legal procedures. Roberts arranged for interviews, through an interpreter, with knowledgeable Zuñi elders, and Smith compiled a corpus of Zuñi "legal procedure, legal principles, the manner of settling disputes, dealing with criminal action, and so on" (Smith 1984a: 295). The resulting report (Smith and Roberts 1954) was "the first published study on problems of legal controls in a Southwestern pueblo... a valuable contribution to Zuñi ethnology in particular and sociolegal science in general" (Hoebel 1955: 1308). Once again Watson Smith had demonstrated his remarkable ability, this time in collaboration with a talented ethnologist, to bring out of a research project a significant and innovative contribution, with importance far beyond its specific subject matter. With his usual modesty, Smith comments on the field interviews, "Virgil would translate my questions for them and then translate their answers. This is the usual anthropological procedure, I guess, but I always felt that it provided a lot of chance for misunderstanding. ... What this means then is... that Virgil Wyaco, the interpreter, in essence wrote the book" (Smith 1984a: 295–297).

HAWIKKU

After the Smiths moved to Tucson in 1954 and Peabody Museum West of the Pecos came into existence, the major focus of work was, as has been described above, reporting on the Awatovi excavations. But an unexpected opportunity arose for work on the results of a much earlier major excavation program. From 1917 through 1923 Frederick W. Hodge carried out what was the largest long-term excavation program in the Southwest up to that time, at the prehistoric and historic Zuñi village of Hawikku (the official Zuñi spelling of what Hodge knew as Hawikuh).

Hodge's first acquaintance with Hawikku had been in 1897 when he was assigned by J. W. Powell, Chief of the Bureau of American Ethnology, to serve as secretary to the director of the Hemenway Expedition, Frank H. Cushing. The Expedition dug first in southern Arizona and later quite briefly at Zuñi. It may be that even then Hodge conceived the idea of digging at Hawikku, located only about 12 miles south of Zuñi. In any case, two decades later, when George Heye, the founder of the Museum of the American Indian in New York, and his friend, Harmon Hendricks, decided to undertake large scale digging at Hawikku, Heye invited Hodge to take charge of the work. Hodge accepted, even though it meant leaving his position at the Smithsonian.

With twenty Zuñi workmen and a staff of five or six, Hodge accomplished an enormous amount of digging and shipped a tremendous collection to the Museum of the American Indian. Although Hodge wrote several short papers on Hawikku and the "History of Hawikuh" (Hodge 1937), a book based on historical documents and almost no archaeology, "the big report on Hawikuh never got done" (Smith 1984a: 331). When the Heye Foundation suffered financial strains in the Depression, Hodge left New York and became director of the Southwest Museum in Los Angeles. He was convinced that the funds for writing and publishing a definitive report on Hawikku had been diverted by Heye to other purposes, but he took the records with him, hoping somehow to prepare the report.

In 1955 Smith, who was acquainted with Hodge, as was nearly everyone in the Southwest, was invited to lecture on the Awatovi kiva murals at the Southwest Museum, and thus began his involvement with Hawikku (Smith 1984a: 333):

> I stayed several days in Pasadena and was invited by Dr. Hodge and his wife to come to dinner, which was all very jolly. . . . Suddenly, and I mean *suddenly*, Dr. Hodge said to me, "Would you be willing to write a report on Hawikuh?" I was astonished. I didn't know how to react, so I temporized by saying, "Well, I know nothing about Hawikuh, I don't have either the expertise or the confidence to do this. Why do you ask?"

Hodge explained that Heye had failed to make funds available for writing a report, and added that since he was now ninety years old, he realized, at last, that he should help someone else to do it. He then showed Smith the extensive notes, drawings, and maps, that would be the basis of the report (the artifacts, however, were still carefully stored in New York at the Museum of the American Indian). To his distress, Hodge could not find the 750 drawings of the pottery. He had forgotten that he had lent them to the artist Don Percival, who later turned them over to Smith.

Next, Hodge requested and received George Heye's approval of the plan to turn the Hawikku project over to Watson Smith. Meanwhile, Smith asked Richard and Nathalie Woodbury to collaborate on the report, since they had recently excavated part of a pueblo ruin at El Morro National Monument that was regarded as ancestral to the later prehistoric Zuñi villages. They were in the midst of studying its pottery, in the hope of improving the classification of late prehistoric Zuñi ceramics. Conveniently, at the start of the work they were in New York and could visit and study the vast collection of Hawikku pottery at the Museum of the American Indian. Equally conveniently, they were then invited to come to Tucson to the University of Arizona, where Richard Woodbury took part in its Arid Lands Research Program.

When Hodge retired and moved from Pasadena to Santa Fe in September, 1956, all the other notes and records went with him, and were there when he died a few weeks later. The question then arose as to whether they belonged to the Museum of the American Indian or perhaps to the Southwest Museum or to Mrs. Hodge. She hoped to sell and keep intact for the use of scholars Hodge's enormous lifelong collection of letters, papers, books, manuscripts, notes, and other documents, including the Hawikku excavation records. Several institutions were making offers to Mrs. Hodge, and Smith and the Woodburys, fearing that once sold, the Hawikku records might be difficult to recover and use, decided that action was essential. Smith phoned Mrs. Hodge, who agreed to make the records available, and Nathalie Woodbury flew to Santa Fe, collected the boxes, rolls, and bundles, and as a snowstorm descended on Santa Fe flew out of its tiny airport and returned to Tucson. Hodge's Hawikku records were ultimately returned to the Museum of the American Indian. The rest of his papers are in the Southwest Museum.

The Director of the Museum of the American Indian was then Frederick J. Dockstader, who assured Smith that the funds for publishing the report on Hawikku were still untouched and available, contrary to Hodge's strongly held belief of many years. As time permitted during the next few years, Smith analyzed and wrote up the mass of detailed architectural information and the Woodburys worked on the pottery and the hundreds of burials. A few unpublished pages by Hodge himself were fitted in, and the architect Ross Montgomery wrote an account of the mission, similar to but shorter than the one he had contributed earlier to "Franciscan Awatovi" (Montgomery 1949).

When complete, the report (Smith, Woodbury, and Woodbury 1966), was perhaps not what Hodge might have written, but it made

*Fig. 1.8. Watson Smith accepting the Kidder Award at a ceremony in the
Arizona State Museum Library. Photo by Helga Teiwes, Arizona State
Museum, University of Arizona.*

available at long last, in organized and accessible form, a large and
unique body of material that even now is being further studied under
the aegis of the Museum of the American Indian. Without Smith's
generosity in acceding to Hodge's unexpected request, as well as his
perseverance, Hodge's pioneering work in one of the most important
regions of the Southwest might still be languishing unreported, un-
used, and largely forgotten.

In 1975 the Smiths moved from their Tucson home of twenty-
one years and Peabody Museum West of the Pecos ceased to exist.
But in their new home, closer to the center of town, Watson Smith
continued to make contributions, although at a more leisurely pace.

He remained active as a trustee of the Museum of Northern Arizona, among other things, preparing an important and much needed long-range plan for the museum. Earlier he had written a detailed but deftly expressed history of the Museum (Smith 1969) for its fortieth anniversary. Beginning in 1975 he had an office in the Arizona State Museum at the University of Arizona, which, with his characteristic view of the world and himself, he describes as "a place to hide, to engage in high-level gossip, to use the library, and to maintain a self-renewing contact with the academic world" (Smith 1984a: 341 [1]). Many of those who have paused and visited in his office would rate it only a little behind the Oracle of Delphi for its combination of wisdom and cautiously phrased but penetrating observations on the passing scene.

In 1983 Smith was honored by the American Anthropological Association with the Alfred Vincent Kidder Award, presented every three years to a person eminent in Southwestern or Mesoamerican archaeology (Fig. 1.8). The award recognized his numerous and significant contributions for many years to Southwestern prehistory and the citation included the statement that, "His writings are distinguished by their clarity and by the fact that, as one colleague has put it, he 'always writes with a twinkle in his eye'" (Kidder Award 1984).

SUMMARY

Although Watson Smith has been interested in (and usually remarkably well informed about) nearly everything, his dedication to Southwestern archaeology in general and to Western Anasazi prehistory in particular has remained his highest concern. His approach has always been a successful combination of science and the humanities, using the minutiae as well as anyone, but never confusing the "facts" with an understanding of the people that they can lead us to (Fig. 1.9). In *One Man's Archaeology* (Smith 1984a: 21–22) he provides what may be the best definition of his position:

> Seen in a broader context, archaeology to me has seemed to be immanent in the soil—not separable from it, but with almost mystical links to the land, the flora, the fauna, and the folk, not only those who lived upon it long ago, fashioning from its body the tools and dwellings that sustained them, and flourishing upon the fruits of its fecundity, but those who in a later day dig them up and ponder them.

Fig. 1.9. Watson Smith, at home in Tucson, 13 March 1985. Photo by Helga Teiwes, Arizona State Museum, University of Arizona.

Watson Smith's field experience, research, and writing have covered much of Western Anasazi archaeology, ranging in time from prehistoric Basket Maker pit houses to the historic Awatovi and Zuñi. He began in 1933 with Paul Martin at the Lowry Ruin, the northwesternmost of the Chaco Outliers, although it was not then recognized as such. Then for three summers he worked with Ralph Beals and others in the Kayenta area, in a program that made a substantial contribution to an area studied much earlier by Cummings, Kidder and Guernsey, and Judd, and then neglected. His experience was next enriched by taking part in the writing of the "Handbook of Northern Arizona Pottery Wares" with Colton and Hargrave. With each of these ventures he added a new kind of experience and gained new archaeological friends and colleagues. These experiences were not planned, but nevertheless led step by step to familiarity with the Western Anasazi region and many styles of archaeological research.

Smith's next role on the archaeological stage was a major one. He had a lead part in the Awatovi Expedition, in the field from 1936 through 1939 and continuing the research and writing for nearly four decades after that. With the publication in 1952 of his report on the Awatovi murals he emerged as one of the major contributors in our day to Southwestern prehistory.

His experience extended in still other directions in 1941 with work in the Gobernador area, and in 1948 with excavations near Wupatki. Then from 1949 to 1954 he learned firsthand about the controversies over the Mogollon culture, working on the Anasazi-Mogollon frontier, in the Quemado area. After his 1952–53 contribution to the ethnology of Pueblo law, and his 1954 diversion from the Southwest to work with Blegen in Greece, he undertook yet one more project, the report on the excavation of Hawikku. This was work that he undertook at another's request, but carried through as conscientiously as if he had directed the original fieldwork himself.

When Watson Smith began fieldwork with Paul Martin in 1933, the Western Anasazi, as a definable culture-historical entity or region, hardly existed. There was still a tendency to think of the Anasazi Southwest in terms of the San Juan, Chaco Canyon, Mesa Verde, Pecos, and not much else. During this half century he and many others have greatly expanded our knowledge and understanding of the northern and western areas of the prehistoric and historic Southwest. Smith has had the good fortune to take part in and to contribute substantially, though not always by plan, to this expansion through his skill in recognizing opportunities and his willingness to make the most of each. His ability to write clearly and elegantly about archaeological matters, his incredible sense of responsibility, and his rare talent for completing what he, and often others, began have resulted in a research record as impressive in its way as the remnants of the prehistoric people whose life and land initially caught his imagination.

Bibliography of Watson Smith

1935   Report on Some Sites Tested Near Marsh Pass. *Rainbow Bridge-Monument Valley Expedition Preliminary Bulletin, Archeological Series* 2. Berkeley.

1936   [With Lyndon Lane Hargrave] A Method for Determining the Texture of Pottery. *American Antiquity* 2(1): 32-36.

1940   Archaeology in the Southwest. *Parents League Bulletin* 5(2):12-18. Providence.

1945   [With Ralph Leon Beals and George Walton Brainerd] Archaeological Studies in Northeastern Arizona: A Report on the Work of the Rainbow Bridge–Monument Valley Expedition. *University of California Publications in American Archaeology and Ethnology* 44(1). Berkeley and Los Angeles: University of California Press.

1945   RB 551. In "Archaeological Studies in Northeastern Arizona," by Ralph Leon Beals, George Walton Brainerd, and Watson Smith, pp. 42-62. *University of California Publications in American Archaeology and Ethnology* 44(1). Berkeley and Los Angeles: University of California Press.

1945   RB 564. In "Archaeological Studies in Northeastern Arizona," by Ralph Leon Beals, George Walton Brainerd, and Watson Smith, pp. 62-66. *University of California Publications in American Archaeology and Ethnology* 44(1). Berkeley and Los Angeles: University of California Press.

1949   [With Ross Gordon Montgomery and John Otis Brew] Franciscan Awatovi: The Excavation and Conjectural Reconstruction of a 17th Century Spanish Mission Establishment at a Hopi Indian Town in Northeastern Arizona. *Papers of the Peabody Museum of American Archaeology and Ethnology* 36. Cambridge: Harvard University.

1949   Mural Decorations of San Bernardo de Aguatubi. In "Franciscan Awatovi," by Ross Gordon Montgomery, John Otis Brew, and

Watson Smith, pp. 291-339. *Papers of the Peabody Museum of American Archaeology and Ethnology* 36. Cambridge: Harvard University.

1949   Excavations in Big Hawk Valley. *Plateau* 21(3): 42-48.

1950   Preliminary Report of the Peabody Museum Upper Gila Expedition, Pueblo Division, 1949. *El Palacio* 57(2): 392-399.

1952   Excavations in Big Hawk Valley, Wupatki National Monument, Arizona. *Bulletin* 24. Flagstaff: Museum of Northern Arizona.

1952   Kiva Mural Decorations at Awatovi and Kawaika-a with a Survey of Other Wall Paintings in the Pueblo Southwest. *Papers of the Peabody Museum of American Archaeology and Ethnology* 37. Cambridge: Harvard University.

1952   Mural Decorations in the Seventeenth-Century Southwestern Missions. *El Palacio* 59(4): 123-125.

1954   Some Aspects of Zuni Law and Procedure. *Plateau* 27(1): 1-5.

1954   [With John Otis Brew] Comments on "Southwestern Cultural Interrelationships and the Question of Area Co-tradition," by Joe Ben Wheat. *American Anthropologist* 56(4): 586-588.

1954   [With John Milton Roberts] Zuni Law: A Field of Values. *Papers of the Peabody Museum of American Archaeology and Ethnology* 43(1). Cambridge: Harvard University. [Reissued by Kraus Reprint, 1973.]

1955   Review of "A Report on the Excavation of a Small Ruin Near Point of Pines, East Central Arizona," by Denver Fred Wendorf and "Four Late Prehistoric Kivas at Point of Pines, Arizona," by Terah Leroy Smiley. *American Journal of Archaeology* 59(2): 193-194.

1955   Review of "Archeological Investigations in Mesa Verde National Park, Colorado, 1950," by James Allen Lancaster and others. *American Journal of Archaeology* 59(3): 360-361.

1956   Review of "The Hopi-Tewa of Arizona," by Edward Pascual Dozier. *American Antiquity* 21(3): 324-325.

1956   George Walton Brainerd, 1909-1956. *American Antiquity* 22(2):165-168.

1957   Review of "Pipeline Archaeology: Report of Salvage Operations in the Southwest on El Paso Natural Gas Company Projects, 1950-1953," edited by Denver Fred Wendorf and others. *American Antiquity* 23(2): 199-200.

1957   Victor Rose Stoner, 1893-1957. *The Kiva* 23(2): 1-3.

1958   Victor Rose Stoner, 1893-1957. *American Antiquity* 23(4): 420.

1958   Alejandro Villaseñor, 1882-1958. *The Kiva* 23(3), inside back cover.

1959   Review of "Pecos, New Mexico: Archaeological Notes," by Alfred Vincent Kidder. *American Journal of Archaeology* 63(4): 416-418.

1959   Review of "Late Mogollon Communities: Four Sites of the Tularosa Phase, Western New Mexico," by Paul Sydney Martin and others. *American Antiquity* 24(1): 93-94.

1959   Review of "Richard Wetherill: Anasazi," by Frank McNitt. *Arizona and the West* 1(3): 295-296.

1959   Harvey L. Johnson, 1904-1959. *The Kiva* 24(4), inside back cover.

1960   Carberry. *Brown Alumni Monthly*, May 1960: 17-19. Providence: Brown University.

1961   Indians and Archaeology of the American Southwest. Presented at a public lecture series at Brown University in Providence, 13 April 1961. MS, Arizona State Museum Archives, University of Arizona, Tucson.

1961   Review of "The Hubbard Site and Other Tri-wall Structures in New Mexico and Colorado," by Richard Gordon Vivian. *American Antiquity* 26(3): 447-448.

1962   [With Jane Gray] Fossil Pollen and Archaeology. *Archaeology* 15(1): 16-26. [Reprinted in Bobbs-Merrill Reprint Series in the Social Sciences A-302, Indianapolis; and in *Introductory Readings in Archaeology*, edited by Brian Murray Fagan, pp. 83-99, Boston: Little, Brown, 1970.]

1962   Robert Frederick Burgh, 1907-1962. *American Antiquity* 28(1): 83-86.

1962   Schools, Pots, and Potters. *American Anthropologist* 64(6): 1165-1178. [Reprinted in Bobbs-Merrill Reprint Series in the Social Sciences A-348, Indianapolis.]

1962   Influences from the United States on the Mexican Constitution of 1824. *Arizona and the West* 4(2): 113-126.

1963   Ansel Franklin Hall, 1894-1962. *American Antiquity* 29(2): 228-229.

1963   Man Against the World. Presented to the Graduate Club of Tucson, 9 January 1963. MS, Arizona State Museum Archives, University of Arizona, Tucson.

1963   Review of "Papago Indian Pottery," by Bernard Lee Fontana and others. *American Antiquity* 29(2): 248.

1963   Review of "The Cerro Colorado Site and Pithouse Architecture in the Southwestern United States prior to A.D. 900," by William Rotch Bullard. *American Journal of Archaeology* 67(3): 326-327.

1964   Review of "Archives of Anthropology, 12-20," edited by David Albert Barreis and others. *American Journal of Archaeology* 68(1): 90-92.

1964   Review of "Archaeological Studies in Tonto National Monument, Arizona," by Charlie Steen and others. *American Antiquity* 29(4): 528-529.

1966   [With Richard Benjamin Woodbury and Nathalie Ferris Sampson Woodbury] The Excavation of Hawikuh by Frederick Webb Hodge: Report of the Hendricks-Hodge Expedition, 1917-1923. *Contributions from the Museum of the American Indian* 20. New York: Museum of the American Indian, Heye Foundation.

1966   Ceramic Studies and Ethnological Investigations. Review of
        "Ceramics and Man," edited by Frederick Rognald Matson. *Science*
        152:927-928.
1967   Review of "Kaiparowitz Plateau and Glen Canyon Prehistory," by
        Florence Cline Lister. *American Antiquity* 32(3): 414-415.
1969   *The Story of the Museum of Northern Arizona.* Flagstaff: Museum of
        Northern Arizona.
1969   Review of "Mound Builders of Ancient America," by Robert
        Silverberg. *American Antiquity* 34(2): 184.
1970   Seventeenth-Century Spanish Missions of the Western Pueblo Area.
        Smoke Signal 21. Tucson: Tucson Corral of the Westerners.
1970   Pots of Gold? *The Kiva* 36(1): 39-43.
1970   [With Bernard Lee Fontana] Religious Sacramentals from Awatovi.
        The Kiva 36(2): 13-16.
1970   Review of "Men Met Along the Trail," by Neil Merton Judd.
        American Antiquity 35(3): 391.
1971   Painted Ceramics of the Western Mound at Awatovi. *Papers of the
        Peabody Museum of American Archaeology and Ethnology* 38.
        Cambridge: Harvard University.
1971   Review of "Men Across the Sea: Problems of Pre-Columbian
        Contact," edited by Carroll Laverne Riley and others. *Science* 1974:
        484.
1972   Prehistoric Kivas of Antelope Mesa, Northeastern Arizona. *Papers
        of the Peabody Museum of American Archaeology and Ethnology*
        39(1). Cambridge: Harvard University.
1972   Review of "White Mountain Red Ware, A Pottery Tradition of East-
        Central Arizona and Western New Mexico," by Roy Lincoln
        Carlson. *American Antiquity* 37(3): 458-459.
1973   Introduction. In *The Cliff Dwellers of the Mesa Verde,
        Southwestern Colorado: Their Pottery and Implements*, by Gustaf
        Eric Adolf Nordenskiöld, pp. xi-xiv. New York: AMS Press [reprint
        of 1893 edition].
1973   The Williams Site: A Frontier Mogollon Village in West-Central
        New Mexico. *Papers of the Peabody Museum of American
        Archaeology and Ethnology* 39(2). Cambridge: Harvard University.
1973   Review of "Anasazi: Ancient People of the Rock," by David Muench
        and Donald Pike. *Ethnohistory* 20(3): 297-298.
1973   Southwestern Indian Pottery. Presented at the 73rd Annual
        Meeting of the National Council on Education for the Ceramic Arts
        at Northern Arizona University in Flagstaff, 29 March 1973. MS,
        Arizona State Museum Archives, University of Arizona, Tucson.
1974   Foreword. In "Prehistoric Ceramics of the Mesa Verde
        Region,"compiled by David Alan Breternitz and others, p. v.
        Ceramic Series 5. Flagstaff: Museum of Northern Arizona.
1974   George Peabody: Forgotten Philanthropist. Presented to the Tucson

Literary Club, 18 November 1974. MS, Arizona State Museum Archives, University of Arizona, Tucson.

1974   Pueblo Indian Bibliography, two volumes, edited by John Vincent Baroco. MS, Arizona State Museum Library, University of Arizona, Tucson.

1975   Review of "Conquistadors Without Swords: Archaeologists in the Americas," by Leo Duell. *Journal of Arizona History* 16(2): 204-205.

1976   Nestor's Palace and How to Become a Godfather Without Really Trying. Presented to the Arizona Archaeological and Historical Society in Tucson, 16 February 1976. MS, Arizona State Museum Archives, University of Arizona.

1976   Review of "Papers on the Archaeology of Black Mesa, Arizona," edited by George John Gumerman and others. *Journal of Arizona History* 17(2): 240-241.

1977   Who Didn't Discover Bernheimer Bridge? *The Kiva* 43(2): 83-87.

1978   [With James Collier Gifford] Gray Corrugated Pottery from Awatovi and Other Jeddito Sites in Northeastern Arizona. *Papers of the Peabody Museum of American Archaeology and Ethnology* 69. Cambridge: Harvard University.

1978   Pueblo Indian Religious Art. Presented to the Tucson Corral of the Westerners, 3 April 1978, MS, Arizona State Museum Archives, University of Arizona, Tucson.

1979   Who Put the Soap in Opera? Presented to the Graduate Club in Tucson, 10 October 1979. MS, Arizona State Museum Archives, University of Arizona, Tucson.

1980   Adventure and Archaeology at Hawikuh. In *Camera, Spade, and Pen: An Inside View of Southwestern Archaeology*, edited by Marnie Gaede, pp. 70-78. Tucson: University of Arizona Press.

1980   The Excavation of Awatovi and Other Archaeology in the Hopi Country. Presented at the Hopi Tricentennial of the Pueblo Rebellion in Oraibi, 15 August 1980, MS, Arizona State Museum Archives, University of Arizona, Tucson.

1980   Foreword. In *Camera, Spade, and Pen: An Inside View of Southwestern Archaeology*, edited by Marnie Gaede, pp. 9-10. Tucson: University of Arizona Press.

1980   Mural Decorations from Ancient Hopi Kivas. In *Hopi Kachina, Spirit of Life*, edited by Dorothy Koster Washburn, pp. 28-37. San Francisco and Seattle: California Academy of Sciences and University of Washington Press.

1981   The Changing Face of Archaeology: A Light Hearted Perspective on a Ponderous Perplex. Presented at the Tucson Menudo Society, 18 June 1981. MS, Arizona State Museum Archives, University of Arizona, Tucson.

1981   Review of "Handbook of North American Indians, Volume 9: Southwest," edited by Alfonso Ortiz. *The Kiva* 46(1-2): 121-124.

1982   Me and Confucius. Presented to the Tucson Literary Club, 19 April
        1982. MS, Arizona State Museum Archives, University of Arizona,
        Tucson.
1983   The Archaeological Legacy of Edward H[olland] Spicer. *The Kiva*
        49(1-2): 75-79.
1983   [With Ralph Leon Beals] Foreword. In "Honoring the Dead:
        Anasazi Ceramics from the Rainbow Bridge-Monument Valley
        Expedition," by Helen Crotty, p. 6. *Monograph Series* 22. Los
        Angeles: Museum of Cultural History, University of California.
1984   *One Man's Archaeology*. Tucson: Privately printed.
1984   *Running, Jumping, and Standing Still*. Tucson: Privately printed.
1984   Review of "Those Who Came Before: Southwestern Archeology in
        the National Park System," by Robert Hill Lister and Florence
        Cline Lister. *Journal of Arizona History* 25(1): 93-94.
1985   Victor Rose Stoner, Founding Father. *The Kiva* 50(4): 183-189.
1985   Kishmus at Wupatki. *Journal of Arizona History* 26(3): 327-334.
1986   Review of "A View from Black Mesa: The Changing Face of
        Archaeology," by George John Gumerman. *The Kiva* 57(2): 129-132.
1987   Emil Haury's Southwest: A Pisgah View. Review of "Emil Haury's
        Prehistory of the American Southwest," edited by James Jefferson
        Reid and David Elmond Doyel. *Journal of the Southwest* 29(1):
        107-120.
1987   *Glimpses through Gossamer*. Tucson: Privately printed by the
        Morgue Publishing Company Resurrected.
1987   *Handy Guide for Doggerelists*. Tucson: Privately printed by the
        Morgue Publishing Company Resurrected.
1988   *Handy Guide for Doggerelists, Supplement "A"*. Tucson: Privately
        printed by the Morgue Publishing Company Resurrected.
1989   Report on the Results of an Etymological Research project: "The
        Functions of Digraphs and Ligatures in the Effective Destruction of
        Mental Equilibrium in the Human Mind (if any)." *Archaeology in
        Tucson, Newsletter of the Center for Desert Archaeology* 3(4): 6–7.
1990   *When Is a Kiva?: And Other Questions About Southwestern
        Archaeology*, edited by Raymond Harris Thompson. Tucson:
        University of Arizona Press.

2. The Vitality of the Hopi Way

Watson Smith spent much of his archaeological career working on sites in present-day or ancestral Hopi territory, as Woodbury has detailed in the previous section. Very early in that career he developed an appreciation for the Hopi people and their culture. In aboriginal times the Hopi met the challenge of their harsh and arid homeland and created a way of life that has sustained them to this day. They successfully resisted Spanish domination and have preserved many of their ancient traditions. They have maintained control of their own affairs in an increasingly interdependent world, and they have become successful participants and high achievers in Anglo culture. They have even adopted the Anglo or Western European practice of celebrating past events by centennial increments.

Most Native American groups shun such celebrations because they not only memorialize events in Anglo culture history, but also often recall the disastrous consequences of those events for the Indian tribes involved. In 1980, however, the Hopi celebrated in full Anglo style an event of great importance in their own cultural history—the Pueblo Rebellion of 1680. The Hopi Tricentennial recalled that three hundred years before all of the Pueblo people in the Southwest had united to expel the Spaniards who had occupied their lands for many years (Brew 1949b: 18). Although the Eastern Pueblos enjoyed only twelve years of independence before the reconquest of New Mexico by Diego de Vargas, the Hopi managed to prevent the Spanish from regaining any control over them (Spicer 1962: 189; Adams 1989). As part of the tricentennial activities, the Hopi invited many Anglos who had studied their culture, including Watson Smith, to a special symposium at Oraibi in mid-August of 1980. Smith, who had many times presented summaries of Hopi culture and history to Anglo audiences, gave the Hopi an overview of the archaeological work that had been carried out on their lands over the previous one hundred years. He provided details about the site of Awatovi where he and other Harvard archaeologists had found archaeological evidence of the Pueblo Rebellion (Smith 1980a).

Smith also took part in 1980 in the development of a major exhibit on Hopi culture, "Hopi Kachina, Spirit of Life," that was dedicated to the Hopi Tricentennial by the California Academy of Sciences, probably the only Anglo institution to participate in that event (Washburn 1980). Smith's role was to summarize archaeological work in Hopi country, again with special reference to Awatovi, for some of the kiva murals that he had recovered from that site were included in the California exhibit. His well-illustrated popular account of the Awatovi work (Smith 1980b), which was published in the catalogue of the exhibit and which appears on the following pages, provides the context for many of the essays in this volume.

R. H. T.

Mural Decorations from Ancient Hopi Kivas

Although the Hopi today occupy several clusters of villages from First Mesa in the east to Moenkopi (Munqapi) in the west, in the late prehistoric period their territory extended farther eastward for about twenty-five kilometers. The major topographic feature of this wider area is Antelope Mesa, below which flows the intermittent Jeddito Wash. Above the steep escarpment of Antelope Mesa were situated at least five large pueblos and several smaller villages, most of them occupied probably into the fourteenth century. Two of them, Awatovi and Kawaika-a, were occupied into the sixteenth century.

The first contact between indigenous peoples of the American Southwest and Europeans occurred in A.D. 1540 with the arrival of Francisco Vásquez de Coronado at the Zuñi pueblo of Háwikuh. Coronado dispatched a small party, under the command of Don García López de Cárdenas, to explore the unknown country northwest of Zuñi. After a few days' travel Cárdenas came upon a pueblo village, which he does not name, but which must have been either Awatovi or Kawaika-a. This meeting apparently did not greatly affect the Hopi, since Cárdenas's most famous accomplishment of this trip was being the first European to discover the Grand Canyon.

For nearly a century afterwards no significant results followed upon this fateful meeting, but in A.D. 1630 a campaign of religious conversion was mounted by the Spanish Franciscan Order based in Santa Fe, and several missions were established in the Hopi villages. Apparently by this time Kawaika-a had been deserted by its populace, but Awatovi, the largest of the Hopi towns, still flourished. Here the

Reprinted with the permission of the California Academy of Sciences from *Hopi Kachina: Spirit of Life*, edited by Dorothy Koster Washburn, pages 28–37, California Academy of Sciences and University of Washington Press, 1980.

friars built their major church and convento and remained in precarious control for fifty years, until 1680, when the resident Spaniards were killed and the church was razed during the Pueblo Revolt. An abortive attempt at reoccupation was made by the Spanish in 1699 but with only momentary success. The entire village was soon destroyed, and in 1700 its people were killed or carried away by noncollaborating Hopi from other villages.

Since this time, Awatovi lay in stately if ruinous peace for two centuries until archaeologists first dug their questing spades into its soil in the 1890s. In 1935 the Peabody Museum of Harvard University, under the direction of J. O. Brew [1952], began a five-year exploration of Awatovi from its unknown beginnings through the period of Spanish dominance.

THE PAINTED KIVAS

Inference from historic pueblo practices and from the actual excavation by Dr. Walter Hough in 1901 of a painted fragment in a kiva at Kawaika-a [Hough 1902] prepared archaeologists for the exciting discovery of a kiva at Awatovi with painted walls dating from about the early fifteenth century. Subsequent investigation at both Awatovi and Kawaika-a uncovered the remains of more than two hundred individual paintings on the walls of about twenty kivas [Smith 1952b]. Many more wall paintings undoubtedly remain undiscovered in these and other ancient Hopi villages.

Kiva walls at Awatovi were then, as now, constructed of roughly coursed sandstone blocks, which were chinked and crudely finished with coatings of coarse mud mortar. Over these were applied thin layers about 1.25 mm in thickness of finish plaster composed of fine homogeneous reddish-brown sandy clay. These coats were renewed from time to time, and in one instance more than one hundred superimposed coats, with a total thickness of about 11 cm, had survived on a single wall.

On these finish coats were painted elaborate designs in a variety of colors. Pigments were mostly minerals readily available in the vicinity, producing various shades of yellow, orange, and red, all from iron oxides; pink and vermilion from mixtures of red ochre and white or gray clays; brown from red ochre mixed with fine particles of charcoal; maroon from red ochre combined with a mineral containing manganese; blue, occasionally from azurite, but much more commonly from a mixture of charcoal and white clay, which surprisingly gave the optical effect of dull gray-blue; green, which was rare, from malachite or sometimes from yellow iron oxide mixed with charcoal. White was derived from relatively pure kaolin; black (the only organic pigment present) was charcoal or bone black.

The vehicle with which the pigments were mixed was probably a vegetable or animal oil mixed with water or saliva. The paints were evidently applied with a stiff brush, such as the frayed end of a yucca leaf, but sometimes with the fingers, as was evident from occasional fingerprints.

It is not possible here to discuss the vast and intricate subject of Pueblo ceremonialism, but it may be said that today most Pueblo ceremonials are conducted in kivas by the members of certain societies. Usually these ceremonials are of several days' duration, and special preparations are made for each one, including sand paintings on the floor, vertical altars with a wide variety of sacred and symbolic objects, and, sometimes ceremonial paintings upon kiva walls. After the conclusion of a particular ceremonial the accoutrements are removed and stored in secrecy, and the mural paintings are obliterated by being washed from the walls.

By analogy to observed and recorded ethnographic examples, it is reasonable to infer that similar procedures were followed in ancient times, except for one very important difference. During the occupation of the Antelope Mesa villages, the kiva wall paintings were covered but not destroyed after the conclusion of a particular ceremonial, by being sealed behind a new coating of sandy-clay plaster. The wall then became available for the application of a new painting appropriate for a subsequent ceremony. This replastering procedure brought a fortuitous reward, since it provided the means for permanent preservation of a graphic record that would otherwise have disappeared forever.

RECOVERING THE PAINTINGS

However, the task of exposing, copying, and removing these treasures was exceedingly difficult. Since there was no exact precedent for working with kiva murals, the task had to be approached pragmatically. It was found that in almost all instances higher portions of the walls had collapsed, leaving an irregular broken edge along the plaster layers. Furthermore, in many cases, the plaster had broken away from the wall behind it and was sustained only by the pressure of the debris that filled the room. The removal of this debris therefore

Fig. 2.1. *Watson Smith making drawing of mural, Awatovi, Room 788, Left Wall, Design 8.*

Fig. 2.2. *Watson Smith applying adhesive to mural.*

Fig. 2.3. *Watson Smith applying muslin to mural.*

Fig. 2.4. *Watson Smith stripping muslin with painting from wall.*

risked the collapse of the plaster integument. By trial and error a simple expedient was worked out for supporting the standing plaster layers by patching and sealing them with a mortar of the very same sandy clay of which the original layers had been composed, and sometimes by erecting a temporary framework set snugly against the plaster face and anchored in the floor. It was then easy to photograph and copy the outermost painting (Fig. 2.1). All details were sketched to scale with the aid of a grid laid over the original, descriptive notes were made, and samples taken of all color variations of the paint.

The most delicate problem was how to expose the next underlying layer without damaging it and without sacrificing the outermost layer. Fortunately the painting technique used was not true fresco, a technique whereby paint is applied to still damp plaster, which absorbs the paint as it dries. Instead, the paint was applied on dry plaster in a manner called *fresco secco*. In this technique the paint forms a thin film with only a superficial bond to the underlying plaster.

The benevolent kachinas (*katsinam*) must have been watching over the puzzled archaeologists at Awatovi, for at exactly this time an identical situation had been discovered at the contemporary Pueblo ruin of Kuaua near Bernalillo, New Mexico. At Kuaua a single kiva had disclosed a wall that bore multiple layers of paintings. By herculean efforts this entire wall was jacketed in a reinforced plaster cocoon and transported to the University of New Mexico in Albuquerque, where a process for the stripping of the successive layers was being developed by Dr. Gordon Vivian, Mr. Wesley Bliss and others. Through their generous collaboration, a similar procedure was adopted at Awatovi, although there the stripping had to be done in the field, with exposure to the uncooperative elements of wind, sun, and rain, since the removal of entire walls to a sheltered laboratory was not feasible.

The stripping was accomplished by applying an acetone-soluble synthetic adhesive to the painted surface and covering this still tacky surface with a sheet of thin muslin (Fig. 2.2). When thoroughly dry the muslin could be peeled from the surface, just as adhesive tape can be removed from the skin, bringing with it the film of paint, which would separate cleanly from its underling plaster.

It is hardly necessary to say that under field conditions many of the requirements were difficult to achieve: the adhesive had to be spread evenly; it had to dry rapidly but not too rapidly; it had to be sufficiently viscous to prevent penetration of the pores within the sandy plaster; it had to resist absorption of moisture from the atmosphere or from the plaster itself; the muslin had to be cut and applied in squares of a size that was manageable under windy conditions; and of course the weather had to be propitious (Fig. 2.3). Under optimum conditions the result was a film of paint adhering face down against a supporting fabric of adhesive and muslin, which could then be stripped from the wall, rolled like wallpaper, and taken to the Peabody Museum in Cambridge for remounting (Fig. 2.4).

Having successfully stripped a painted layer, it was then necessary to remove the underlying and now sterile plaster in order to expose the next painted layer behind it. This was done by means of that technological workhorse, the Boy Scout knife, which had to be neither too sharp nor too dull, so that the granular plaster could be gently abraded and separated from the paint beneath it. Then for each successive painted layer the procedure began all over again, until the bottom and earliest layer had been recovered.

In Cambridge the stripped painting was mounted on a permanent backing for preservation and display. In some cases the stripping was mounted directly on tempered Masonite, which provided a fairly close match for the color of the original plaster. In other instances a thin coating of plaster composed of the actual sandy clay of the originals was spread upon the Masonite and the stripped section was mounted thereon.

To accomplish this the surface of the permanent support was coated with an adhesive different from that used in the field, and upon this the muslin sheet was spread so that the reverse of the original paint film adhered to the new support. The original adhesive was then dissolved in acetone, thus freeing the muslin sheet from the paint film, and it could then be removed, exposing the remounted painting safely supported by its new backing. The success of this operation required that the final mounting adhesive be insoluble in acetone—otherwise it would be removed with the muslin.

In this instance a water-soluble animal-derived glue was used, but one potential problem with animal-derived glues is that fungus will attack and ultimately destroy the glue. However, addition of a chemical fungicide to the adhesive solution during its preparation will suppress fungus growth. It is gratifying that forty years later the remounted specimens show no evidence of deterioration.

In practice not all of the more than two hundred paintings or fragments thereof were actually stripped and remounted. Since this was a tedious task and time was a vital factor in the field, a hard decision had to be made between the competing ideal of complete preservation of all paintings and that of uncovering and recording as many different examples as possible. Only those most nearly complete or most spectacular and interesting in detail were preserved intact. All others were carefully copied in scale drawings amplified by photographs, notes, and paint samples, and these were later reproduced at the Museum. The reproductions were done at half scale on heavy illustration board, the surface of which was prepared by a flocking process, whereby a liquid of glue sizing containing a reddish-brown pigment was sprayed on the board in such a manner as to produce a fine granular surface that closely resembled the texture and color of the original wall plaster. On this surface an exact rendering of the painting was then executed in opaque watercolor, using the field sketches, notes, paint samples, and photographs as basic data.

THE PAINTINGS

The artistry and craftsmanship of the ancient Hopi mural paintings are of several styles, which show changes over the centuries from comparatively simple geometric, almost abstract beginnings to detailed representational compositions portraying the personages, animals, and paraphernalia involved in particular ceremonies. The execution, while precise and balanced, was usually static, sometimes almost like the frozen instant of a single frame in a moving picture.

However, a few of the later compositions possess a more fluid style in which the feeling of movement was more effectively achieved. Several of the latter portrayed scenes of symbolic combat between two anthropomorphic figures, some of which can, with a degree of certainty, be identified as representing actions that are still carried out today in certain ceremonials.

Both styles contained essentially the same elements, principally kachinas and human figures; a wide assortment of plants, such as corn, beans, squash, and cactus; animals, including badgers, rabbits, deer, snakes, lizards, birds, fish, and frogs; pahos (*paavaho*), tiponis (*tiitiponi*), crooks, feathers, animal skins, bows, arrows, shields, clouds, lightning, and other features symbolic of the purposes and requirements of a particular religious observance. It seems quite clear that paintings of this kind were mimetic of the living scene that was acted out either in the kiva or at an associated dance in the village plaza.

Among the best-preserved mural paintings at Awatovi were those from a kiva designated Room 788, which was found directly beneath the sanctuary of the Franciscan church [Smith 1972]. As was often their practice, the Spanish fathers had purposely positioned their most sacred structure over an existing shrine of the Indians as a visual symbol of the supplanting of the old faith by the new [Montgomery, Smith, and Brew 1949]. The kiva was deliberately filled with clean sand, and its roof and walls were left intact, so that the paintings had suffered much less deterioration than had those in other kivas.

While the representational style became more intricate during later years, geometric and abstract compositions never died out. Some of the most complex and involved patterns occurred contemporaneously with explicitly representational scenes and were the most beautiful and carefully planned of all. Several of these were designed and executed in the convoluted manner of the Sikyatki style of decoration that appeared on certain pottery vessels current in the late sixteenth century, which were probably the most elaborate and beautiful ceramic achievement of the prehistoric Pueblo peoples. An outstanding example is shown in Figure 2.5.

The name is derived from the discovery of many examples at the excavation of the ruined pueblo of Sikyatki, just east of First Mesa, by J. W. Fewkes in the late nineteenth century. Nothing comparable to them had been made for almost four centuries until a well-known potter named Nampeyo, then living in the village of Hano (Haano) on First Mesa, inspired by these ancient designs, created a revised version of the old Sikyatki style, adapted and modified by her own genius. This tradition has been carried on by several of Nampeyo's descendants and other recent potters and has come to be known by her name.

Although these designs appear at first glance to be entirely geometric, they were in fact composed of many abstract renderings of elements from Nature: birds' feathers and tails, mythical beasts, cloud forms, stars, lightning, growing plants, water symbols, prayer plumes, tiponis, and the like.

In some cases portrayals in particular paintings can be equated with personages in modern ceremonies. An example is shown in Fig-

Fig. 2.5. Sikyatki mural, Awatovi, Test 14, Room 3, Front B, Design No. 11.

ure 2.6, which depicts a combat between costumed antagonists. This may be a rendering of the symbolic combat that occurs at the Soyal (Soyalawgwu) ceremony to compel the sun to reverse its southward retreat after the time of the winter solstice—an effort which is, of course, successful.

In Figure 2.7 the central figure may represent one of several Hopi supernaturals, including Avachhoya (Avatshoya), Spotted-corn Kachina or Shula-witsi (Solaawitsi), a hunter. Both appear in various ceremonies and are characterized by painted circles or spots on their torsos.

In Figure 2.8 a fully caparisoned warrior, similar to some shown in modern paintings and ceremonies, appears to the right of a sinuous "squash maiden," who dances behind him. That she is an unmarried woman is indicated by the whorls of hair at each side of her head. She may perhaps be associated with Patun (Patang), the Squash Kachina, although the latter is always male.

In Figure 2.9 the central figure, wearing a conical cap embellished with the imprint of a bear paw and carrying a shield, with bow and arrows, may represent one of the twin Hopi War Gods.

In Figure 2.10 is almost certainly shown Ahöla kachina, who ap-

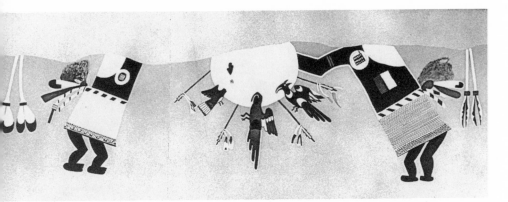

Fig. 2.6. Symbolic combat, possibly Soyal ceremony, Awatovi, Test 14, Room 3, Front B Wall, Design No. 2.

Fig. 2.7. Supernatural figures, Awatovi, Room 788, Left Wall, Design No. 3.

pears at the Powamu (Powamuya) ceremony and symbolizes the coming of the sun. Powamu (or "Bean Dance") occurs in February, and its purpose is the renovation of the earth for another planting season and the celebration of the return of the kachinas.

In Figure 2.11 is a group of several personages. The one at the lower left is identifiable as Kokopelli (Kookopölö), a character who appears widely throughout the New World, and is distinguished by his humped back and his phallic ostentation. He is often depicted playing a flute and is then referred to as the Humpbacked Flute Player, but his more ribald role in Hopi ceremonials is that of a comic seducer of girls and a bringer of babies.

The upside-down figure above Kokopelli probably represents his

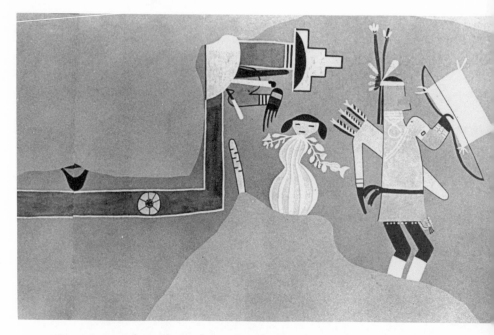

Fig. 2.8. *Squash maiden and warrior, Awatovi, Room 529, Right Wall, Design 1 (right half).*

Fig. 2.9. *Possibly one of the twin War Gods, Awatovi, Test 14, Room 2, Right Wall, Design No. 6.*

Fig. 2.10. Ahöla kachina, possibly Powamu ceremony, Awatovi, Room 788, Right Wall, Design No. 4.

female companion, Kokopell Mana (Kokopöl Mana), whose mask is decorated in the manner shown here.

The technology used in rendering the various styles of design seems not to have changed with time or among different craftsmen, although variations in skill can be noted. Paint was almost always applied as solid cover over areas which were usually outlined with narrow borders of a contrasting color. The outlining was apparently applied after the body of the element had been completed. Rarely was a spatter technique used and almost never was there an attempt at shading or perspective.

It was not possible to determine whether a preliminary layout was scratched on the surface as a guide in constructing the design. The symmetry and balance with which most designs were arranged within the available field might seem to demand such advance planning, but in the light of the skill shown by modern Pueblo potters in painting their vessels wholly by eye and without preliminary guidelines, it seems probable that the ancient muralists may also have worked freehand.

OTHER PAINTED KIVAS

The practice of painting kiva walls is old and widespread in the Pueblo Southwest. The earliest recorded samples, dated at around A.D. 900–1100, are very elemental series of geometric figures and hardly compare with the intricate pictorial murals of the sixteenth and seventeenth centuries found in Hopi and other Pueblo kivas in the Rio Grande area.

*Fig. 2.11. Kokopelli and Kokopell mana, Awatovi, Room 529, Back Wall,
Design No. 1 (detail).*

At Kuaua, now maintained as Coronado State Monument, twenty well-preserved mural paintings were recovered and copied at the University of New Mexico, and a definitive report has been written about them by Dr. Bertha P. Dutton (1963). The paintings from Kuaua were usually more freely drawn and more loosely arranged than were their Hopi counterparts, and they exhibited less static and carefully planned patterns. Dr. Dutton has connected them with prehistoric events at Zuñi and has interpreted them in terms of Zuñi legend and folklore.

By far the largest and most spectacular assemblage of kiva wall paintings, however, was found at a sixteenth-century pueblo called Pottery Mound in the valley of the Rio Puerco northwest of Albuquerque. At this village a mass of more than 800 individual design fragments from seventeen kivas was excavated under the direction of Dr. Frank C. Hibben (1975). The paintings at Pottery Mound resembled those in the Hopi villages much more closely than did those at Kuaua, and in some instances the identity was so close as almost to suggest ex-ecution by a single artist or at least by one belonging to the same school.

While it is not possible or appropriate here to attempt detailed analysis, it is enough to emphasize the widespread cultural and ceremonial dynamics that have pervaded the Pueblo world from early times until the present. The practice of kiva wall painting survives today at least among some Pueblos. One of the most comprehensive monographs on the subject is the *Hopi Journal* of Alexander M. Stephen [1936], who lived among the Hopi for several years during the 1880s and 1890s. It is largely on the basis of Stephen's drawings and descriptions that interpretations by analogy have been made of the ancient paintings from Awatovi and Kawaika-a. In addition much insight has been derived from comparing direct observation of kachina costumes and activities during the public phases of modern Hopi dances with the ancient kiva mural portrayals of kachina figures. Fur-thermore, valuable testimony was gathered from the Hopi men who worked at the Awatovi excavation, other Hopi, such as Fred Kabotie and Elizabeth White, who have bridged the Indian and white worlds and want to help us understand the Hopi way, and many other "sidewalk superintendents" who came to watch.

CONCLUSION

The discovery of ancient kiva mural paintings has provided a uniquely illuminating insight into the long continuity of Hopi religious symbolism and practice. These imaginative renderings emphasize the intimately dependent associations in the Hopi cosmos between mankind and Nature in all her forms—the animals, the plants, the winds, the rain—and the overpowering concern with fertility and life. Essential to human survival is the intercession of the kachinas, and the precarious balance between fulfillment and want is constantly reiterated through the realization of their annual retirement to their mountain home and their promised return in the coming spring.

But that their beneficent services may not be taken for granted is evident from the emphasis on mimetic actions and compulsive magic—to turn the sun around and to propitiate the forces of Nature. Without these things the delicate balance between Man and his world would collapse, and The People could no longer be.

3. Pit House and Kiva Pitfalls

Southwestern archaeologists have known *what* a kiva is for almost a hundred years, ever since Victor Mindeleff (1891: 111), following the advice of John Wesley Powell, first used the Hopi word *kiva* for the ceremonial chambers of the Pueblo Indians. Archaeologists were, of course, already familiar with the chambers themselves, which had been known to Europeans since the earliest Spanish explorations of the Southwest.

Within less than fifty years after Columbus stumbled onto the New World while on his way to the East Indies and less than twenty years after Cortez conquered the Aztec of Mexico, Spaniards had reached the Pueblo lands in the present states of Arizona and New Mexico. The Coronado expedition of 1540 observed kivas in Pueblo towns at Cíbola (Zuñi), in the Tusayan (Hopi) region, and along the Rio Grande.

Pedro de Castañeda, the chief chronicler of that expedition, even provided a fairly detailed description of a large kiva at Taos (Winship 1896: 511). The Spaniards apparently believed that kivas were northern counterparts to the sweatbaths that they had encountered in central Mexico and called them *estufas*, or steam rooms (Brew 1946: 203; Kidder 1958: 143).

The pioneer archaeologists followed the Spanish terminology until Mindeleff introduced the Hopi term. According to the huge etymological dictionary being compiled by Emory Sekaquaptewa and his colleagues, *kiva* has the general meaning of "underground room" or "basement" as well as the more specific meaning of "an underground ceremonial chamber." With the adoption of the clearly more appropriate Hopi word, the turn-of-the-century archaeologists satisfied their terminological and classificatory needs and turned their attention to chronological matters in an attempt to trace the history of the development of these Pueblo ceremonial structures.

In very short order, the semi-subterranean, domestic pit house of the earlier Basket Maker culture was identified as the ancestor of the kiva. Brew (1946: 203–214) provides an excellent summary of the resulting architectural developmental sequence that is both widely accepted and frequently challenged (Lekson 1988). The first Pecos Conference had trouble defining the identifying features of kivas and settled for the simple statement that "a kiva is a chamber especially constructed for ceremonial purposes" (Kidder 1927: 490). Because of this failure to produce objective criteria (Lekson 1988: 215), it was not long before Southwestern archaeologists were having taxonomic difficulties with ceremonial structures. When is a pit house a proto-kiva and not just another pit house? How many "kiva features" must be present to identify a structure as a kiva?

Watson Smith was confronted with these and similar questions in 1936–37 when he excavated RB 551 for the Rainbow Bridge–Monument Valley Expedition. This small site with four or five surface rooms and a large circular, semi-subterranean structure of early-to-middle Pueblo II times provided Smith (1945: 52) with an opportunity to mention briefly his ideas about what constitutes a kiva:

> Throughout the foregoing description this large circular subterranean room has been called a "kiva." Perhaps a few words should be added in justification of the use of this term instead of the more general term "pit house." Many writers prefer to apply the word kiva only to structures which can be indubitably regarded as having been used for ceremonial rather than for dwelling purposes. In accordance with this usage, the evidence here pretty conclusively justifies the use of the word kiva. First, it existed in close relation to and was obviously contemporary with the surface structure, which must have been a combined dwelling and storage house, large enough to shelter a population sufficiently numerous to require, or at least desire, a kiva. Second, no evidence that the circular room had been lived in was forthcoming; no pots, no metates

or mealing bins, very few sherds, and almost no bones were found in it. Third, certain features suggestive of ceremonial use did exist. These were the rabbit burial, the rectangular box in the position usually occupied by the sipapu in most kivas, and the long box on the eastern part of the banquette. Moreover, its position, to the east and south of the surface house, is consistent with the usual orientation of kivas in the San Juan area.

Smith (1952a) had to address these same questions a decade later in 1948 when he excavated a series of sites in Big Hawk Valley on Wupatki National Monument in northern Arizona. This region is on the prehistoric frontier between the Kayenta Anasazi territory where there were "real" kivas and the lands of the Sinagua and Cohonina cultures where the presence of kivas had not been adequately demonstrated.

Smith attacked the problem of whether there were kivas in his frontier sites by using the same classical archaeological methodology involving comparative method and judgments about context that he had employed at RB 551. His seminal essay (Smith 1952a: 154–165) was the first, and is still the best (Peckham 1979: 56), attempt to deal with the problem of "When Is a Kiva?"

R. H. T.

When Is a Kiva?

There are many pitfalls for the unwary Southwesternist, but perhaps the easiest to fall into and most difficult to climb out of is that of the kiva. Almost anyone can stumble into a kiva but unless he is like the Monarch of Mo he cannot usually extricate himself with dignity and grace. The Monarch of Mo once fell into a very deep pit from which he was unable to climb; but, being a resourceful fellow, he picked up the pit, turned it upside down, and thus finding himself at the top, brushed himself off and walked away (Baum 1900: 44).

In Big Hawk Valley three subterranean structures were excavated that might be regarded either as kivas or as pit houses, depending upon the definition thereof to be adopted. The kiva, defined as a specialized ceremonial room, with few or no functions of a domestic nature, is apparently limited to the Anasazi area, and seems always to have been one of the basic criteria of Anasazi culture. It has certainly not been recognized in the Hohokam or on the Plains and the determination of its presence or absence in intermediate areas occupied by peoples of such clouded legitimacy as the Sinagua and the Mogollon becomes obviously a matter of great importance to the establishment of their proper social status. If they had kivas, perhaps they were culturally affiliated with the people on the right side of the tracks; if they lacked them, perhaps with those on the other, since presumably a feature so intimately integrated into the usually conservative religious and ceremonial pattern of a culture would likely be both consistent and persistent throughout the extent of that culture in both areal and temporal dimensions.

Reprinted with the permission of the Museum of Northern Arizona from "Excavations in Big Hawk Valley, Wupatki National Monument, Arizona," by Watson Smith, pages 154-165, *Bulletin 24*, Museum of Northern Arizona, 1952.

The objective of research in this regard, therefore, especially in frontier areas such as the Big Hawk Valley, is to determine the presence or absence of kivas at particular sites by establishing their associations in terms of other traits. If kivas were objectively identifiable through their universal and exclusive possession of some one or more constant features, the problem would be simple. Unfortunately there seems to be no such feature or combination of features that can be depended upon automatically to provide the answer, despite the fact that in certain areas and at certain times the architectural arrangement of kivas did indeed become remarkably well standardized. Over a wider range, however, the criteria for kivas seem not always to have been expressed in terms of structural pattern, but rather in the mental concepts of those who used them as such. As with the Christians, whose communal workshop in any place where a number are gathered together makes that place *ipso facto* a church or shrine, even if used at times for other purposes as well, so I suspect that with the Anasazi a place was a kiva if they said it was and even despite its occasional use for secular purposes.

But since we cannot read the minds of the Anasazi we must attempt to interpret their way of life by means of their material remains, and when we analyse those remains for a common denominator for kivas we find the problem rather more complex than has often been realized. The use of words as descriptive symbols is very convenient, but we must constantly be on watch against the danger of confusing the word with the thing. If the kiva is peculiar to the Anasazi culture, then it is sound deductive logic to conclude that a site plainly containing a kiva had Anasazi affiliations. But to call a particular room a kiva will not make it such, unless we can isolate some recognizable and universal feature of kivas generically. When we examine the record critically we shall see that the quest for this essential determinant is not a happy one, and in making an investigation we should be concerned not only with the objective or physical character of the rooms reported as kivas but also with collateral factors that may have influenced the reporters in making their determinations.

DEVELOPMENT OF KIVAS IN THE SAN JUAN

It is generally accepted now, I believe, that the kiva as finally evolved in its most highly standardized form at Mesa Verde, the Hopi country, Chaco Canyon and the Rio Grande, during Pueblo III and later, was at first an outgrowth of an earlier form of pit house that had originally served simply as a dwelling. This subject has been thoroughly explored by J. O. Brew with great clarity (Brew 1946: 203–214). His historical outline is quite convincing, and my purpose here is neither to add to nor to modify it, but rather to seek a handy means of determining in individual cases "When is a kiva and why?" For the purposes of this investigation it will probably prove sufficient to confine ourselves to the San Juan and lower Little Colorado areas, since the variety of what have been called kivas in those areas is probably as great as in the Anasazi region as a whole. And we shall not attempt an exhaustive survey, but consider only a representative selection from published material.

Since the Chinle-Kayenta-Tsegi-Marsh Pass area was one major center of the San Juan Stem's development, where undoubted kivas did exist in Pueblo III times, and because any intrusion of the kiva concept into the San Francisco Mountain area would probably have come from there, let us see what standards, if any, have been applied there to the recognition and identification of kivas. For convenience and brevity I propose to summarize the published descriptions of rooms in this area whose possible function as kivas has been considered, giving also in each case the location, the reporter's determination of function and the bibliographical reference. If from these data we can isolate any one feature or group of features that is possessed in common by all alleged kivas and that at the same time is not possessed by other rooms, then we may see that a determinant has been established. If, on the other hand, we can find no such feature we shall be forced to the conclusion that, in its absence, we have no reliable key whatever to the definitive recognition of a kiva, and that the ascription of ceremonial function in a given instance must rest largely on an inferential basis and will be only a more or less convincing hypothesis. Since the published descriptions are in most cases woefully incomplete it is possible that additional information might further elucidate the problem, but in the present state of the literature this cannot be had without extensive fieldwork and reappraisal. In the following summary some abbreviation and rearrangement of data have been made but no available information has been omitted. Whenever specific features are not mentioned as either present or absent, it may be assumed that the original authority was silent on that point. Since the excavations of Kidder and Guernsey were the pioneer work in the area, and were also the most widespread, we shall begin with them, and follow with the reports of other investigators.

PUBLISHED DATA ON PARTICULAR KIVAS

Kidder and Guernsey 1919.

Hagoé Canyon, Flute Player House (Ruin 5), pp. 43–44; Fig. 18. Subterranean, circular, 10 feet by 11 feet. Not masonry. Lacked firepit, sipapu, ventilator. Pueblo III. *Not a kiva.*

Hagoé Canyon, Ruin 6, p. 46, Fig. 19. Rounded rectangle, 9 feet by 9 feet. Masonry, plastered walls, central firepit. Lacked bench, sipapu, deflector, niches. Wall where ventilator might have been collapsed. Pueblo II–III. *"Probably" a kiva.*

Comb Ridge, Olla House (Ruin 7), p. 49, Fig. 21, Pl. 15. Subterranean, circular, diameter 11 feet. Masonry; recess with bench half way around on northeast side opposite ventilator; deflector, firepit. Lacked niches and wall plaster. Pueblo III. *Kiva.*

Marsh Pass, Ruin 8, Kiva 1, pp. 59–60, Fig. 24. Semi-subterranean rounded rectangle. Masonry; "back" wall slightly bulging; "front" wall, which might have had ventilator, missing; bench all across back wall; firepit; two holes in floor that might have been sipapus. Lacked niches. Pueblo III. *"Probably" a kiva.*

Marsh Pass, Ruin 8, Kiva 2, p. 60, Fig. 24. Semi-subterranean, rounded rectangle, 10 feet by 12 feet. Masonry; one side wall bulging; "front" wall, which might have contained ventilator, missing; central firepit, sipapu, 2 rows of loom holes. Lacked deflector, bench niches. Pueblo III. *Kiva.*

Marsh Pass, Unnumbered Ruin, pp. 64–65, Fig. 25. Subterranean, circular, diameter 10 feet. Masonry, bench all around, recess at southeast with ventilator tunnel beneath it and shaft outside; deflector, firepit, sipapu. Pueblo II or III. *Kiva.*

Chinle, Waterfall Ruin (Ruin 9), pp. 72–73, Fig. 27. Subterranean, rounded square. Masonry, ventilator on south side, rectangular firepit, sipapu(?), "probably" a deflector, 2 rows of loom holes, 3 posts set into wall. Pueblo III. *Kiva.*

Sayodneechee, Ruin 2, Kiva 1, pp. 20–21, Figs. 3, 5. Semi-subterranean, circular, diameter 14 feet. Masonry; firepit; sipapu and deflector "cannot be determined"; ventilator outside south wall. Lacked bench, niches. Pueblo II(?). *Kiva.*

Sayodneechee, Ruin 2, Kiva 2, pp. 22–23. Semi-subterranean, circular, diameter 12 feet. Masonry, recess on north side opposite ventilator; firepit. Lacked sipapu, deflector. Pueblo II(?). *Kiva.*

Monument Valley, Ruin 4, pp. 37–38, Fig. 14. Semi-subterranean, rounded square, 7 feet by 7 feet. Masonry, plastered walls, firepit, sipapu, deflector, ventilator at southwest corner. Lacked bench, recess, niches. Pueblo II(?). *Kiva.*

Guernsey and Kidder 1921.

Comb Ridge, White Dog Cave, pp. 23–24, Fig. 7, Pl. 10, a. Subterranean, flattened circle, diameter 12 feet. Masonry, ventilator, firepit, probably 4 posts. Lacked deflector, bench. Area of possible sipapu not excavated. Pueblo II(?). *Kiva(?).*

Guernsey 1931.

Chinle, Poncho House, p. 53, Fig. 18. Not subterranean, roughly rectangular, 15 feet by 11 feet. Masonry, fireplace, deflector, ventilator, 4 loom holes. Lacked bench, sipapu. Pueblo III. *Kiva.*

Bubbling Springs Wash, Cave 1, p. 5, Fig. 2. Two kivas are said to exist in this Pueblo III ruin, but they are not described, beyond being circular and of masonry.

Bubbling Springs Wash, Cave 2, p. 12, Fig. 3. Oval, ventilator on south. Not further described. Pueblo II. *Kiva.*

Chinle, Ford House, pp. 43–44, Fig. 16. Semi-subterranean, circular, diameter 12 feet. Masonry, firepit, ventilator. Lacked bench. No other features mentioned. Pueblo III. *Kiva.*

Subsequent re-use as secular room determined by presence of two mealing bins directly over firepit.

Keet Seel Canyon, Cave 2, pp. 62–64, Fig. 23. Early occupation: subterranean, circular, diameter 15 feet. Masonry, firepit, ventilator, southeast recess. Lacked bench. Pueblo III. *Kiva.*

Later occupation: subterranean, circular, flattened on one side, diameter 11 feet by 12 feet. Masonry, firepit, deflector, ventilator, 4 loom holes, 3 other holes that might have been sipapu, 2 posts set in wall. Lacked bench, recess. Pueblo III. *Kiva.*

In the Navajo Mountain region, several kivas have been reported:

Morss 1931.

Gishi Canyon, Site 31, p. 6. A "broken-down kiva of the simple circular type." No other features mentioned. Early Pueblo III. *Kiva.*

Gishi Canyon, Site 36 (same as West's Ruin 2), p. 6, Pl. 4. A two-story circular structure. "The lower story contained a slab deflector and had perhaps served as a kiva." No further description. *Kiva?*

Segito Canyon, Site 13, pp. 6–7. All rooms rectangular, but some much larger than others or than "nine-tenths of the secular rooms in the cliff-dwellings of this region." No special features. Early Pueblo II. *Kivas?*

Segito Canyon, Site 16, p. 11. Circular, "small," and ". . . remarkable for a free-standing inner shell of adobe, the 6-inch space between it and the outer wall of the kiva being filled with clean straw." Late Pueblo III. *Kiva.*

Segito Canyon, Site 17, (same as West's Ruin 3), Room 3, pp. 12–13. Rectangular, 13.5 feet by 8 feet, not subterranean. Roof with 2 main beams like others in ruin, manhole in center, bordered with stone slabs; "appears to be no banquette"; opening in front wall 2.5 feet above floor and 9 inches in diameter; rectangular firepit; sub-floor rectangular vault with circular opening in floor covered by slab; tunnel from vault under floor and wall. Late Pueblo III. *Kiva.*

Segito Canyon, Room 8, p. 13, Pl. 7. Circular, apparently not subterranean. Plastered wall; probably had frontal semilunar recess and banquette; roof supported on single large, beam; sub-floor vault and tunnel like that in Room 3. Late Pueblo III. *Kiva.*

Forbidden Canyon, Site 19, p. 6. Circular, diameter 13 feet, not subterranean. Plastered wall, slab deflector, square firepit, ventilator opening through wall. *Kiva.*

Navajo Mountain, unidentified sites, p. 11. Two large open pueblos with large circular rooms having banquettes all the way around. No further description. *Kivas.*

West 1927.

Navajo Canyon, Ruin 3, p. 23. Circular, diameter 10 feet, ventilator at southeast. No further description. Pueblo III. *Kiva.*

Inscription House, 3 rooms, p. 31. One was oval with battered walls, 13 feet by 10 feet; two were circular, diameter 7 feet. No further description. Pueblo III. *Kivas.*

Cummings 1915.

"On the Kayenta," p. 276. Circular, diameter 15 feet, bench half way around. No further description. *Kiva.*

Water Lily Canyon, Twin Cave House, p. 276. Circular, diameter 20 feet, bench all around, firepit, deflector, ventilator, wall niches, rectangular box 4 inches by 8 inches in floor that might have been a sipapu. *Kiva.*

Nitznoeboko, Pine Tree House, p. 278. Circular, diameter 8.5 feet, semi-subterranean, firepit against wall, ventilator 3 feet to its right. No further description. *Kiva.*

Nitznoeboko, p. 279. Square, 10 feet by 10 feet; firepit, sipapu, 24 inches by 10 inches by 5 inches, covered with plank. No further description. *Kiva.*

Beals, Brainerd, and Smith 1945.

Black Mesa, Site RB 551, pp. 49–52, Fig. 10, Pls. 9, b, 10, a. Circular, diameter 21 feet, subterranean. Masonry, bench all around; firepit, deflector; ventilator at southeast; rectangular box covered with board that might have been sipapu; 4 posts in face of bench. Lacked niches, recess. Pueblo II. *Kiva.*

Tsegi Canyon, Site RB 1006, pp. 69–70, Fig. 13. Roughly circular, diameter 11 feet, subterranean. Masonry; recess on east side with ventilator tunnel beneath it; bench a third of the way around opposite side; deflector, firepit, one niche. Lacked sipapu. Pueblo II. *Function not certain.*

Kaycuddie Canyon, Site RB 568, Room P, pp. 82–83, Fig. 17. Semi-subterranean, rounded rectangular, 8 feet by 7 feet. Masonry, plastered walls, ventilator, firepit, deflector. Lacked sipapu, bench, recess. Pueblo II–III. *Function not certain.*

Kaycuddie Canyon, Room Q, pp. 82–83, Fig. 17. Rounded rectangle, 7 feet by 9 feet, semi-subterranean. Masonry, deflector, ventilator at southeast corner. Lacked firepit, sipapu, bench, recess. Pueblo II–III. *Function not certain.*

Farther to the West but still within the area of the San Juan Stem is the Tusayan Ruin on the South Rim of the Grand Canyon, which was excavated by Haury and in which were two rooms that are of interest here.

Haury 1931.

Tusayan Ruin, Grand Canyon, Kiva A, pp. 6–12, Fig. 2. Partially subterranean, crudely circular, diameter 19 feet. No masonry. Firepit, sipapu, ventilator on southeast, bench half way around opposite ventilator; 4-post roof support. Lacked deflector. Pueblo III. *Kiva.*

Tusayan Ruin, Kiva B, pp. 15–20, Fig. 3. Partially subterranean, flattened circular, diameter 20 feet. No masonry. Firepit, ventilator to east, bench all around, 4-post roof support. Pueblo III. *Kiva*.

BETATAKIN

At Betatakin, a Pueblo III ruin in the Tsegi Canyon system, a thorough investigation was carried out by Neil M. Judd and room-by-room descriptions were published (Judd 1930). These data are not always complete or adequate but they include Judd's identifications as kivas of five rooms out of a total of 135. It is interesting to study his notes and to analyse the characteristics of his putative kivas in comparison with those of other rooms in this ruin, as well as with alleged kivas in other ruins of the general region. It will serve no useful purpose here to recapitulate in detail all the specifications of each room at Betatakin, but an attempt to isolate those features that conceivably might be diagnostic in identifying a kiva will be valuable.

In describing the 135 rooms in the ruin, Judd classified them in six groups: kivas, dwelling rooms, storage rooms, open courts, unidentified rooms, and unexcavated or destroyed rooms. For the purposes of this inquiry we may ignore the storage rooms, which were usually small and relatively featureless, the open courts and the unexcavated and destroyed rooms. There remain twenty rooms that Judd called either kivas or dwelling rooms. The data for sixteen others were too incomplete for their functional identification. Figure 3.1 presents in concise form the features of these rooms to the extent provided by the original report; where a particular item was not mentioned as present there was usually no positive statement that it was lacking but since Judd's notes were pretty carefully compiled its omission from them may probably be taken as evidence of its absence.

A study of Figure 3.1 will reveal several things. First, there were no circular rooms in Betatakin, so that if there were kivas at all they must have been rectangular. Secondly, the five alleged kivas have only one characteristic certainly common to all of them, namely plastered walls. Four of them also possessed firepits, deflectors and a ventilator hole in the wall, and it is very likely (but not stated) that the fifth, Room 55, also had those features, since Judd thought it was "obviously a ceremonial chamber. Like other Betatakin kivas, its special function is evidenced by certain furnishings never present in secular structures." Moreover its walls were smoked (Judd 1930: 35–36).

Room Number	Dimensions in meters	More than 3m. in one dimension	Less than 3m. in both dimensions	Mealing bins	Plastered walls	Sipapu	Door or hatch	Platform	Firepit	Deflector	Wall ventilator hole	Bench	Loom holes	Shelf or niche	Decorated walls	Cist	Remarks
"Kivas"																	
11	3.3 × 2.6	✓			✓		H		✓	✓	✓				✓			
14	2.8 × 2.7		✓		✓	✓	D		✓	✓	✓							Also in Cummings; 1915, p. 277
18	3.5 × 2.8	✓			✓	✓	D		✓	✓	✓							
22	3.0 × 2.2	✓			✓		H		✓	✓	✓	✓			✓			
55	3.8 × 2.2	✓			✓							✓	✓	✓				
"Dwelling Rooms"																	
3	2.9 × 2.1		✓		✓		D		✓	✓			✓					
7	2.6 × 1.8		✓		✓													
27	2.5 × 2.4		✓		✓		D		✓	✓				✓				
29	2.8 × 2.4		✓		✓		H		✓	✓	✓	✓	✓					
30	? × ?													✓				
35	3.2 × 3.1	✓			✓				✓		✓			✓				
39	2.7 × 2.1		✓		✓		D		✓	✓			✓	✓				
43	1.9 × 2.1		✓				D		✓									
66	2.4 × 2.1		✓			✓	D		✓	✓								
79	2.2 × 2.1		✓			✓	D		✓	✓	✓			✓				
81	2.3 × 1.5		✓															
89	1.9 × 1.8		✓				D		✓	✓				✓				
93	2.1 × 1.6		✓				D		✓									
95	2.8 × 2.4		✓			✓	D		✓	✓			✓					
121	3.3 × 2.6	✓					D		✓							✓		
"Unidentified Rooms"																	
4	1.9 × 1.8		✓		✓		D		✓	✓								
16	3.3 × 1.7	✓											✓				Long and narrow
23	1.8 × 1.6	✓							✓								
25	2.8 × 2.6	✓					D		✓	✓	✓		✓			✓	
41	3.6 × 2.1	✓					D		✓	✓							
46	3.2 × 3.1	✓															
48	1.2 × 0.8		✓														
49	4.2 × 1.4	✓					D		✓				✓				
56	3.3 × 1.7	✓		✓													Long and narrow
57	2.9 × 2.1	✓															
75	3.0 × 2.4	✓				✓	✻						✻	✓			✻ Shallow hole 2" diam. in floor near East wall
80	2.0 × 1.8		✓						✓								
82	2.5 × 2.4		✓		✓		D		✓	✓	✓						
117	3.4 × 2.2	✓		✓													
126	2.5 × 2.2	✓							✓			✓					
127	? × ?						D										

Fig. 3.1. Chart of all features of "kivas," "dwelling rooms," and "unidentified rooms" at Betatakin, as reported by Judd (1930), showing room numbers, dimensions, and all recorded characteristics.

Four of the five "kivas" were relatively large, being more than 3 meters [10 feet] in at least one dimension, and the fifth was not much smaller. No other single feature was common to more than two. We might, then, conclude tentatively that a kiva at Betatakin was characterized by relatively large size, plastered walls, firepit, deflector and ventilator. But when we investigate the fifteen alleged "dwelling rooms" we will see that a good many of them possess one or several or, in some cases, all of those same characteristics.

Although in general the "dwelling rooms" are smaller, two of them are of sizes comparable to the "kivas." At least six are definitely stated to have had plastered walls, and very likely others had them also, since that was a general characteristic of Pueblo II and III architecture everywhere. Twelve rooms had firepits, which certainly cannot be regarded as peculiar to kivas anyway, seven had deflectors, and four had ventilators. Two "dwelling rooms" had benches, while only two "kivas" had them. Four "dwellings" and only one "kiva" had loom holes. Five "dwellings" and only one "kiva" had wall niches. One "dwelling" had a floor cist, whereas there was none among the "kivas." Walls decorated with incised markings existed in two "kivas" and not in any "dwelling." Two "kivas" had hatchway entrances, but this occurred in only one "dwelling." Only a single questionable "sipapu" occurred, and this in an unidentified room that also was larger than normal and had some incised decoration on its wall. It would seem that this room was thus as much entitled to be called a kiva as any of the others, especially by reason of its possible sipapu. This is a feature whose presence, if positively established, should serve beyond question to identify a room as a kiva, since its ceremonial significance is such that it could not occur in a purely secular room. But it is not, on the other hand, an essential feature of a kiva (Brew 1946: 211), many of which, in both modern and ancient Pueblo villages, lack them. Furthermore its identification is in many instances open to question, since we cannot be sure that any little hole toward the center of the floor was really a sipapu. Conceivably it might have been a posthole, a ladder socket, a floor cist or something else, and consequently a published identification categorically identifying a sipapu without further description is always suspect; there was certainly a hole in the floor, large or small, round or rectangular, but that it was a sipapu is purely inferential. In many cases doubtless it was such but we should be very careful not to jump to conclusions (Smith 1952a: 72–74).

Even allowing for some incompleteness in the descriptions, it is very difficult to see on what standard Judd based his identifications, for his classifications are certainly not mutually exclusive. Only three rooms, Nos. 11, 22, and 29, possessed hatchways, a feature peculiar to kivas in the Mesa Verde area and elsewhere, but they did not have all the other features in common, and Judd has called two of them kivas and one a dwelling. It looks as if he had had in mind the notion that in a general way kivas were relatively large and tended to possess certain other features, none of which was, however, conclusively diagnostic, and that his estimates were largely subjective or intuitive, as he himself frequently implies by the use of expressions of uncertainty.

This is said in no wise disparagingly. I have pointed out the discrepancies in the Betatakin data only in order to emphasize the belief that even in this highly evolved Pueblo III village the diagnostics of kivas are practically impossible to recognize.

Little else pertinent here has been published for the Kayenta–Marsh Pass–Tsegi–Lower Chinle area but some writers have expressed general views as to the characteristics of kivas there. Cummings thought that the earliest kivas were circular and that the later ones were rectangular (Cummings 1915: 275, 279) and he seemed also to believe that they had to be subterranean and to possess a sipapu (Cummings 1915: 272). Guernsey and Kidder (1921: 26) at one time wrote that ". . . the mere presence of a ventilating apparatus. . . and the subterranean situation. . . are all features perfectly normal in Cliff-dweller kivas." Normal, perhaps, but certainly not universal or exclusive. They added, however, that kivas in the western San Juan area, during Pueblo II and early Pueblo III, were notable for their "variability and characterlessness (Kidder 1924: 72; Kidder and Guernsey 1919: 201; Guernsey and Kidder 1921: 26).

This last observation, originally made over thirty years ago, remains valid, and I am convinced that no workable definition or trait list can be compiled on the basis of present knowledge whereby a kiva can certainly be recognized in the western San Juan area, at least during Pueblo II and early Pueblo III.

ALKALI RIDGE

Because of the great thoroughness with which the data have been amassed and presented, it is also helpful to consider here Brew's report on pit houses and kivas on Alkali Ridge (Brew 1946: 204–205, Table 5). The variability during the Developmental Pueblo Period is nowhere better shown than there, where fourteen kivas and fifteen pit houses are analysed for forty different characteristics. In the majority of cases these characteristics occur in some but not all of the rooms of each class. There are several features that occur in some pit houses but never in kivas: slab or post-supported walls, partitions, floor ridges, and southern antechambers. Two features occur in some kivas, but never in pit houses: coursed masonry and benches. In terms of shape all kivas are round, whereas pit houses are both round and rectangular, and pilasters occur in all kivas but never in pit houses. Even at Alkali Ridge, then, there was a good deal of kiva variability, which will appear much greater when these kivas are compared with those already described from farther west and south. The one feature that was limited to kivas at Alkali Ridge, namely, pilasters, certainly was not a criterion across the San Juan River, where it did not occur at all.

THE PROBLEM OF IDENTIFICATION

As a consequence of this lack of uniformity in kiva architecture even in this part of its homeland there is therefore no acceptable standard by which particular rooms, either above the surface or subterranean, can be certainly identified as kivas in frontier areas like that of the San Francisco Mountain region, where the situation is further complicated by foreign influences. That does not mean, however, that hypothetical identifications cannot be made on consideration of a balance of numerous factors. Looking back over the data already adduced from the home grounds of the Kayenta Branch, it seems to me that the most convincing determinant in most cases lies not in the specific features of any particular room taken in the absolute, but rather in that room's relationship to other rooms in the architectural unit of which it was a part. There is not one architectural feature that is either universally present in all kivas and universally absent from all non-kivas, or vice versa. Every single recognized feature of the rooms described in the preceding pages either may often be absent or may occur reasonably often in rooms of the other class. While I have spelled out the situation at Betatakin most fully, a similar analysis of the other instances listed will produce comparable results. This is not to say that reasonable identifications are not possible, or even that those heretofore made are incorrect. It does imply, however, that the assigned reasons for the determination may often not have been the actual reasons.

It is my feeling that in a large number of cases a given room may have served for both secular and ceremonial uses, and that in most of those cases there is no way whatever of certainly determining the fact. On the other hand, there are many cases in which the relationships of a particular room within its architectural complex, its difference in shape or size from other associated rooms, and its positional relation to them, will be of greater significance in its identification than any or all of its internal features as such. A critical examination of the original reports that have been summarized above will reveal that nearly always the room called a kiva was regarded as such because it differed in some way from the other rooms of its unit, or stood apart from them positionally; and not primarily because it possessed or lacked any particular internal feature or complex of features. For example, in many of the ruins considered, one room was perhaps circular while all the others were rectangular; it was subterranean while the others were built upon the surface; it was relatively larger than most of the others; it stood apart from the others, perhaps to the south or southeast; although obviously contemporary, it possessed the only ventilator or the only bench or recess in the unit. Thus it was set apart; to be a kiva it did not have to be square or round, subterranean or surficial, to be equipped with any particular kind of roof, to possess a ventilator or a bench or even a sipapu. It merely had to be different. Guernsey and Kidder (1921) had this idea in mind, I think, in discussing a room at White Dog Cave in Comb Ridge. A Basket Maker site occupied the cave, but there was also a circular, masonry, subterranean room, equipped with a firepit and ventilator, which pretty clearly represented a much later occupation of what they then called "Cliffdweller" type. They saw that it resembled other rooms that had been called kivas. "On the other hand we have never seen, nor have we read of, a kiva built as is this room all by itself with no living chambers in the vicinity. All kivas with which we are familiar form integral parts of house clusters" (Guernsey and Kidder 1921: 26–27). In other words they were reluctant to regard it as a kiva on its morphological features alone, in view of its peculiarly isolated position.

POSSIBLE KIVAS IN SAN FRANCISCO MOUNTAIN AREA

If the San Juan kiva was evolved during Pueblo II out of an early pit house type of dwelling and did not reach any high degree of specialization or standardization until well into Pueblo III, as is usually believed and very convincingly expounded by Brew (1946: 203–214), then it seems probable that, when this kiva concept, during its transi-

tional period, was introduced, as apparently it was, into an area like
that of the San Francisco Mountains in which one or two differing cultures were also present, it would become manifest in a spectacular galaxy of mutations.

In that region there existed traditions of variously shaped pit
houses both shallow and deep with either side or top entrances, and
with and without ventilators, as well as surface structures of various
sorts. The impingement of a still uncrystallized kiva concept on this
situation could only result in something rather variable and unstable.
Let us look at those rooms or houses in the region that for one reason
or another have been called kivas by their excavators.

At Elden Pueblo, near Flagstaff, a Sinagua site in a cultural position corresponding to Pueblo III, there was a rounded rectangular
room, much larger than any of the other rooms in the pueblo, with a
bench all around, but lacking any other very distinctive features. Dr.
Fewkes, who excavated and partly restored Elden Pueblo, reported
that this room was "half-underground" and that it had a ventilator tunnel through the east wall at floor level. "The vertical portion of this
shaft is enclosed by stone masonry bulging from the external wall of
the room." He found no deflector or firepit, but observed that the
room had "great similarity" to kivas at Marsh Pass (Fewkes 1927: 213,
Fig. 207). Perhaps it had, but no more than to many dwelling rooms.

Since the existence of kivas in Sinagua sites has not up to this
time been established, the proper identification of the large room at
Elden Pueblo is of considerable importance. Fortunately there is additional direct evidence available. Dr. Colton, who was present at the
site during the period of Dr. Fewkes' excavations, says that the room
was not in fact below the level of the ground, and that in the position
at which Fewkes depicts a ventilator there was merely a pile of stones.
He adds, however, that since Dr. Fewkes strongly felt the need for a
kiva somewhere in the ruin, he felt justified in postulating a ventilator
because he thought there ought to be one. It thus becomes apparent
that the evidence for a kiva at Elden can be made to depend only on
the large size of the room in question and the existence of the bench
within it. These features do distinguish it from the other rooms in the
Pueblo, and it may well have had ceremonial function. But its positive
designation as a kiva is obviously quite unwarranted.

At NA 1814, a site of mingled cultures, three miles south of Big
Hawk Valley, there were two surface masonry houses of nine and four
rooms respectively. A short distance to the east of each surface unit

was a subterranean rectangular masonry structure. One (NA 1814E) was unusually large, and had an eastern recess with ventilator beneath it, deflector and firepit (Smith 1952a: 77–80; Colton 1946: 151–152). The other (NA 1814F) had an alcove in the northeast corner, but no recess or bench, a ventilator at the southeast, a firepit, a probable sipapu covered with a board like that at NA 537 and two rows of loom holes (Colton 1946: 152–154, Fig. 87). Again I believe this room may well have been a kiva, not only because it had an apparent sipapu, but because of its positional relation to the surface structure nearby. If the latter was a dwelling, as it seems to have been, then it does not seem likely that a contemporary subterranean structure in close association with it would also have been a dwelling.

At Lebarron Ranch on the rim of Walnut Canyon is situated site NA 521, consisting of a surface pueblo of seven rooms and a rectangular subterranean room of masonry. The latter had a central fireplace, deflector and ventilator, but no bench, recess or other special features, except a round hole in the floor approximately where a sipapu might have been. It was closely similar to Padre Focus pit houses, but its relation to the pueblo strongly suggests that it was a kiva (Colton 1931: 28; 1946: 67–68, Fig. 35).

Heiser Spring Ruin (NA 1754), a site several miles east of Big Hawk Valley, contained a Kayenta component consisting of a masonry surface structure of three rectangular rooms, all large enough for dwelling purposes, and east of it an oval subterranean room, also of masonry, with a bench all around, an eastern recess beneath which passed a ventilator, a firepit, a deflector, possible loom holes, two wall niches and four posts set against the face of the bench; a rectangular hole in the floor west of the firepit might have been a sipapu. That this was a kiva seems almost certain, both because of its internal features and because of its position and association (Hargrave 1933b: 58–64, Figs. 20, 23; Colton 1946: 130–131, Figs. 70, 73). That the features in themselves, however, were not sufficient for identification of the room as a kiva was emphasized by Hargrave, who pointed out that any or all of them are known to have occurred in pit houses that were certainly not kivas. And he adds that "we must look outside the structure for an explanation of its use" (Hargrave 1933b: 64).

The Citadel (NA 355), two miles northeast of the Big Hawk sites, another Kayenta pueblo of about thirty rooms, has never been fully excavated, and in two published descriptions by Colton no reference is made to possible kivas (Colton 1932: 33–36, Fig. 15; 1946:

52–53, Fig. 25). On the other hand an earlier report by Barrett mentions a "rectangular kiva" 13 feet by 11 feet; it had a wall niche but no bench; and no further details are supplied (Barrett 1927: 46–47, Figs. 34, 40). Since this pueblo belonged to the Klethla Focus of middle Pueblo III, however, it would seem likely that it did have a kiva, even though its objective features were not very distinctive.

At Nalakihu, near the Citadel, King reports that one room "displayed features which hint strongly the room had once been used as a kiva: e.g., firepit, hole for deflector, hole possibly for ladder base, and possible sipapu. Other floor features exist, but it is significant that the above named, and those only, were plastered over, presumably when a second story was added and Room 2 was converted into a storeroom; (King 1949: 22, 50). With reference to another room King points to the presence of ventilator, firepit and loom holes as possibly suggesting its use as a kiva, but adds cautiously that those features "are not sufficient to establish" it as such (King 1949: 30).

The only other sites in the general region in which possible kivas have been described are Wupatki (NA 405) and Crack-in-Rock (NA 537). The latter pretty certainly had a kiva (Smith 1952a: 70–75). At Wupatki, a mixed site with a Klethla focus component, there was a very large circular surface structure of masonry, 50 feet in diameter, with a northeast entrance, a bench all around and a firepit. No means for supporting a roof were found but this room may have served as a kiva (Colton 1946: 57, Figs. 28, 30).

In recapitulation, then, it seems to me that the certain determination of any given structure as a kiva during Pueblo II and early Pueblo III in the San Francisco Mountain area is a well-nigh impossible task, but that reasonable hypothetical identifications can be made by a broad consideration of the morphological features of the room in connection with its positional relationships. On this basis I believe that very likely the three subterranean structures at NA 680, NA 681 and NA 682 were all kivas. That at NA 682 was most convincingly so, because it had most of the features, excepting only the bench, that might be expected in a kiva, and it bore an appropriate relation to its surface pueblo. That at NA 680 is slightly less convincing, since its possession of a sipapu was not certain, though in other respects it was kiva-like and it too was properly located with reference to the surface structure. That both of these rooms were quite unlike the rectangular masonry pit house of contemporary Sinagua sites provides additional evidence that they were kivas. The subterranean room at NA 681 is more problematical. It possesses no feature that could not have been found in a contemporary Sinagua pit house of the Padre Focus, and in fact was strikingly like most of them. On the other hand there was almost no ceramic or other evidence of Sinagua origin at NA 681, and the entire site seemed to belong to the Kayenta Branch. That being so, and the positional relationship of the subterranean room to the surface pueblo being identical with that at NA 680 and NA 681, I feel that it was very likely used as a kiva.

4. D-Shaped Features

Although there are some differences of opinion as to when, or even whether, the pit house became a kiva (Lekson 1988), there seems to be general agreement that there were three kinds of kivas. During the sixteenth century, the Spanish explorers observed that a circular kiva was typical of the Eastern Pueblo region and that a rectangular kiva was characteristic of the Western Pueblos. The fourteenth- and fifteenth-century kivas of the late prehistoric periods were comparable to the historically recorded structures (Kidder 1958; Hodge 1939; Smith 1972). However, the thirteenth-century forms of the Pueblo III period were either circular (Brew 1946) or D-shaped (Smith 1972).

The D-shaped kiva may be nothing more than a circular kiva with one side flattened and some of the D-shaped kivas may have served more domestic than ceremonial purposes (Lekson 1988). Other D-shaped buildings, though, exhibit so many "kiva features" and stand out so distinctly from other structures at the sites where they are found that it seems appropriate to many to consider them as kivas. As a result of these differing views of kiva development, the D-shaped kiva has a unique place in the history of Southwestern archaeology. Among the various excavated structures that have contributed to this special historical status of the D-shaped kiva, none can claim the fame that is enjoyed by two such kivas excavated by the Awatovi Expedition. Although no D-shaped kivas were discovered at Awatovi itself, several were found at other sites on Antelope Mesa.

The first important D-shaped kiva, Room 8 at Jeddito Site 111 about 2.5 miles northeast of Awatovi, was being excavated in

August of 1939 when Alfred Vincent Kidder visited the Awatovi
Expedition. Kidder, the first professionally trained North American
archaeologist (Ph. D. at Harvard in 1914), had moved American
archaeology away from its antiquarian beginnings toward a more
systematic approach to the study of the past (Woodbury 1973). His
many years of exploration and excavation in the Southwest led to
the first synthesis of the archaeology of that region (Kidder 1924).
He then turned his attention to Mesoamerica where he directed
the Maya program of the Carnegie Institution of Washington. In
1939 he was visiting Awatovi and other archaeological sites with
Vannevar Bush, the new President of the Carnegie Institution, who
was in the process of reducing Carnegie's investment in archaeology
(Willey 1988: 304). Watson Smith (1984a: 192) said of the visit that
he thought "Kidder felt that our camp was an exemplary demon-
stration of archaeological endeavor that would appeal to Dr. Bush
and induce in him a mental climate of kindliness toward the sort of
thing that Carnegie was doing in archaeology."

Kidder did not dissuade Bush from ultimately terminating the
Carnegie Maya Program, but he did bestow on the D-shaped kiva
at Site 111 a permanent place in the history of Southwestern
archaeology by making it the subject of one his famous stick-figure
cartoons. He had developed these cartoons to entertain his children, but soon found that they were also enjoyed by his professional colleagues (Wauchope 1965: 164–165; Woodbury 1989:
xi–xii). Watson Smith (1972, Fig. 92) wisely included Kidder's
Awatovi cartoon in his account of the D-shaped kiva at Site 111. It
is reproduced here (Fig. 4.1) as evidence that both Kidder and
Smith derive part of their legendary status from their ability as
practitioners of the lighter side of archaeology. Their writings are
replete with delightful reminders that archaeologists should not
take themselves too seriously. Kidder's cartoon also serves as an
affectionate tribute to John Otis Brew, the portly Director of the
Awatovi Expedition, who, years later, was the director of my doctoral dissertation (Thompson 1958), as he had been of Richard
Woodbury's (1954).

The second important D-shaped kiva found by the Awatovi
Expedition is the well-preserved structure at Jeddito Site 4 excavated by Charles Avery Amsden of the Southwest Museum in Los
Angeles. Amsden began his archaeological career in 1914 as a teen-
ager with Kidder on a trip into the San Juan country. His very

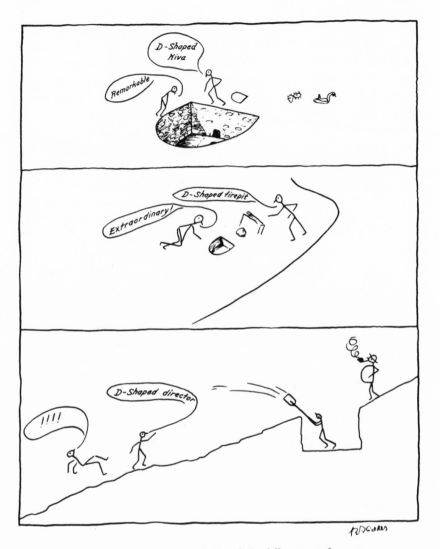

Fig. 4.1. D-shaped director. Smith offered the following information as caption for the final illustration in his "Prehistoric Kivas of Antelope Mesa" (Smith 1972, Fig. 92): "In August, 1939, Dr. A. V. Kidder visited the Jeddito excavations. At Room 8 of Site 111, accompanied by the Field Director, Dr. J. O. Brew, his keen archaeological eye noted certain remarkable morphological coincidences, which he recorded in the field drawing reproduced herewith."

promising archaeological career was cut short in his forty-second year after a long illness. Kidder (1949) wrote eloquently of Amsden in an Introduction to his posthumously published popular book on Southwestern prehistory (Amsden 1949). In an effort to describe the kind of archaeologist Amsden was, Kidder (1949: xi, compare De Laet 1957: 13–14) identified two famous archaeological stereotypes:

> In popular belief, and unfortunately to some extent in fact, there are two sorts of archaeologists, the hairy-chested and the hairy-chinned. Happily, the hairy-chested variety rarely occurs save in the rotogravure sections of the Sunday papers and in the advertisements of a certain well-known brand of whiskey. There one sees him as a strong-jawed young man in a tropical helmet, pistol on hip, hacking his way through the jungle in search of lost cities and buried treasure. His boots, always highly polished, reach to his knees, presumably for protection against black mambas and other sorts of deadly serpents. The only concession he makes to the difficulties and dangers of his calling is to have his shirt enough unbuttoned to reveal the manliness of his bosom.
>
> The hairy-chinned archaeologist exists, for the greater part, in the *Saturday Evening Post* and *Colliers*, usually as the father of a beautiful girl in jodhpurs. He is old. He is benevolently absent-minded. His only weapon is a magnifying glass, with which he scrutinizes inscriptions in forgotten languages. Usually his triumphant decipherment coincides, in the last chapter, with his daughter's rescue from savages by the handsome young assistant.

Kidder went on to explain that Amsden was neither a hairy-chested adventurer seeking only things nor a hairy-chinned epigrapher interested only in translations, but rather an archaeologist who prized "the product of his excavations not as curious or beautiful or rare objects. . . , but as documents that throw light on the lives of human beings."

Charles Avery Amsden was a valued but, because of his poor health, an irregular member of the Awatovi Expedition. It was he who suggested (Brew 1949c: xix; Smith 1984a: 152) that Ross Montgomery, a Los Angeles architect interested in the Spanish missions in northern New Spain, be invited to assist in the excavation and interpretation of the ruins of the Franciscan mission at Awatovi

(Montgomery 1949). Montgomery, Smith, and Brew (1949) dedicated their monograph on "Franciscan Awatovi" to Amsden's
memory. Amsden's primary responsibility at Awatovi was the
supervision of the excavations at Site 4. His careful and detailed
notes on the D-shaped kiva there were the basis of Watson Smith's
published description of it (Smith 1972: 126–131). The Smith-
Amsden collaboration is probably the best report on a D-shaped
kiva in the archaeological literature of the Southwest.

R. H. T.

The Kiva at Site 4

A small pueblo II–III site designated Jeddito 4 was situated near the southeastern escarpment of Antelope Mesa, a short distance downstream from the Jeddito Trading Post and about 100 meters northeast from Site 4A. It consisted of a single row of at least ten masonry surface rooms arranged in a northeast-southwest orientation, with three or four small outlying masonry structures that may have been either dwelling units or storage rooms. Its excavation was supervised by the late Dr. Charles A. Amsden, and the following description is adapted from his field notes.

Approximately in front of the third room from the northeasterly end of the main row and about 9 m southeasterly from it was a subterranean kiva, the floor of which was just over 1.50 m below the modern surface. This kiva was markedly D-shaped, one of several examples of this unusual form discovered in the Jeddito region (Figs. 4.2, 4.3). The rear boundary of the floor area, which was defined by the face of a rear bench, was straight and measured 3.60 m across. The front and sides were defined by a continuously curved wall which splayed slightly outward from the two rear corners, in arcs of relatively long radius, to opposite points approximately 2.25 m from the rear boundary where they were 3.90 m apart. Thence these side walls converged toward the front along arcs of somewhat shorter radius until they merged at a point 4.00 m from the rear boundary of the floor

Reprinted with the permission of the Peabody Museum from "Prehistoric Kivas of Antelope Mesa, Northeastern Arizona," by Watson Smith, pages 126-131, *Papers of the Peabody Museum of American Archaeology and Ethnology*, Volume 39, Number 1, Harvard University, 1972.

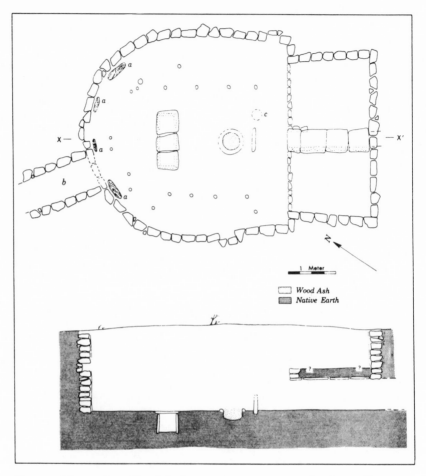

Fig. 4.2. Plan and profile of the kiva at Site 4. Four wooden battenlike objects (a) lay on the floor near the front wall, and a gray corrugated jar had been set into a cavity beneath the floor (c). A subterranean passage-way (b) led from the kiva to a point below one of the rooms of the asso-ciated pueblo, to which a vertical shaft gave access through the floor of the room.

area. The rear boundary coincided along most of its length with the face of a bench, although the bench itself measured only 2.90 m along its face. This was 70 cm less than the full length of the rear boundary of the floor area, which thus extended about 35 cm beyond the bench at each end. The bench thus occupied what might be called an alcove or recess. It extended rearward to a breadth of 1.70 m, but its ends diverged slightly so that its rear wall was 3.15 m long.

Fig. 4.3. Rear portion of the D-shaped kiva at Site 4, showing bench with ventilator tunnel, deflector, and clay-lined, basin-shaped firepit with raised coping. Adjacent to the deflector was a pit containing a broken utility jar. Note characteristic Pueblo II masonry of the walls, and the loom-anchor holes set into the hard clay floor.

The floor of the kiva was approximately 1.50 m below the modern ground surface and the surface of the bench was between 85 cm and 1.00 m above the floor. The kiva was oriented about N 38 W.

The face of the rear bench was constructed of well-laid masonry of about seven courses of sandstone blocks similar to those used in the main walls of the room. No paving slabs were found on the surface of the bench except a row that formed the roof for a ventilator tunnel. The tunnel lay almost exactly along the midline of the bench and perpendicular to its face. Its side walls were of masonry and its cover, as stated, was formed of stone slabs laid horizontally across the tunnel and supported by the side walls. These covering slabs were slightly lower than the topmost course of the masonry in the face of the bench, and had probably not constituted a part of the original surface, which must have been at a higher level and may have been formed of earth or other slabs. The tunnel was rather narrow, being only 30 cm wide by about 65 cm high. No investigation was made of the vertical ventilator shaft outside the rear wall.

The floor of the kiva itself was of hard, light-colored, mud plaster about 2 cm thick laid over a bed of clean sand. A firepit was located 1.00 m in front of the face of the bench, 1.60 m from the left wall, and 1.90 m from the right. It was almost circular, 40 cm in diameter by 20 cm in depth, with vertical sides and a slightly concave bottom, and was completely lined with clay. It was surrounded by a convex coping 7 cm high and about 12 cm wide at floor level. The firepit contained only wood ashes. A stone slab serving as a deflector was set upright in the floor between the mouth of the ventilator and the firepit and 20 cm from the latter. Its exact dimensions were not recorded.

About 45 cm forward from the firepit a rectangular box was sunk through the floor. It was 1.10 m long by 30 cm wide by 45 cm deep, its longer dimension transverse to the midline of the room. This box was lined with upright stone slabs and had an earth bottom. It was covered with stone slabs inset into the kiva floor so that their upper surfaces were flush with it. It probably represented a sipapu and may have served as a resonator or footdrum, as in many kivas at Awatovi and Kawaika-a as well as in modern Hopi kivas.

About 15 cm to the right of the deflector a gray corrugated jar had been set into a cavity in the floor about 30 cm deep. It appeared to have been already broken at the time of its emplacement, and had probably once served as the lining for a storage cist.

At least eighteen small, neatly made, circular holes, varying between 5 cm and 8 cm in diameter, penetrated the earthen floor. Two rows of five each, which must have been used as receptacles for loom anchors (Smith 1972: 121–123), extended parallel to the midline of the kiva and from 65 to 80 cm from left and right walls, respectively. Intervals between holes varied from 25 to 70 cm, and each row was about 2.20 m long. The other eight holes were haphazardly distributed and are shown in Figure 4.2.

The purpose of these latter holes was not clear. Similar haphazard distribution has been referred to in descriptions of Pueblo IV kivas, where they occurred in large stone paving slabs. The hypothesis has been proposed that they had originally been drilled as loom-anchor holes in slabs located elsewhere, and that their irregular arrangement resulted from the removal of the slabs from their original positions, and their later installation in other kivas where their earlier and more orderly arrangements were lost. This hypothesis can hardly apply, however, to holes in an earth floor without separable segments that can be moved about independently like paving slabs. Another explanation must, therefore, be sought. Some of the holes might have served as postholes; others possibly as receptacles for prayer sticks (pahos) or standards such as are often used in modern Hopi ceremonials, although there has been found no convincing evidence of the latter usage.

The roof of the kiva had burned, probably at or just after the time of abandonment because its charred remnants lay directly upon the floor. Although the exact form of the original roof structure could not be ascertained, the surviving fragments provided clues that suggested its arrangement. Two main beams had extended across the kiva, and since there was no evidence of supporting pilasters or posts, they must have rested directly upon the walls. Judged from the position of the remnants lying on the floor, one beam had apparently been placed just above the face of the bench, and the other about midway between it and the extreme front of the kiva. These beams appeared to have been from 20 to 25 cm in diameter, and of course must have been at least 4.50 to 5.00 m long.

Two similar beams about 1.00 m apart may have spanned the area between the two main beams at right angles to them. On these secondary beams was probably erected the frame for a hatchway. In a rough radial pattern over the main and secondary beams were laid numerous smaller poles perhaps about 6 to 7 cm thick, extending outward from the beams to the masonry walls. Upon these poles was a mat of coarse grass, sometimes in double layers at right angles, and from 2 to 3 cm thick. This mat was chinked here and there in its low spots with bundles of juniper bark, evidently to provide an even surface. The whole fabric was then covered with a layer of clay 4 to 10 cm thick. A hypothetical reconstruction of the roof is shown in Figure 4.4, although it is admittedly imprecise in detail.

The walls of the entire structure were of unusually good masonry of evenly coursed sandstone blocks, most of them approximately rectangular though some were trapezoidal or trapeziform. The blocks were not artificially dressed but had been selected and laid so that naturally straight edges formed the exposed surface of the wall, while the unexposed edges remained irregular. The blocks varied in size around an average 30 cm long by 20 cm thick by 20 cm broad. They were laid

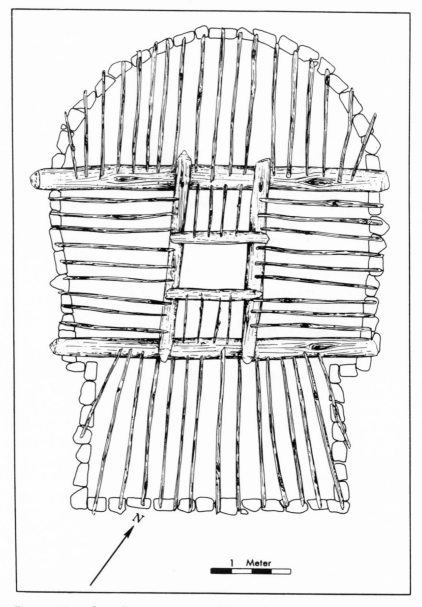

Fig. 4.4. Hypothetical reconstruction of the roof framework on the kiva at Site 4. This pattern was inferred by Charles A. Amsden from charred remains found upon the floor, where they lay in essentially their original relationships.

in a bedding of adobe mortar from 2 to 10 cm thick and without spalls. The surfaces of the walls had been plastered with a brownish silty material to a thickness of about 1 cm, but no evidence of painted decoration was found.

Three niches had been let into the walls, all of nearly the same dimensions. They were formed simply by the removal of one component block in the masonry although sometimes vertical slabs had been set to form the sides and to support the top. One was almost exactly at the center of the frontal curve of the room, 80 cm above the floor and 23 cm high. Another was in the right wall almost at its rear corner, 92 cm above the floor and 20 cm high. The third was in the left wall, about 1.00 m from the rear corner, 91 cm above the floor and 20 cm high. The depth of the niches was not recorded. All were empty.

An opening through the front wall, about 50 cm to the left of the foremost point in the curve, led into a passageway that extended northwesterly to a point beneath one of the row of surface rooms that formed the pueblo, where a pit through the floor provided access to it. The bottom of this passageway was about 1.00 m above the floor of the kiva and it was about 60 cm wide, supported by parallel masonry walls, which had partly collapsed, however. Its height was indeterminate, and there remained no trace of a roof or lintel. This tunnel must have been a communicating link with the domestic rooms of the pueblo.

Several artifacts were found on the floor of the kiva, including a slab of sandstone with abraded channels, as if used for sharpening bone awls, a fragment of an ovoid mano, a roughly rounded hammerstone, and two squared stones suggesting floor smoothers. Beside these nondescript items were four badly charred wooden objects that somewhat resembled weaving battens. They were all elongated, flattened, and rounded along their edges and at their ends. Two were almost 50 cm long and two considerably shorter, although the latter may have been fragmentary. All lay on the floor, very close to the curved front wall and parallel to it. They are shown in situ in Figure 4.2.

Of the numerous charred remnants of the roof that lay upon the floor, Edward T. Hall dated thirty-six specimens (some of which may have come originally from the same log) at dates between 1253 + 3 and 1257 + 2. He noted that outside rings were well preserved and that the logs had perhaps been cut and stock-piled over a short period of years before being incorporated into the structure, a custom that prevails among the Hopis and other Indians in the Southwest today.

Five of the same specimens were dated by the Laboratory of Tree-Ring Research of the University of Arizona at 1235, 1253, 1255, and 1275, respectively (Bannister, Robinson, and Warren 1967: 31). The authors of that report express the opinion that construction probably occurred just after 1255, and that the date of 1275 may represent later repair. They are thus in almost exact agreement with Hall.

Three small charred branches found in the firepit were dated by Hall at 1282–83. He remarked that in each case the outer rings were present and the surfaces showed no effects of prolonged weathering, suggesting that they had been used in the firepit very soon after having been cut. Thus it may be inferred that the kiva was in use for approximately thirty years.

Although some components of the site may have been built and occupied during Pueblo II, it seems clear that the D-shaped kiva was built and used during middle or late Pueblo III.

5. *The Kiva Beneath the Altar*

The closing decades of the twentieth century have not been good years for the preservation and continuity of American Indian traditions, languages, and religions. The inexorable forces of change have caused the loss or serious deterioration of many of the traditional ways of life that had survived reasonably intact into this century. Many Indian communities are understandably concerned and justifiably alarmed about the rapid pace of the change that has caused massive loss of their cultural heritage.

At a time in the history of this country when Americans of diverse origins are vigorously and successfully searching for their roots, Native Americans find themselves at a frustrating disadvantage in dealing with their past. Some communities have developed culture centers and museums, sponsored oral history programs, and stimulated interest in learning and recording their native language. Others, with little or nothing of their culture remaining to preserve, have tried to rescue whatever is left in order to recreate their heritage. In those cases in which the isolation from traditional culture is extreme, they have even set about to re-invent their past, their traditions, and their religion.

Fortunately, there are some striking exceptions to this generally bleak situation, especially among the Indian cultures of the Southwest. The Hopi Indians, who live in the mesa country of northern Arizona, are an interesting example of a people who have achieved great success in the majority culture without giving up their traditional practices or losing the vitality of their culture. They were uniquely successful during the Spanish Colonial period in resisting the efforts of both civil and religious authorities to bring them under Spanish control (Brew 1949b; Adams 1989). Spicer (1962: 189) has emphasized the uniqueness of the history of Spanish-Hopi contacts: "It is the story of an Indian group... able to fend off further contacts and go its own way."

The isolation of the Hopi from the center of Spanish settlement in the Upper Rio Grande valley, the lack of surface water for irrigation, and the diplomatic skill that their leaders displayed in dealing with the Spanish protected them from outside domination until almost the end of the last century, when the United States government began to extend its influence into the Hopi towns (Spicer 1962: 200–205; Adams 1989). By that time, the Hopi, more than any other group of Pueblo Indians, had learned how to adjust to the outside world without abandoning their values, losing their faith, or sacrificing their traditions.

That the Hopi should have achieved and maintained this somewhat unusual degree of control over their lives and their heritage comes as no surprise to anyone who is familiar with the history of Awatovi (Brew 1949b). It was at this easternmost of the historic Hopi towns that the Franciscan missionaries were able to establish a precarious foothold in Hopi country early in the seventeenth century. Only the people of Awatovi requested the return of Spanish missionaries after the Pueblo Rebellion of 1680. According to both Hopi and Spanish accounts, before the Franciscans were able to reestablish their mission, warriors from other Hopi villages destroyed Awatovi, killing many of the men and placing some of the women and children in the remaining Hopi villages (Brew 1949b: 19–23; Spicer 1962: 192–193; Adams 1989: 83–84). This decisive action in 1700 ended effective Christian missionary activity among the Hopi for almost 200 years, allowing Hopi religious beliefs and practices to survive to this day with a remarkable degree of vitality and integrity.

The clash between the Hopi and Christian religions was strikingly documented by the archaeological discovery of the "kiva beneath the altar" at Awatovi. The Franciscan missionaries, following an old Spanish tradition of superposition (Montgomery 1949: 134–137, 265–672), built their church on top of a kiva, which they left undisturbed and filled with clean sand (Brew 1949a: 65–67). That action on the part of the Spaniards assured that the superimposed kiva would be the best preserved of the thirty-odd kivas excavated by the Awatovi Expedition almost three hundred years later. The roof and the walls were essentially intact and the paintings on the walls were the most complete of the many paintings found at Awatovi and Kawaika-a. Despite the Spanish intentions, the kiva beneath the altar is now a symbol of the persistence rather than the replacement of the Hopi religion.

Ruined structures have long enjoyed a special place in our romantic notions of the past (Lowenthal 1985: 168–169; Macaulay 1953), but they usually stand as reminders of the demise of ancient glories (Stoneman 1987: 144, 301). Smith, whose description of the "kiva beneath the altar" follows (Smith 1972:59-66), knew that ruins also serve as symbols of continuity from the past. He began to become aware of some of that symbolism as expressed in poetic form during a return by steamship from a European tour in 1923. He spent a good deal of time on that trip reading in a newly acquired book of English verse that he reported "was opening new vistas to my mind" (Smith 1984b: 670). These vistas included an appreciation for the powerful and suggestive imagery of poetry.

Armed with this appreciation, Smith later discovered the evocative view of the past presented by Percy Bysshe Shelley in a sonnet written in 1818 just before he left England for Italy where he spent his final years (Drabble 1985). The sonnet was devoted to the ruins of a monument to Rameses II at Thebes that had been identified as the tomb of Ozymandias by Diodorus Siculus, a Roman author who compiled a world history in Greek during the first century B.C. (Harvey 1981; Hammond and Scullard 1970). In the sonnet "Ozymandias," Shelley, inspired by the awesomeness of the ruined monument, commented on the fragility of ancient grandeur. Smith (1972: 125) called upon that same imagery to emphasize the continuity of the Hopi way: "Ozymandias has fallen on his face, but the Hopi kachinas still stand erect in their ancestral kivas."

R. H. T.

Room 788

The kiva designated room 788 (Fig. 5.1) was the most exciting and revealing among those excavated at Awatovi and Kawaika-a. Its very location was provocative, situated as it was directly beneath parts of the sanctuary and sacristy of the mission Church of San Bernardo. Before discussing the significance of this fact, however, we shall describe the kiva objectively.

Room 788 was almost precisely rectangular, and was thus more nearly accurate in shape than were most rooms or kivas at Awatovi. It measured 3.40 m across the front wall, 3.55 m across the rear, 4.65 m along the left, and 4.75 m along the right, and was oriented about N 20° W. The left-front and right-rear corners were very slightly more than right angles, the other corners slightly less. The floor was 3.15 m below the floor of the predella in the sanctuary of the superimposed church, and 2.50 m below the floor of the nave (Fig. 5.8). About 1.90 m above the floor of the kiva and well below that of the church was the kiva roof, which had survived almost intact.

Across the rear (southeast) end of the kiva was a bench from 1.10 m to 1.20 m broad and 37 cm high (Fig. 5.2). The face of this bench was made of fairly substantial masonry composed of sandstone blocks of varying sizes, but mostly rectangular and carefully laid in a manner approaching regular courses. The surface of the bench was completely paved with large sandstone slabs of irregular shape and varying size, but their generous dimensions are indicated by the statement that only twelve slabs served to cover the entire area (Fig. 5.1).

Reprinted with the permission of the Peabody Museum from "Prehistoric Kivas of Antelope Mesa, Northeastern Arizona," by Watson Smith, pages 59-66, *Papers of the Peabody Museum of American Archaeology and Ethnology*, Volume 39, Number 1, Harvard University, 1972.

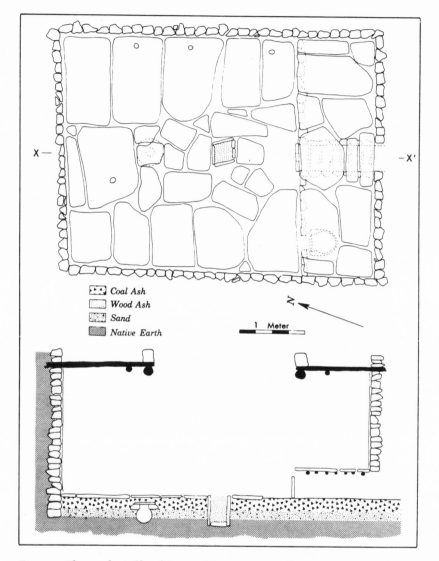

Fig. 5.1. Plan and profile of Room 788 at Awatovi, showing positions of a utility jar beneath the left-hand side of the rear bench, and a jar-shaped pit (sipapu?) below the floor near the front wall. The positions of the roof beams and hatchway coping are also indicated.

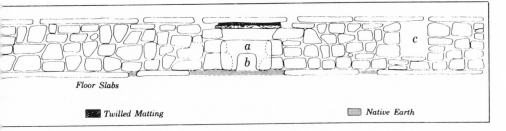

Floor Slabs

▓▓ Twilled Matting   ▦ Native Earth

Fig. 5.2. Elevation of the rear bench in Room 788 at Awatovi. The mouth of the ventilator tunnel was partly closed by a vertical stone slab (a), which was pierced by a rectangular hole (b). A twilled mat of rushes lay upon the roof beams of the tunnel. Access to a cist beneath the bench was provided by the opening (c).

Transversely beneath the bench and exactly along the midline ran a ventilator tunnel 36 cm wide and about 25 cm high. Its sides were formed of irregular masonry, and its floor was not paved. The tunnel extended through the rear wall beyond which rose a vertical shaft, the details of which were not precisely recorded.

Across the mouth of the tunnel and snugly against the face of the bench was set a rectangular slab of stone about 38 cm wide by about 20 cm high with a rounded rectangular hole through its lower portion about 12 cm high by about 15 cm wide, very closely similar to the analogous arrangement in Kiva A. The effect was to reduce the size of the opening and thereby also to reduce the volume of air admitted through it (Fig. 5.2).

Within the tunnel were eight accurately ground stone balls. Similar collections occurred in the ventilator tunnel of Test 31, Room 1, and in the jar that was set under the rear bench in Test 14, Room 5. Their possible significance and use [in kicking races, for imitating thunder, or as clubs] are discussed by Woodbury (1954: 171–173). The tunnel was roofed by seven wooden beams set irregularly across it and supported by its masonry side walls (Fig. 5.3), and directly upon the beams lay a mat of rushes woven in a twilled pattern exactly like other mats that were sometimes used on walls to support the overlying plaster (Smith 1972, Figs. 68 *e*, 69). These mats will be discussed below. Over the mat was a coating of adobe from 2 to 5 cm thick, and upon this rested the surface paving slabs. This arrangement was used also in the other kivas, notably in Room 529.

A cist penetrated the left (or southwest) half of the face of the

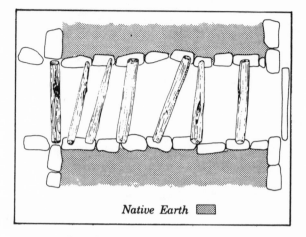

Native Earth

Fig. 5.3. Plan of roof structure of ventilator tunnel through the rear bench of Room 788 at Awatovi.

bench, about 40 cm from its left end, and about 20 cm wide by 25 cm high (Fig. 5.4). Its sill was formed of a thin slab of sandstone and the paving slabs on top of the bench formed its cover. Behind this cist was emplaced a large globular yellow corrugated jar, 32 cm deep with a mouth 30 cm in diameter. It was set at an angle of about 45° to the horizontal, upper and lower points of the rim being in contact with the sill and roof of the cist. It contained only a few seeds, apparently squash. This feature was homologous to similar arrangements in several other kivas (Smith 1972, Figs. 12, 34, 52, 56). No benches existed along the left, right, or front walls.

The entire floor of the kiva was paved with large slabs of sandstone, neatly fitted, most of them roughly rectangular. About 1.00 m from the mouth of the ventilator tunnel, and midway between the right and left walls, a firepit was let into the floor. This pit was a rhombus in plan, each side measuring about 28 cm long. Each of three sides was formed by a single, upright slab, but the north side consisted of two adjacent slabs. The pit was 44 cm deep, paved with a single slab, and filled with wood ash and charcoal. A tubular clay pipe with an incised decoration was found in the fill.

No deflector was found between the firepit and the ventilator tunnel, but its function was probably served by the slab that was placed, as already mentioned, across the mouth of the tunnel, partially blocking the inflow of air.

Below the floor toward the front of the room, 1.10 m from the

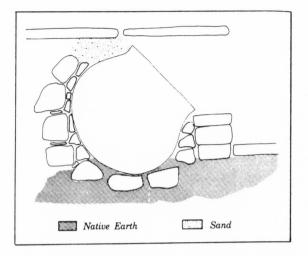

Native Earth   Sand

Fig. 5.4. Profile of a cist containing a globular utility jar under the rear bench in Room 788 at Awatovi.

front wall and midway between the right and left walls, was a construction that must have represented a sipapu. At first this was not discovered because it was completely obscured by the paving slabs of the floor. On subsequent investigation, however, one such slab was removed, and a few centimeters beneath it was found a thin triangular slab measuring between 40 and 50 cm on each edge, and only about 1 cm thick. This thin slab lay directly upon a circular collar of modeled but unbaked clay, flat on its lower surface but rounded on its outer and upper surfaces, exactly like the upper half of a doughnut. This collar was about 40 cm in outer diameter by about 8 cm high. The orifice was almost circular, 14 to 15 cm in diameter. Below the orifice a globular pocket had been excavated into the underlying strata, its profile closely approximating that of a large-mouth jar, although no actual jar had been emplaced.

The rounded bottom of the pocket had been dug into pure native clay to a depth of about 12 cm. Over the clay was a thin stratum of clean sand about 2 cm thick, above this a layer of mixed sand and black coal ash about 6 cm thick, then a second stratum of clean sand about 4 cm thick, and finally about 16 cm of red coal ash. The floor slabs of the kiva lay directly upon this uppermost ash layer, and the clay doughnut and its cover slab were surrounded by it. Below the doughnut, where the excavation penetrated the successive layers of sand and ash, a clay lining or facing had been modeled to support the loose surrounding

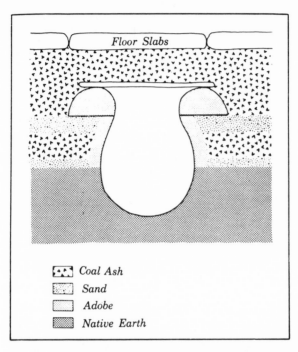

Fig. 5.5. Profile of probable sipapu beneath the floor of Room 788 at Awatovi, showing a jar-shaped pocket and doughnut-shaped clay ring forming its neck.

material and prevent its collapse into the pocket. No supporting lining was necessary in the underlying clay bed. The height of the pocket was about 26 cm and its maximum diameter, which occurred at the contact between the clay bed and the immediately overlying sand, about 22 cm. This sipapu, if indeed it was one, is illustrated in profile in Figure 5.5. It contained nothing. The whole thing was puzzling because it had been completely covered by the uppermost ash layer and sealed by the floor-paving slabs, periodic removal of which had clearly not been intended. Nor was there surviving evidence of an earlier floor, flush with the orifice of the sipapu, although such a floor might once have existed and have been entirely removed before the installation of the surviving floor found at the time of excavation.

Numerous circular holes were drilled through the slabs of the floor and of the surface of the bench. These had probably been for the purpose of inserting loom anchors. Five were arranged in a straight row about 25 cm from the left wall, at intervals of between 20 and 30 cm. Three holes were in a similar row about 15 to 25 cm from the right wall, spaced about 70 cm and 1.00 m apart, respectively. Other holes were randomly placed and probably had been drilled when the slabs in which they occurred had been in use in another room, from which they had been robbed for placement in Room 788. On the floor was found a small fragment of turquoise.

The walls of this kiva were of the usual rather slovenly masonry characteristic of all the late pre-Spanish rooms of the village, but they were rather more nearly straight and vertical than most. This condition was probably due to the fact that the roof remained almost intact, and the walls beneath it had not collapsed.

The walls on all interior faces had been heavily plastered, and although the extreme upper areas of plaster had fallen in irregular patches and a few centimeters along the base had eroded away, this room exhibited by far the most extensively preserved mural coverings and painted decorations that were found at Awatovi or Kawaika-a. The method of construction by which plaster was applied and supported was perfectly exemplified here. Directly over the masonry surface had been applied a thin coating of gray adobe mortar of variable thickness to produce a fairly even surface over the irregular stones of the masonry. Into this mortar was pressed a mass of grass and reeds, arranged horizontally and composed mostly of reeds from 2 or 3 mm to 6 or 7 mm in diameter. More adobe was then applied over the reeds and grass and firmly consolidated with the underlying material.

After application of the outer coatings of adobe, long sections of roots or vines up to 1.50 m long and from 5 to 15 mm in diameter were pressed into the fresh adobe in a generally vertical position. These roots or vines were usually laid in pairs, not twined but snugly parallel, or sometimes singly, and extended from floor to roof, at horizontal intervals of from 25 to 35 cm. Over this reinforced undercoat was then applied the reddish sandy plaster that was used generally on all kivas as a finish coat for the application of painted designs. Similar reinforcement was used in Kiva A, Test 22, Room 10, and other kivas (Smith 1972, Fig. 68 f).

In the corner areas, where two contiguous walls intersected, a different sort of reinforcement was used. Here were strips of matting woven in a rectangular twill in a two-over-two-under pattern, apparently to provide a strong and continuous backing for the plaster as it rounded the corner. The fabric was formed of groups of four or five parallel reeds, each about 1.5 to 2.5 mm in diameter (Smith 1972, Fig. 69 a). Similar mats had been used on the walls of Kiva A, Room 529, and Test 19, Room 3, but the elements of the fabric in those kivas lay diagonally with relation to one another. Furthermore in Test 19, Room 3, the mats were used not only in corners but along the entire lower parts of the right and left walls to a height of from 15 to 20 cm above the floor. Bundles of reeds had been used also in Test 22, Room 10.

No vestige of the underlying reinforcement of grass and reeds nor of the twilled matting had survived in any case, but clear impressions of both occurred in many places (Smith 1972, Fig. 68 e; 1952b: 14–15, Figs. 5, 34 b, d). Some of the vertical vines or roots however, were preserved, but have not been botanically identified.

Numerous coats of finish plaster covered each wall and, although the total number was not exactly determined, those that had carried painted decoration were recorded and numbered. Of these, there were fourteen on the left wall, nine on the right wall, one on the front wall, and two on the rear wall. Of those that were sufficiently well preserved for classification, all belonged to Layout Group 1. They were among the most nearly complete and complex designs found in any kiva and have been fully discussed and reproduced in Smith (1952b, Figs. 35 a–d, 38 a, b, 39 a, 67 a, 71 b, 76 c, 77 a, 78 a, b, 79 a, b, 80 a, b, 81 a, 82 a, 85 d, 86 c, 87 b, 89 a, c, 90 f, 92 b–d, Plates B, F, I).

After excavation of the sanctuary of the Franciscan Church of San Bernardo, it was suggested by Mr. Ross G. Montgomery, who was acting as consultant on the ecclesiastical structures of the village, that it had often been the custom of the Spanish missionaries to build the altars of their churches above or upon the sacred fanes of the pagan tribes whose conversion to the Faith they sought to accomplish. In order to test this thesis, a small pit was dug through the floor of the sanctuary near the steps that led up to the predella, and at a depth of about 1.25 m below that level there came to light the top of a masonry wall with the butt of a wooden beam emplaced in a socket extending through it. Realizing that the structure was probably the kiva that we sought, we removed the altar of the church and the north wall of the sanctuary in order to permit its complete excavation.

Gradually the entire roof structure was exposed and, although the central area had subsided about 30 to 40 cm from its original position, the method of its construction was apparent (Fig. 5.6). The major support consisted of two heavy main beams that had been emplaced across the shorter dimension of the room, resting in sockets in the left and right walls, with their ends extending through and somewhat beyond the exterior faces of the walls. The front (northwest) beam was about 1.10 m from the front wall, the rear (southeast) beam about 1.20 m from the rear wall. That portion of the left (southwest) wall, in which the rear (southeast) beam had been socketed, had been destroyed by the Spaniards to provide a footing for the north wall of the sanctuary, thus also destroying a portion of the beam itself, but in no other respect had the construction of the church significantly damaged the kiva roof or walls.

The diameters of the two main beams were not recorded, but the interval between them was about 2.25 m, although this varied slightly because they were neither perfectly straight nor exactly parallel. These beams were about 1.90 m above the floor.

The secondary roof component consisted of several smaller beams or stringers. Two of these were placed approximately parallel to the main beams and each lay between one main beam and its nearest parallel wall. They were perhaps one-third the diameter of the main beams and like the latter extended fully across the kiva, their ends resting in sockets in the side walls. Spanning the interval between the two main beams, lying upon them at right angles but not extending beyond them, were five other secondary beams or stringers, each about 2.70 m in length and irregularly spaced between the right and left walls of the kiva. The central pair were about equidistant (approximately 1.00 m) from and parallel to the left and right walls, respectively, and were almost as thick as the main beams themselves. Between them and the side walls lay three other and thinner secondary beams or stringers, one on the right side, two on the left.

The intersections of the two main beams and the central pair of secondary beams embraced a rectangular aperture about 2.40 m long by 1.10 m wide, which formed a hatchway for access to the interior of the kiva. Surrounding the hatchway and directly upon the framing beams had been erected a masonry parapet (Figs. 5.6, 5.7). This structure was about 30 to 35 cm high by about 20 to 25 cm thick and was formed of small, irregularly shaped stones set in a matrix of copious adobe mortar.

A third component of the roof skeleton consisted of a series of closely spaced sticks or poles arranged in parallel sequences along each side of the structure. The butt ends of these members were socketed into interstices between the stones of the masonry walls, and they extended outward at right angles to the walls toward the main and secondary beams that supported the parapet. In most cases, how-

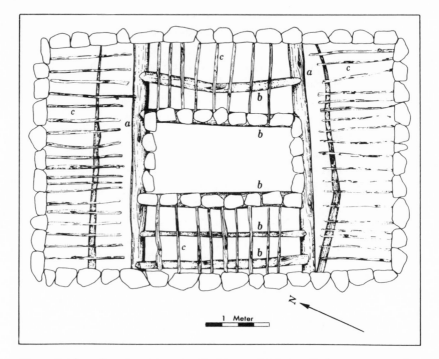

Fig. 5.6. Plan of roof construction for Room 788, beneath the sanctuary of Church 2 at Awatovi. The frame consisted of two main and two secondary transverse beams (a), at right angles to which and across the two main beams lay five secondary longitudinal beams (b). The main beams and two central secondary beams supported a masonry parapet framing a hatchway, and numerous close-set savinos (c) spanned the areas on all sides of the central opening. Although this roof had sagged considerably from its original level, its members remained intact and in proper relation to one another.

ever, they did not quite reach these beams, but were actually supported by the secondary stringers that have been mentioned above as lying outside but parallel to the heavy beams that supported the parapet. There were twenty poles along the front sector of the roof and nineteen along the rear, both groups extending from wall to wall. The sets of poles along the right and left sides were shorter, since they filled only the areas between the two main beams. There were eight on the right side and perhaps a few more on the left, although some of the latter had been destroyed by the construction of the footings for the wall of the sanctuary.

All members of this roof structure were found in their original

Fig. 5.7. *Roof of Room 788, beneath the sanctuary and sacristy of the second Franciscan church. In the center is part of the masonry coping surrounding the hatchway, the remainder of which had been destroyed by the building of the north wall of the sanctuary, the end of which appears at the upper left.*

relation to one another, but the entire fabric had slumped downward about 30 to 40 cm below its original level and rested upon the debris that filled the kiva (Fig. 5.7). The roof skeleton had probably been covered with grass and brush topped off with earth, but no evidence of such material was found.

The fill of the kiva below as well as above the level of the roof was composed of almost pure sand. That below the roof appeared to have been poured through the hatchway, since its strata sloped downwards in all directions from the center. There were very few potsherds, stones, or other material within the sand and the inference was very strong that the kiva had been deliberately and rapidly filled by human agency. If this was so, it may be explained by consideration of certain practices known to have been frequently followed by Spanish missionaries.

In Mexico and elsewhere in the New World, one of the first actions of the religious was to erect an altar to their Christian Faith. Usually this was done in a native village within which was a shrine or

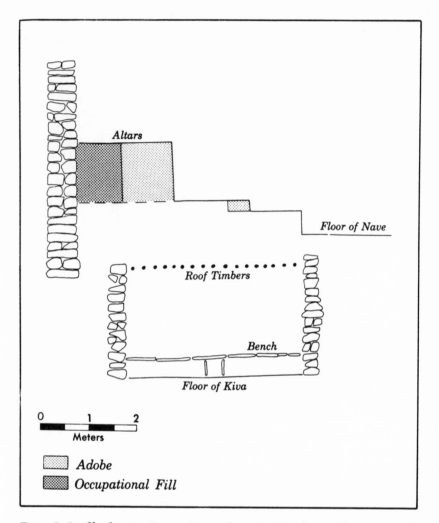

Fig. 5.8. Profile showing Room 788 in relation to the altar and sanctuary of Church 2 at Awatovi. The section is along the longitudinal dimension of the church and the transverse dimension of the kiva, and indicates the depth of the latter beneath the superimposed Franciscan structure. (See Montgomery, Smith, and Brew 1949: 62-67.)

holy place that was already venerated by the inhabitants. The Christians wished to obliterate the pagan shrine and in its stead to erect their own. It was reasonable to accomplish both purposes by superimposing the Christian fane upon the pagan counterpart, thus demonstrating the dominance of the new Faith over the old, and at the same time perhaps translating the established sanctity of the particular locale into the substitutional structure.

This was apparently done at Awatovi (Fig. 5.8). Of the many kivas that were excavated there and at other villages in the vicinity, only two still retained their roofs intact. These were Rooms 788 and 908, which adjoined each other, and both of which lay beneath the sanctuary and sacristy of the mission church. Generally in the Pueblo Southwest, roof timbers were removed from abandoned rooms for use elsewhere, for they were too precious to be left behind. Rarely, except in cases of fire or when the entire village was abandoned, have such timbers been found still *in situ*. The two exceptions at Awatovi argue strongly for the hypothesis that the missionaries sought to supplant the kivas as foci for religious observances but not to destroy them, and thereby to identify their new sanctuary with the old. This subject has been more fully discussed in Montgomery, Smith, and Brew (1949: 65–67, 134–136, Fig. 10).

Certain other objects found in the fill included scattered small fragments of charcoal, a three-quarter-grooved axe, a chert blade, two polishing pebbles (Woodbury 1954, Figs. 14 *k*, 27 *a*, 40 *l*, *o*), four pecking stones, two stone loom blocks, a human femur, fragments of six painted wooden pahos, or prayer sticks, and two fragmentary animal skulls with straight tapering horns that may have belonged to goats. If so, they had certainly arrived with the Spaniards.

The sherds within the fill of Room 788 were mostly of post-Sikyatki types with small components of Jeddito Black-on-yellow and Sikyatki Polychrome, characteristic of the late phase of Ceramic Group A-1.

Four of the roof timbers were dated by Hall at 1382 ± 5, 1502 ± 5, $1504 + x$, and $1564 + x$, and by the Laboratory of Tree-Ring Research at 1385vv, 1412vv, 1498vv, and 1503vv (Bannister, Robinson, and Warren 1967: 11). The outer ring of each specimen was an undeterminable distance from the bark, but we may reasonably infer from them collectively that the kiva may have been built well after the beginning of the sixteenth century. From other considerations discussed above we may also infer with confidence that it was abandoned very shortly after 1630, when the missionaries arrived.

If these inferences are correct, the kiva would have been in use for a period of between seventy and one hundred years, but the presence of only fourteen coats of painted wall plaster would account for ceremonial renewals at intervals of roughly every five to seven years, which seems too long between drinks. It may thus be warrantable to hypothesize a later date of construction, say about 1580 or so, on the supposition that the beam dated $1564 + x$ was nearer to the actual date than were the others, and that the latter had been taken from earlier structures for reuse here. It is also possible but not very convincing to suppose that the surviving mural paintings were all executed during the latest years of occupancy, perhaps following a renovation and removal of possible earlier ones.

6. *"Ethnology Itself Carried Back"*

As early as the 1840s, travelers from the eastern United States to the Southwest (then Mexican territory) observed the similarity of the ancient ruins to the villages of the Pueblo Indians (Schuyler 1971: 387–394). In fact, the Southwest provided the American public with the first obvious and easily appreciable evidence of the connection between archaeological remains and living Indians (Thompson 1989: 219). The pioneer archaeologists in the Southwest were very much aware of this living connection with the past. Cushing (1890: 160) considered archaeology to be "ethnology itself carried back" into the past. Fewkes (1900: 579) anticipated present-day terminology by describing himself as an "ethno-archaeologist." Longacre (1970: 2) has characterized the mood of the times: "Since the prehistoric cultures were broadly similar to the modern Pueblos, one could interpret prehistoric societies by direct analogy to the living peoples."

Although the Pueblo Southwest is a classic case of the direct historical (Steward 1942) or continuous (Gould 1974: 39) model of the use of ethnographic analogy, the application of the approach has not been limited to this region. Archaeologists everywhere have long depended on ethnohistorical records and ethnographic accounts as a comparative resource for enriching their interpretations of the past. There are several early examples of ethnographic work done by archaeologists in order to supplement the archaeological record (Fewkes 1900; Guthe 1925; Wauchope 1938), but the active participation of archaeologists in the ethnographic enterprise and the emergence of ethnoarchaeology as an important subfield of archaeology (Schiffer 1978: 154) are post-World War II phenomena (Thompson 1958; Longacre 1974; Gould 1978; Binford 1978).

Ethnographic analogy, however, has not been universally welcomed into the archaeological fold. From the very beginning there have been critics who have cast methodological or theoretical doubt on the validity of the approach. Others have claimed that various flaws in the ethnographic relationship severely limit the value and even the trustworthiness of any archaeological interpretation derived from ethnographic analogy. There is, in fact, a substantial literature in which the issues are explored: the passive resistance of informants; deceit and falsification on their part; the differential and limited knowledge of individual informants; the inability of some ethnographers to distinguish between the real and the false; many questions about the strength of the linkage between the past and living cultures; and wishful thinking and related self-deception on the part of some archaeologists.

In the 1880s Stephen (1936: 294) complained about the uncooperative and deceitful behavior of Hopi informants and Bourke (1984: 181–182) recorded the reluctance of his Hopi contacts to reveal esoteric information. Parsons (1936b: 14), who experienced difficulties in obtaining information from Indians in both the Southwest and southern Mexico, took the somewhat more optimistic view that "in a conservative, secretive community the social detective learns much from the efforts to conceal." Passin (1942: 235), writing about "Tarahumara prevarication," bemoaned the fact that "lying on the part of informants is a persistent and irritating problem." On the other hand, Evans-Pritchard (1976: 247), reflecting on his field experience among the Azande in Africa, took the position that natives do not lie to those they trust except when they want to conceal esoteric information. However, Ellen Basso (1987) shows that deceit in the form of both "verbal and visual fabrication" plays an important role in interpersonal relations among the Kalapalo of the Amazon Basin.

The continuing controversies surrounding the books of Carlos Castaneda (1968, 1984; Spicer 1969; Wilk 1977; Sebald 1987) and the attacks on the Samoan research of Margaret Mead (1928; Freeman 1983; Brady 1983) not only raise questions about the quality of the data and the interpretations of them, but also suggest that various ruling hypotheses (Chamberlin 1890) may govern the interpretations (Clifford 1986). That contemporary anthropologists consider "truth in ethnography" to be a significant issue is demonstrated by a series of essays on authenticity and deception in a

world-wide sample of cultures assembled by Hans Peter Duerr
(1987).

When Watson Smith undertook the formidable task of
recovering, describing, and interpreting the kiva murals from
Awatovi, he was immediately confronted with the full range of issues surrounding ethnographic analogy. He was already aware not
only of the value of the extensive ethnographic literature on the
Hopi and other Pueblo groups for the interpretation of the
prehistoric record, but also of the potential of the ancient murals
themselves to contribute to the solution of ethnographic problems
(Smith 1952b: 3):

> A knowledge of modern Pueblo ceremonial practices provides
> us with keener insight into the lives and even the minds of
> the dwellers in ancient towns, those once mysterious people
> whom the Navajos call Anasazi, the ones who have gone
> before. And reciprocally, the material remains of those old folk
> can explain to us much that is obscure in the patterns of
> religious mysticism and social sanctions that govern the lives
> of their inheritors.

This enthusiasm notwithstanding, he approached the ethnographic record with a measure of caution. He recognized that the
huge corpus of ethnographic data available to him had its problems.
Of special concern to him as an archaeologist was the question of
the chronological significance of that loosely defined period, the
"ethnographic present." He knew from his archaeological experiences at Awatovi and elsewhere that whatever else culture may do,
it changes and sometimes quite rapidly. He not only had to assess
the quality and the value of the ethnographic information collected
before the turn of the century by Stevenson, Cushing, Stephen,
Voth, Fewkes, and others, he also had to decide whether the
"ethnographic present" of the 1890s was a true, or at least an adequate reflection of the conditions of the 1400s, or of the 1950s, or
neither (Upham 1987).

He was again reminded of this type of problem when he collaborated with Jack Roberts on a study of Zuñi law (Smith and
Roberts 1954). He found that the very act of recording the details
of Zuñi legal philosophy and practice during a particular point in
time violated the continuity of the process of change. Some years
later, Smith (1984a: 297) discovered that the monograph had not

only been assigned as a college text, but that "it was also used by the Zuñi Tribal Council as an authoritative reference." He feared that this formal use of his summary of Zuñi law might place serious constraints on the ability of the Zuñi legal system to change as it faces the need to adjust to new situations. A similar concern was expressed by Emory Sekaquaptewa (1984: xv), when he commented that the Hopi who had permitted Bourke to record ceremonies in 1884 "failed to realize the eternal nature of the printed word that. . . left us with a written account of some esoteric knowledge that weighs upon present-day members of the Snake Ceremony as they try to maintain its ritual dignity." Smith addressed many of these problems in his detailed analysis of the ethnographic record. His essay on the "Extent of Ethnographic Studies among the Pueblos," which appears on the following pages, is a classic statement of some of the key problems of ethnographic analogy (Smith 1952b:163–173).

R.H.T.

Extent of Ethnographic Studies Among the Pueblos

The vast subject of Pueblo Indian religion is far beyond the scope of the present discussion, and in any case has been exhaustively studied and described by numerous investigators of unquestioned capacity and integrity, armed with a mass of objective factual data almost staggering in its enormity. Since the inception of modern ethnographic studies about seventy years ago, the bibliography of Pueblo ceremonial, ritual, and folklore has fairly outstripped the parabled mustard seed in its fruitfulness, and the zeal of successive generations of anthropologists has rendered the inoffensive peoples of the terraced villages of the Southwest perhaps the most intensively studied and continuously harassed cultural entity on earth. The ratio of anthropological effort, in terms of man-hours of study plus pages of published discussion, per unit of population in the Pueblo villages, must surely already have established some kind of record. And with each new season that ratio continues to increase.

One might suppose, therefore, that almost everything knowable about the Pueblo Indians would already have been discovered and given to a sated public, and that the last secret of ceremonial practice and social organization would have transpired. But one would be quite wrong. The error would derive from a failure to take into account the important factor of Pueblo passive resistance to any very far-reaching attempt at an invasion of their privacy by inquiring anthropologists, their disapprobation of Quisling activities among their own number,

Reprinted with the permission of the Peabody Museum from "Kiva Mural Decorations at Awatovi and Kawaika-a," by Watson Smith, pages 163–173, *Papers of the Peabody Museum of American Archaeology and Ethnology*, Volume 37, Harvard University, 1952.

and the persistent, almost pathologic, nurturing of the things of the spirit as the last cherished possessions of a people compelled by the logic of circumstances to accept the political and cultural compulsions of a dominant race, but steadfastly refusing to render unto Caesar those things that are not his to demand.

Thus, although literally thousands of white men have had more or less intimate contacts with one or another of the Pueblo groups, and numerous professional ethnologists have carried out systematic studies of all phases of their lives and thoughts, with the resultant tangible product of tens of thousands of printed pages, the amount of real understanding that we have of Pueblo thought and ceremonial practice is in proportion startlingly small. There are some villages in which there is no record of an outsider ever having seen an esoteric religious ritual; there are others in which observers have witnessed and recorded entire ceremonies or parts of ceremonies; but there is no village in which any one white man or all of them together can report fully on the complete ceremonial pattern. In fact, it is perhaps true that in some cases archaeology has told us more of the Pueblo past than ethnology does of its present.

Against such a background, then, in which the data are indeed voluminous, but in which they are also quite incomplete, we must project the Jeddito wall paintings and seek to determine from analogy to modern ceremonialism their possible meaning and cultural significance. It may appear that we are herein accepting gratuitously the assumption that our mural paintings are in fact of a hieratic character, but I think that such a conclusion is amply justified by several considerations. First, it is clear that without exception the paintings occurred in kivas, the ceremonial character of which throughout the later periods of Pueblo development is hardly open to question. Secondly, in nearly all recorded instances of comparable wall paintings in other villages, both prehistoric and modern, they have also been found in kivas. An exception to this rule, wherein examples of wall paintings have been reported in rooms other than kivas, is more apparent than real, as at Zuñi or Hano on First Mesa, for example, where such rooms are sometimes used on special occasions for ceremonial purposes, although not reserved exclusively therefor. The existence of wall paintings in such rooms, therefore, does not suggest that the pictures are in any sense themselves secular. And thirdly, the unanimous testimony alike of investigators and informants reporting on modern ritual practices so identifies them.

IDENTIFICATION OF JEDDITO MURALS
WITH MODERN RITUAL

If our hypothesis is true, that the kiva wall paintings were of a ceremonial nature, they provide us then with a source of data looking toward the partial solution of several specific problems of basic interest in Pueblo ethnology and archaeology. The ultimate problem, and the one to which we shall advert from time to time after we have laid a groundwork of its adequate consideration, is that of the history of cultural interchanges between the several Pueblo and non-Pueblo groups in the Southwest. Before we can employ for that purpose, however, the evidence afforded by these mural decorations, we must first essay to identify and interpret them in terms of their similarities and apparent kinships with the ceremonial practices, costumes, and paraphernalia of other Pueblo groups, both prehistoric and modern.

To a large extent, this procedure can be accomplished only by indirection, for, while we can compare directly our murals with those reported elsewhere, and thus achieve an immediate basis for determining similarities and differences, the actual number of comparable paintings in other sites is so small as to provide relatively little data. Of far wider application will be the study of our murals or elements in them together with the records of ritual practices expressed in other media, such as ceremonial dance costume, masks, symbolic signs, sand paintings, altars, and sacred paraphernalia.

In many cases this will present no great difficulty or controversy, whenever a particular detail of one of the murals is of such a degree of realism as to warrant its equation with some object actually in use in observed ceremonials. But in many instances it will be found that elements in the paintings are so highly conventionalized or abstract that they can be interpreted not by direct comparison with natural objects, but only by inference through a study of comparative symbolism or representational convention. Furthermore, although a particular design feature may be quite naturalistic, it still may possess a ritual significance quite apart from its representational aspect. Thus, for example, a realistically painted feather in a wall painting may indeed be directly correlated with a feather of identifiable genus or species known to be used in actual ceremonials; it may, however, be not merely a feather but an abstract or simplified symbol of a bird; and finally the ritual significance of the feather (or the inferential bird) may be something quite esoteric and unsuspectable from its objective characteristics alone.

In the analysis and discussion that follows, therefore, we shall proceed first to the actual morphological identification of the several elements or details that occur and recur in the artistic vocabulary of the paintings, secondly to their equation with their prototypes as used in known ceremonies among particular Pueblo groups, and finally to the rarefied plateau of inferential affinities between the ritual symbolism of painters of the Jeddito and the inhabitants of other villages throughout the Pueblo area.

In considering the particular design elements that are presented to us, it will be feasible to organize them into groups having essentially similar though not always identical features, and then to indicate correlative instances of the occurrence of like objects at other villages, both in the representational form of mural or other types of painting and in their actual physical employment in a living ceremony. Before entering upon this systematic analysis, however, I should like to expand briefly upon two fundamental subjects, both of which must be kept constantly in mind, though they are often sadly forgotten, in any investigation of this nature. The first of these considerations has already been touched upon, namely the inadequacy of our knowledge and understanding of Pueblo religion and the difficulties in the way of expanding it. The second is akin to the first, and might be called the Slough of Symbololatry, which may become a bottomless pit of confusion and misconception yawning for the unwary whose lively imaginations impel them irresistibly toward the imputation of hidden meanings in every daily doodle and of sermons in every rolling stone.

DIFFICULTIES OF INTERPRETATION

Lo, the Inscrutable

Although the Pueblos have been exposed to European impingement of varying degrees of intensity for over four centuries, it is only within relatively recent years that systematic anthropology has been imposed upon them, with the view to studying the intimate features of their lives and thoughts. In the main, they have responded with a passive resistance that has baffled the most avid ethnographers, as the testimony of the latter makes abundantly clear. Much of this has undoubtedly been intentional, but perhaps also some of it has stemmed from actual ignorance on the part of informants, every one of whom cannot be expected to be familiar with every abstruse detail of the ceremonialism of his village.

The Hopi have undoubtedly been more thoroughly studied than any other Pueblo group, and through the journals of Alexander M. Stephen and H. R. Voth, both of whom actually lived with the Hopi for extended periods of years, rivaled only by the sojourn of Frank H. Cushing at Zuñi, we have a vast compendium of data on all phases of Hopi life at the end of the 19th century. But even Stephen and Voth, speaking the language of the Hopi and enjoying their confidence, were unable to penetrate fully into the mysteries of local religion.

Stephen, whose patience seems at times to have been sorely tried, wrote during the early period of his life at Walpi: "I am constrained to admit that the amount of really comprehensive knowledge I have gained of their religious system and laws of conduct is still tantalizingly small" (Stephen 1940: 1). Seven years later he was still baffled: "A lifetime is not long enough to learn all these complicated details and mystic acts, and how these dull [sic!] creatures can themselves apprehend the infinity of routine and preserve the sequences of these multitudinous rites, I cannot divine, unless, as I am at times inclined to believe, they have developed some specialized brain convolutions with this particular function" (Stephen 1936: 1003). Still later, Stephen's patience was exhausted, and he exploded: "Damn these tantalizing whelps, to the devil with all of them. I have been bamboozled from pillar to post all day, have received no scrap of information" (Stephen 1936: 294).

This attitude was confirmed by Captain Bourke, who visited the Hopis in 1881 with Frank H. Cushing as interpreter. He was later told by a Zuñi man that the Hopi had refused to tell him many things about the Snake dance, and his informant added: "We tell all sorts of stories to outsiders. . . . Of course that is lying, but if we adopted any other course our secrets wouldn't be kept very long" (Bourke 1884: 181–182). And in recent years Mischa Titiev has emphasized the same situation among the Hopi by noting: "It is by no means certain that any of the interpretations of specific ritual acts are correct. No informant is entirely trustworthy when the subject deals with sacred matters" (Titiev 1944: 117, note 48).

At Zuñi, also, there has been a characteristic reticence in divulging information, as indicated by the statement already quoted by Bourke. Mrs. Matilda Stevenson noted that from 1891 to 1902 a particular ceremony was not performed "owing, the Indians said, to their wish to keep the sacred ceremony from the eyes of the Americans" (Stevenson 1904: 180, note c). The veteran trader at Zuñi, Mr. R. L.

Wallace, has been quoted as believing that "even the most elaborate study of Zuñi has not touched on some of their ceremonial practices" and he added that night after night there occurred esoteric ceremonies and chanting, about which he was able to learn nothing (Kirk 1943: 13).

Coming eastward to Acoma, we have the testimony of Leslie White, who has done more work at that village than any other person, that the Acomans "are suspicious, distrustful, and unfriendly. . . . They are ever on their guard to prevent any information concerning their ceremonies to become known lest they be suppressed (or ridiculed) by the whites." He notes that sentinels are posted to prevent aliens from seeing masked dances, and sums up in despair: "At times their conservatism seems to be organic, below the level of thought entirely" (White 1932: 29, 45, 53; Parsons 1920b: 56, 69).

The other Keresan villages conform to the same pattern. At Laguna whites are not permitted to see secret dances (Parsons 1920a: 98, note 1; Parsons 1920b: 56 says her informants were "all reluctant to talk"), nor are they at Cochiti, where Father Nöel Dumarest lived for some years and enjoyed cordial relations with the inhabitants. Even he apparently never saw a sacred ceremony and he cites several instances of the precautions taken to prevent strangers from coming within sight even of dances held in the open (Dumarest 1919: 208, driving away of a shepherd; 197, strangers compelled to remain indoors).

At Santo Domingo the same conditions are emphasized by White, who notes that "Santo Domingo. . . is bitterly opposed to telling white people, ethnologists above all, anything," and he adds that the Government school "is closed on days when masked dances are held, and the teachers required to vacate the pueblo until the dance is over" (White 1935: 7–8). It may also be noted that Bandelier was not able to learn anything at Santo Domingo, and that Bourke was thrown forcefully out of a kiva there.

The Tewa villagers, according to Mrs. Parsons (1929: 7–8), "are past masters in the art of defeating inquiry," and her information came from informants, some admittedly ill-informed and one a "three-fold liar." She adds that "systematic description of the mask dances is. . . out of the question" (Parsons 1929: 179), and that while the Keresan townspeople are secretive "they are easily outdone by the Tewa" (Parsons 1929: 150; Whitman 1947: v, 117). Even at Isleta, Mexicanized or Americanized as it is, Mrs. Parsons noted in 1921 a fear of revealing anything: "A woman. . . resisted all endeavors to learn from her not only words of ceremonial import, but clan names," and "the leading man of the town. . . was equally timid" (Parsons 1921: 49). Some years later, after further attempts, Mrs. Parsons concluded that "Isletans are particularly secretive, and what information is received from them contained contradictions." Two of her informants were "absolutely closemouthed" on the subject of ritual, because the giving of informa-tion about customs is "strictly taboo." As at other Rio Grande villages, Mexicans and Anglo-Americans are excluded from knowledge of the ceremonial life (Parsons 1932: 201–207).

At Taos, Mrs. Parsons (1936c: 104) says that the information about altars "is given so reluctantly that it is not at all reliable," and she dedicates her monograph on that village "To my best friend in Taos, the most scrupulous Pueblo Indian of my acquaintance, who told me nothing about the pueblo and who never will tell any white person anything his people would not have him tell, which is nothing" (Parsons 1936a: 3). Mrs. Blanche C. Grant said that when she dis-cussed with a Taos Indian some falsehoods told by him to an inquirer, he had replied with a smile, "Oh he likes it." Another Taos informant told her that even if she recorded her data correctly, other Indians "will say it is not true" (Grant 1925: 7–8).

LIMITATION OF RITUAL KNOWLEDGE
TO A FEW INDIVIDUALS

While a studied reluctance to divulge information thus appears to be endemic among the Pueblos, another ethnographic obstacle is undoubtedly that of simple ignorance on the part of many individual Indians, especially those who do not hold hierarchical positions. There is at least some evidence of a tendency on the part of priests in Pueblo religious orders to cherish certain esoteric elements from the knowledge even of their own lay fellow townsmen, and particularly from women. Priestcraft is, after all, a closed shop in all lands, and one would not expect a lay Christian to be particularly well informed upon all the tenuous intricacies of the dogma of his own faith.

For example, the Christian reader might imagine himself asked by a visiting Antelope Chief why the pelican is often depicted in Cath-olic churches. Just possibly he might be able to explain that when the pelican presses its red-tipped beak against its crop in order to induce regurgitation of the fish that it has caught as food for its young, the red tip, resembling a spot of blood on its breast, suggests that the bird is actually drawing its own blood with which to feed its young, and that from this semblance arises the symbolism of the pelican, particularly in connection with the Holy Eucharist, as an emblem of Him Who shed His Blood for all men.

Antelope Chief might further inquire concerning the very fish that the Pelican had captured, and Christian might or might not be able to tell him that the fish is also a symbol of the Saviour because its name in Greek, $I\chi\theta\hat{v}\varsigma$, is the acrostic of the initial letters of the Greek phrase ᾿Ιησοῦς Χριστός Θεοῦ Υἱός Σωτήρ (Iesous CHristos THeou Uios Soter, Jesus Christ, Son of God, Saviour). Of course, he might say further that it is also emblematic of the miraculous draft of fishes with which Jesus fed the multitude and thus symbolizes the vocation of the apostles as "fishers of men." If Christian were unusually well informed, he might add that the dolphin, a notably nimble aquatic creature rather resembling a fish, signifies the swiftness with which the Christian pursues his Saviour.

But if now the Bishop should happen by, Antelope Chief might be impelled to wonder at his crook, and Christian perhaps could tell him that its curled upper end symbolizes the duty of the bishop to recapture those who have wandered; that its pointed lower end provides an effective goad with which to prod the indifferent; and its sturdy shaft a support for the weary and the weak. If Antelope Chief were to remain to witness the ordination of a priest, he would see the latter hang a chasuble over his shoulders, and he would be interested to know that this act represented the assumption of the Yoke of Christ, and was further emblematic of humility and charity.

He would also be edified to learn that the cherubim surrounding the portrait of the saint in the chapel represent angels of the second highest of nine celestial choirs, and that their name derives from a Hebrew term signifying the fullness of knowledge, with which they are filled by virtue of their favored position in being permitted so closely to behold the sublime Glory of God.

Indeed, Antelope Chief might go on to inquire into a great many more subjects of like nature in the Church's symbolism, but I wonder how much Christian would really be able to tell him. To no greater extent should we expect from every Indian an exegesis of the cult ritual in which he may take an active but probably a non-critical part. With reference to Cochiti, for example, Goldfrank (1927: 5) expressed the belief that much of the detailed ceremonialism was "held secret by the shamans and has not reached the commoners." And Titiev (1944: 177, note 48) at Oraibi says that "the true explanation for certain actions is as much a mystery to the performers as it is to us, and they make up 'explanations' to answer one's question." Fewkes (1922: 591, note 4) was even of the opinion that Hopi priests themselves possessed limited knowledge: "No one but a snake priest knows anything about the snake altars, and some of them are unfamiliar with many details." He points out further that "the priests who now control different ceremonials in each of the five pueblos know little, save by hearsay and tradition, of the secret rites of the religious societies of their neighbors. The Snake chief at Walpi had never seen the altars and secret rites of the Snake Dance in any pueblo but his own. . . . The Flute chiefs at the Middle Mesa, although old men, never saw the Flute altars at Walpi, and the priests of the Flute Society at Walpi refused to go into the Flute House at Oraibi" (Fewkes 1896: 242). Under such circumstances, it becomes inevitable that the testimony of any one individual, however honest and well-intentioned, must be limited in its scope and should not be used uncritically as a basis for generalizing. At best it can represent only the knowledge of one man with reference to a special set of circumstances, and inferences drawn from it are very definitely subject to the rule of *caveat emptor*. At worst it can be completely and designedly misleading. Perhaps the whole matter is well summed up in Leo Crane's rueful observation that "when an Indian of the pueblo type. . . knows nothing, he knows it with a thoroughness and mental vacuity that is profound" (Crane 1929: 13).

SUBJECTIVE LIMITATIONS OF THE INVESTIGATOR

The potential dangers in ethnographic and archaeological research are not entirely encompassed by the limitations of informants, however, for the entire process is a two-way affair, in the give-and-take of which the investigator's personal equation is also a significant factor. Raw data do not express or explain themselves; their implications are subject to interpretation; and often to distortion by hyper-fanciful presentation. While a degree of rational inference and logical interpretation is always desirable and even necessary on the part of the expositor, there are often tendencies toward fine-spun and remote analogies that are quite unwarranted. There is also a tendency, of rather frequent occurrence, to interpret ethnographic or archaeological evidence in terms of the familiar psychological processes of the investigator and his own cultural pattern instead of in those of the vastly more difficult and unfamiliar framework of the people who created the evidence. The ideal in this matter is admittedly a very difficult one to achieve, and we may as well admit at the outset that almost no white man, for example, is capable of thinking like an Indian; but we can be on guard against obliviousness of that very fact, and so constantly remind ourselves that conclusions that appear quite reasonable by our own intuitive or rational standards may not even remotely represent the inferences that would be drawn by the Indian creator of the object or even by another person of the same cultural complex.

REPRESENTATION AND SYMBOLISM

Two closely related fields in which examples of this danger are readily available are those of representational art and of symbolism. Although these words are frequently used as if they were synonymous, such lack of precision presents semantic difficulties of a major magnitude. In this volume a careful distinction will be maintained in their usage and the fact will be kept in mind that a representation is properly a likeness, picture, model, image, or reproduction of an object, whereas a symbol is rather a sign by which one knows or infers a thing or an idea. It stands for or suggests something else without having intentional resemblance to it; thus a pattern or a design element may stand for an intangible idea or quality or perhaps for some other object, which, by reason of outward similarity, familiar association, or arbitrary convention is brought to the mind of the observer when he beholds the symbol. Moreover, while every symbol is expressed in the form of a design or tangible object, it does not follow that every usage of those same designs or objects carries the same symbolism, or that in every case it is symbolic at all.

The mental association between the symbol and its significant implications must derive wholly from within the cultural framework in which it occurs, and for it to achieve a successful conveyance of meaning, both the creator of the intended symbol and its observer must be able to think within the limits of the same framework. A drawing of a fish, for example, may *represent* a fish and nothing more; on the other hand, it may *symbolize* any one of several things, depending upon the associational complex mutually shared by the creator and the observer. For example, to a Zuñi it may symbolize water and consequently fertility (Cushing, quoted in Matthews 1898: 110); to a Hopi, the supernatural being of fire and death, Masaú wû, who cut his tail into little pieces, each of which became a fish (Stephen 1936: 150); to a Navajo, the idea of danger from something forbidden by a powerful taboo (Matthews 1897: 239, note 169; Luomala 1938: 45; Kluckhohn and Leighton 1946: 139); to a Christian the idea of salvation through faith, from the parable of Jesus' feeding of the multitude; or perhaps to a resident of Massachusetts the majesty of his political cosmos. But perhaps the whole matter is best dealt with by Sancho Panza: "Good your Lordship, this is no time for me to mind niceties, and spelling of letters: I have other Fish to fry."

Unwarranted Imputation of Symbolism. Not only, however, is genuine symbolism liable to misinterpretation by reason of the incommensurable thought process of the creator and the observer, but further danger lurks in a potential error of a slightly different sort. Because of the cherished, but probably baseless, legend that attributes devious and subtle processes of thought to the Indian, many persons succumb to the irresistible impulse to read symbolic meanings into almost every product of the Indian's artistic urge. I suspect that a very large number of these supposed symbols are parthenogenetically conceived in the mind of the observer, and that he is gratuitously imputing mysticism to the obvious. His mental gyrations are closely similar to those of witch doctors, witch hunters (in Salem or any other place), and superstitious cultists of any land and clime, who mask their ignorance and take refuge from their fears by discovering supernatural significance in whatever they do not understand.

Many authorities have recognized this difficulty and have recorded as their opinions the incorrectness of the belief that all Indian design "means something." It has been remarked by one writer that "many designs are used only for decoration, and if by chance they symbolize an object, quality or idea, it is merely by association" (Roediger 1941: 94–95). Virgil Hubert, in a careful consideration of the subject, says that the Hopi or other Pueblo artist, in working out a decoration, will often conventionalize life forms in order to reduce them to the requirements of the design. He points out that this process does not necessarily produce symbolism although in some cases it may, and he adds that "in some cases there is a very deep symbolical meaning connected with a given design, especially when it is used on a ceremonial object, but that design may also be used at another time and place and have no symbolical meaning" (Hubert 1937: 2).

Douglas (1934: 43–44) discusses the matter from a slightly different point of view, in connection with the practice of giving names to particular designs, which he regards as a "purely practical action to make easy the discussion and description of the patterns. . . .

"Naming a design does not make it a symbol. . . . Often the designs. . . are not supposed to be representations of the objects named, but because of a real or fancied resemblance to some natural object were given the names after they were first completed.

". . . It must be realized that purely decorative designs are very common among the Indians. They are made only to gratify an esthetic impulse and have absolutely no message to give or philosophy to expound. Symbolism and decoration exist side by side."

He further points out that very often the creations of Indian artists are "determined only by their individual wishes. . . . Unless the student receives from the maker of each design accurate information about it, it is impossible for him to know whether it is decorative, or, if symbolic, what its meaning may be." Dr. Bunzel (1932: 862) quotes a Zuñi informant as follows: "Sometimes the painting on the mask means something, sometimes not. . . . They paint something on the mask to please the earth and something to please the sky, and so on. The painting on Lelacoktipona's face [a line of alternate black and white squares] does not look like the Milky Way, but they call it that anyway to please the Milky Way." It is just possible also that they "call it that" to please the ethnologist.

Spinden (1931: 3, 5) also emphasizes that symbolic intent is not to be too readily inferred, as do Wissler (1938: 97–101), Boas (1910: 662–664), and Stephen (1936: 390, note 1). That sufficient caution is not always observed, however, is evident from many examples, in which the fecund imagination of the writer has been given pretty full play.

Perhaps an outstanding exemplar of the symbololators was Dr. Fewkes, whose active mind was probably not content with a mere colorless representational interpretation of Pueblo design, and who purported to see the most complex symbolism inherent in almost every stroke of the Indian's brush as well as in his architecture and the other elements of his material culture. No simple triangle was safe from metamorphosis into a bird by Dr. Fewkes, who thought that "the main subjects chosen by the native women for decoration of their pottery are symbolic (Fewkes 1898a: 658), and who went the limit in saying, "The Moki cultus is one of symbols, and every figure on their altars has a symbolic meaning connected with their worship" (Fewkes

1896: 243). I am convinced that that is an overstatement of Paul Bunyanian magnitude. That Dr. Fewkes was not to be denied by the reticence of informants, however, is indicated by his recounting that "when questioned in regard to the meaning of [a highly conventional-ized curvilinear design on a particular pottery vessel] the best in-formed Hopi priests had no suggestion to offer." Their non-co-operation did not prevent Dr. Fewkes from identifying it, however, as a bird (Fewkes 1898a: 687, Pl. 139 f). Dr. Fewkes strong penchant for birds could sometimes lead even him into confusion as indicated by his discussion of a design on a Sikyatki Polychrome bowl (Fewkes 1898a, Pl. 167b), which on page 688 is a bird, but which on page 703 mysteriously metamorphoses into a "compound star."

Dr. Spinden, too, sometimes forgot his own advice and ran amok in this happy hunting ground, as for example in his interpretation of a decorative device commonly used on modern Pueblo pottery, consist-ing of a simple scroll on the convex side of which are painted a series of solid triangles. This, he said, was an irrigation ditch running beneath little hills (Spinden 1931: 9, Fig. a). Actually, this pattern is only a form of the "Rain Bird" design, which has been very comprehensively studied by Dr. Harry P. Mera (1937), and which probably had no sym-bolic significance whatever.

Particular Symbols. At the risk of falling into what James Thur-ber (1947) called "the obscurantism of the explicit," we shall proceed to a detailed consideration of certain specific symbols or representa-tions, as they occur in the Jeddito murals.

Even given a willing and knowledgeable informant and a cau-tious investigator, however, there still exist the facts that particular symbols and conventions do not at all times and places and under all circumstances convey identical or consistent meanings, and con-versely that very dissimilar graphic expressions are sometimes in-tended to convey identical meanings. When this is the case, we can minimize error by limiting our interpretation to the frame of reference of the creator of the design, provided we can definitely determine what it was. But probably more often than not absolute certainty is im-possible. Thus, we must always avoid assigning to a particular design element a fixed significance in all its occurrences, merely because an informant so identified it in one particular association. Dr. Parsons has remarked: "It is characteristically Pueblo to compare ceremonies or organization on the basis of some minor feature. I have yet to meet a Pueblo, even a man of travel, who has any comprehension of comparative organization" (Parsons, in Stephen 1936: 945, note 1). If this is true, as I suspect it is, modern Hopi identification of ancient mural paintings would tend to be rather unreliable. Partly for emphasis in support of this cautionary credo, and partly to indicate the specific uncertainties inherent in the attempted interpretation of Pueblo design, it will be worthwhile to consider intimately certain examples.

Color Symbolism. Perhaps the simplest and most fundamental feature of decoration is color. Frequently, it is said that, at least within a given cultural group, each color is arbitrarily and consistently endowed with a fixed symbolism, and that whenever that color is used in a painting its significance is reliably inferable. How far this is from the truth can be strikingly demonstrated by a tabulation of the variety of implications ascribed to particular colors in different places and under different conditions, or even in the same place and under similar conditions.

Such a tabulation was actually made in the course of this study, comprising one hundred and fifty instances of the ascription of specific symbolism to particular colors, from Hopi, Zuñi, Acoma, Cochiti, Santa Ana, Rio Grande Tewa, and Hano Tewa, as reported by thirteen different investigators over the past sixty years (Smith 1952b: 170, note 44). In a large number of cases, to be sure, there was corroboration, but in a smaller though significant number the variation was striking indeed. A very general summary with a few illustrative examples will suffice here to point up the proposition that while color certainly carries symbolic imputations, these are not by any means entirely consistent, even within a particular village.

The directional symbolism of color is most frequently encountered, and is very consistent within each Pueblo group, although not throughout all the villages. Hopi, Acoma, and Zuñi all follow the usage of yellow for north (or northwest), blue or green for west (or southwest), red for south (or southeast), and white for east (or northeast). The Tewa, on the other hand, use yellow for the west and blue or green for the north, although they do not differ in the colors symbolic of south and east. For the zenith and nadir, Hopi, Acoma, and Tewa use black and all colors, respectively, while Zuñi reverses that order.

When the colors are used with other than directional significance, however, all rules are suspended. For example, yellow at Hopi stands for pumpkins and "prayers for flowers" as well as north; at Zuñi it stands for "the waters around the world," an eldest sister, flowers, corn pollen, "yellow-breasted birds, butterflies, and all beautiful things," "days of sunshine and rain without wind," and the rainbow; at Acoma it represents the earth as well as the sun; at Cochiti it brings rain; and with the Tewa it is said to refer to the time "after the autumnal equinox."

A comparable galaxy of meanings is ascribed to the other colors, mention of only a few of which will suffice. Blue is the second eldest sister at Zuñi, and is the sky at Acoma. Green is for good crops and for corn at Hopi; for grass at Zuñi; whereas at Acoma, it represents summer crops, mountains, sky, water, day, life, and fecundity.

Red is the warrior's color at Hopi, where it also symbolizes peaches, death, and corn. At Zuñi it is red-breasted birds, the third eldest sister, and "to make him see well." At Santa Ana, it is blood.

White is the sun at Zuñi, the earth at Acoma, and the winter rainbow among the Tewa. Black is the raincloud and the warrior (but so is red also) at Hopi. It is the earth, the sky, and the youngest sister at Zuñi; night and smoke at Acoma.

Mixed colors suggest blossoms as well as "the maker of Life" at Hopi, whereas at Zuñi they are raindrops, blood, and "all kinds of flowers for a fine summer." Black and yellow together are the oriole at Zuñi, and red and yellow there are for "all beautiful things."

The foregoing summation indicates most significantly for our purposes the impossibility of ascribing precise color symbolism to any features of the Jeddito murals on analogy to modern documented Pueblo decoration or design. It seems obvious that any color is susceptible of such a wide variety of particular implications that the correct one can often be inferred only by reading the mind of the original creator. We can make a few general observations, however, by noting that color is used in two basic ways, first as a purely abstract or conventional symbol of direction, and secondly to suggest, by a fairly obvious process of correlation, the appearance of natural objects that are associated with the weather or with plant life, and that thereby suggest ideas of fructification and growth.

The directional symbolism is quite abstruse, and probably arbitrary. It is significant, however, and may be useful to us, that it differs slightly among the various Pueblo groups, conforming to one convention among the Hopi, with a partial variant at Zuñi, and another partial variant among the Tewa, for example. The mimetic use of color, on the other hand, is usually simple and often fairly obvious, in its association of green with growing things, yellow for pumpkins, blue with the sky, red with the sunset, white with the sun, black with night, and so on. But in some of its connotations it fairly defies analysis and simply has to be taken on faith. Why yellow should suggest rain, or black one's youngest sister is hardly apparent. And even in those cases where the gross meaning is pretty obvious, the particular signifi- cance often is not. For instance, green readily suggests growing things and therefore life, but whether it is to be interpreted in a given case as grass, water, corn, daylight, life, summer, or whatnot is impossible to determine objectively.

Furthermore, it is not at all certain that the use of particular colors in particular connections is prescriptively fixed, except prob- ably in direction symbolism. That Pueblo painters exercise a degree of artistic freedom untrammeled by totalitarian authority is indicated by numerous reports of ethnologists. For example, in repainting four cloud symbols on the body of a figurine, a priest at Oraibi used colors different from those that had been used before. He said that it was "good" anyway and gave as his reason "that he did not happen to have all the paints there" (Voth 1912b: 45). In another instance red was omitted in painting some gourds at Oraibi, concerning which Voth writes: "I do not believe that this was omitted intentionally. The men probably did not happen to have that color" (Voth 1912b: 60–61). Stephen (1936: 210) reports that wall paintings were made "by two or three young men of the kiva" but that the colors were "suggested" by the elder men, which sounds as if a good deal of variation was permis- sible.

A number of similar instances of the casual substitution of one color for another are recorded. At Walpi, for instance, in 1893, the bodies of one group of participants in a kickball race bore the "prescribed decoration" of white crosses, those of another group solid red, and still others solid blue-green. Six days later, in a repetition of the race, the crosses were blue "as they had no white," the red was omitted because "they had no red pigment," and the blue-green was applied in stripes (Stephen 1936: 263, 267). And two weeks after that the crosses were both white and blue (Stephen 1936: 280). With fur- ther reference to the last group, an informant is quoted as stating that within his lifetime a change had occurred in the method of decoration of his group, "whose mark used to be a white diagonal band across the body, passing over the right shoulder" (Stephen 1936: 354).

As to kachina masks, while certain key devices are probably constant, the use of color appears to be pretty flexible. Colton (1947: 43) makes the general observation that "kachinas are difficult to classify, not only because the Hopis have rather vague ideas about their appearances and functions but because these ideas differ from mesa to mesa, pueblo to pueblo, and clan to clan." Colton might have added, I think, that these ideas also must have differed from time to time, further widening the gap between those of the sixteenth century and the present. Several observers have reported that most kachina masks are painted in at least four color variants, apparently suggestive of the cardinal directions (Fewkes 1903: 95; Douglas 1935: 60; Colton 1947: 42; Stevenson 1904: 219–220).

One further comment on the use of color by Pueblos should be made, as indicative of the fact that they do not always recognize the same distinctions of hue and intensity that we do, with a resulting possibility of confusion in the translation of native words into English. For example, there is generally no distinction made between green and blue and their various blendings (Stephen 1936: 1191, 1288; Hough 1902: 466), although in one case it is reported that at Oraibi all shades of blue and the darker greens were grouped together, while light grass green was referred to by another word (Voth 1901: 75, note), and at Zuñi separate words are used respectively for pale-blue and gray, turquoise and light green, bright green, dark blue (Bunzel 1932: 861, note 21). It has also been reported that with the Hopi orange is not differentiated from yellow or red and that red and violet are not distinguished (Hough 1902: 466). It is also well to observe that in Pueblo cosmology the "above" is distinct from the "sky" and the "below" from the "earth," so that the use, for example, of blue for the sky and black for the zenith is not in itself a contradiction (Bandelier 1890: 292).

[*Summary.*] It would be possible to multiply examples of contradictory interpretations of a wide variety of decorative or "symbolic" devices as used in Pueblo art and ceremonialism, but to do so comprehensively would lead us very far afield and would serve only as additional emphasis for the point we are trying to make, namely that the process of interpretation is a very tenuous thread connecting a graphic element with its imputed meaning. We can do as well, I think, by confining our attention to the Jeddito murals as a point of departure, and since the inventory of design features embraced within them is limited, it will be convenient to consider those features that do occur there, and to attempt to identify their representational character or their symbolic significance, if any. In order to achieve these purposes, we shall have recourse to analogy throughout the Pueblo area, insofar as comparative material is available, either from archaeological or ethnological sources, and in whatever form it occurs, whether as tangible objects, such as pottery, masks, ceremonial paraphernalia and costume, or in the form of graphic art.

In some cases there will be found little or no doubt as to the identity of an object represented in the murals, on the basis of its recognizably realistic portrayal or on the consistence of its formalization with documented examples from modern times. In other cases, however, the variability of convention or the conflict in interpretation will render accurate identification almost if not quite impossible. It might make an impressive case to marshal in a single mass all the evidence of inconsistence throughout the recorded data on Pueblo ethnography, but I believe that the cumulative impact of this evidence will be as effective when discussed in relation to particular features considered independently.

7. Birds of a Feather

The Peabody Museum of American Archaeology and Ethnology was established at Harvard University in 1866 (Brew 1968: 12), back in the days when people knew the proper way to spell "archæology." Those guardians of knowledge across the Charles River from the Athens of America that was nineteenth-century Boston knew that for some time conventions had been established for using Greek and Latin roots to create new words for English. They rejected the shortened spelling of "archeology" proposed by Noah Webster, America's first lexicographer who was laboring in the hinterland of western Massachusetts. They let him know what they thought of his application of Yankee efficiency to spelling (Woodbury 1984) when they refused to follow John Wesley Powell's adoption of the new form for the federal anthropological establishment. They were no more interested in the new-fangled spelling being promoted by Webster and Powell than they were in the several earlier British variations in spelling, such as "archaeiology," "archaiology," and "archiology" (Woodbury 1984; Daniel 1968: 1). Nor did they accept the Gallic logic of *archéologie*, despite the influence of France in the Athens of America. Whether the umlauted German version, *Archäologie* or *Archaeologie*, had any influence on proper spelling is not known.

In any event, the early Harvard archaeologists were loyal to the "ae" spelling. They not only used the digraph (ae), two letters written together pronounced as one sound, but also the ligature (æ), the single-letter symbol made by joining the two letters. To its credit, the Peabody Museum has never abandoned the digraph, but there is evidence of serious backsliding on the use of the ligature shortly after the publication in 1896 of the first numbers of the *Papers of the Peabody Museum of American Archaeology and Ethnology*. By 1910, the ligature had disappeared from the Peabody publications, not to reappear until 1951 when Watson Smith came to its rescue. The ligature returned in Volume 35, Number 3 (Lawrence 1951) and remained through Volume 59, Number 1 (Dincauze 1968). Volume 59, Number 2 (Gunnerson 1969) marks the beginning of the present ligature-free era of the Peabody Museum.

Thanks, however, to the influence of Smith, the ligature enjoyed almost two decades of borrowed glory in the pages of the venerable Peabody Museum publications. Although a passionate proponent of the use of the ligature, Smith did not ride to its rescue, nor did he campaign aggressively for its adoption. Rather, like so many other episodes in his life, the renewed use of the ligature just happened. He got involved in the recovery of the kiva murals because he happened to arrive at Awatovi a few days after kivas with painted walls had been discovered. All other staff members were occupied with other projects, so Smith was given responsibility for the murals (Smith 1984a: 179–180, 205). Donald Scott, then Director of the Peabody, happened to invite Smith to complete the mural research, including the report writing (Smith 1984a: 205–206, 208).

Scott and Smith had become good friends and they happened to share an interest in matters antiquarian, such as the use of the ligature in the preferred spelling of archaeology. Scott happened to have worked in the world of publishing, holding a position in the Century Company, prior to his return to his alma mater and his new career at the Peabody where he "established the beginnings of a separate publications department" (Smith 1984a: 228). He hired and trained an editor, Cordelia Galt, and "ingrained in her a deep devotion to syntactical and orthographic nicety" (Smith 1984a: 240).

In the late 1940s, Smith, encouraged if not actively supported by Scott, happened to suggest that archaeology be presented in its ligatured form in his monograph on the Awatovi kiva murals which was nearing completion. It was natural for an editor of Galt's competence and experience to demand a justification for such a departure from an accepted practice that had been honored since 1910 (Smith 1984a: 240– 241). Smith (1984a: 241–243, 1987: 132–136) responded by producing for her an essay that he has described as "a dubious contribution to scholarship." Entitled "Report on the

Results of an Etymological Research Project: The Functions of
Digraphs and Ligatures in the Effective Destruction of the Mental
Equilibrium of the Human Mind (if any)," it ended in poetic form
(Smith 1984a: 243, 1987: 134–136, 1989; Woodbury 1984) as
follows:

APOSTROPHE TO A DIGRAPH

Oh lovely Digraph, ligatured with grace,
Though you have fallen from your wonted high estate
And all but lost the orthographic race,
There yet remains one chance ere Time cries out, "Too late!"

Your body rises phœnixlike from death
Despite diurnal efforts of the vulgar tongue
To pour upon't contemnatory breath
As if you were but obsolescent verbal dung.

You once disported with the Olympian band,
With brave Æneas, on the wings of Æolus,
An ægis held in mighty Cæsar's conquering hand,
The vibrant symbol of æsthetic animus.

But, lo! What ugly orthographic fate
Has torn from you your lovely ligature,
And left you like a clod to æstivate
Until the Fates in time shall work a cure?

How pitiful a plight! Your graceful form
Thus split asunder from its wedded glee
And made mere vowels of undistinguished norm,
Or worse, reduced to just a lonely "e."

What sorrow that the charm of formulæ
Should be supplanted by the ugly barrenness
Of formulas! That rounded harmony
Give place to crass vainglory of the sinuous "s."

But all is not yet lost—a Goddess stands
Who holds within her strong, resuscitating palm,
The healing balm to reunite your failing hands
And weld your moieties once more in classic calm.

Refulgent glory in her face we see,
She is the Færie Archæology!

Thus did Watson Smith, Cordelia Galt, and "Færie Archæology" restore proper spelling, "ligatured with grace," to the pages of the *Papers of the Peabody Museum of American Archaeology and Ethnology*. It is interesting to note, however, that at the very time that this orthographic success was in the making, the forces of modernism were already at work. J. O. Brew replaced Donald Scott as Director of the Peabody Museum in 1948 and almost immediately unleashed those forces. Smith (1984a: 238–239) has chronicled Brew's early effort to "modernize" the Peabody Museum publications during one of the regular monthly luncheon meetings held at the Harvard faculty club by the Peabody staff:

> At one of his first luncheons [Brew] confidently brought forth a revolutionary proposal. For an understanding of its effect, one must be aware that since time immemorial the Peabody Museum *Papers* had been issued in paper covers of a color irreverently referred to by some observers as "medium horse manure." Jo's proposal was for the use of cover-papers of differing colors, distinctive and varied, . . . including brilliant . . . reds, blues, yellow, greens. A stunned silence ensued. Tozzer, Hooton, and Scott looked at each other in disbelief. To change the venerable style of the *Papers*? . . . It was unthinkable. And so the old cover-papers remained unchanged, until Burton Jones came to reinvigorate the publications program many years later, and began to produce coats of many colors for the New Day.

Even when the New Day arrived, however, not all of the *Papers* appeared in the new colors. At least at first, it was mostly the reports on Southwestern archaeology, Brew's special area of interest, that suffered modernization. And modernization meant more than just color for the covers. It involved the removal from the digraph of the ligature and from every letter the serifs, those elegant finishing lines with which Roman stone carvers adorned the graceful predecessors of our capital letters.

It is ironic that these lapses in the maintenance of high standards of purity in printing at 11 Divinity Avenue resulted in a special kind of poetic justice for Watson Smith, who just happened to have conspired with antiquarian birds of a feather to impede progress some twenty years before. Among the very first *Papers* to appear with covers of

rich desert tones of orange and gold were two of his Awatovi monographs, the first (Smith 1971) minus ligatures and the second (Smith
1972) stripped of both ligatures and serifs.

Nevertheless, it was a great triumph for all concerned that the
long-awaited study of the kiva murals at Awatovi appeared in the
traditional format complete with proper digraph and ligature (Smith
1952b). Of course, that exhaustive study of painted kiva walls is also
important because of the skill and success with which Watson
Smith presented and interpreted the kiva murals themselves. The
following discussion of the feathers depicted on the murals is an
outstanding example of his systematic and perceptive approach to
scholarship (Smith 1952b: 173–183).

R.H.T.

Feathers

Perhaps the most basic and widely used class of objects in the entire field of Pueblo ritual is that of feathers, which are used both independently as well as for appendages on almost all the different objects used ceremonially. They appear on altars, masks, headdresses, prayer-sticks, aspergills, *tiponis*, rattles, whistles, gourds, road markers, society standards, and a variety of other paraphernalia (Fewkes 1898a: 689), and any compilation of instances of their use in particular cases would be virtually interminable. There is no need to labor that point, but a brief consideration of the purposes of their use may be appropriate. Their primary significance would seem to be that of serving as conveyers to the supernatural powers of petitions for rain. This is implicit in much of the ritual, though it is not often broadly stated in ethnographic reports, which in most cases are concerned with the particular rather than the general. For example, it is said of a Zuñi kachina that he wears owl feathers "to bring the rain," and of another that he wears parrot and downy eagle feathers down his back "to make the clouds come" (Bunzel 1932: 1041, 1012). Eagle-tail feathers in certain Hopi costume "are the white cloud wings," and on the staff carried by a Hopi kachina they are "to waft or carry the prayer, any, all prayers" (Stephen 1936: 853, 216). Furthermore, a feather attached to a string and laid across a trail in Hopi ritual observances is "the trail over which travel all the prayers of all the people" (Stephen 1936: 782). In some instances, feathers are suspended

Reprinted with the permission of the Peabody Museum from "Kiva Mural Decorations at Awatovi and Kawaika-a," by Watson Smith, pages 173-183, *Papers of the Museum of the American Archaeology and Ethnology*, Volume 37, Harvard University, 1952.

beneath cloud symbols "depicting falling rain" (Stephen 1936: 85–86). The use of feathers on prayer-sticks is of course consistent with what has just been said, and is considered elsewhere (Smith 1952b: 189–198). Although most of the evidence indicates a characteristic preoccupation with rain in connection with the use of feathers, some writers have ascribed more sophisticated or fanciful concepts to their use, for example, Nequatewa (1946: 16), where the use of the eagle "breath" plume is said to be a "prayer that the language of the Hopi be soft and cheerful, and also that the lives of people may be long without trouble or sickness."

It is generally supposed, and I think would usually be stated by an informant, that the feathers of particular birds possess special significance or symbolism, and that their use in particular circumstances is prescriptive. While this is undoubtedly true within limits, I believe that the observation of such distinctions is actually not always honored in practice, and that we cannot therefore depend with assurance upon the presence or absence of a given kind of feather as a diagnostic for the identification of a particular ceremonial or kachina impersonation. This hypothesis is borne out by a number of authorities. On describing the making of *hihikwispi*, or feathers with strings attached, for the Oraibi Soyal observance, Voth lists the feathers of five different birds as having been used, but he adds that others are substituted "if any one is out of one or the other feather" (Dorsey and Voth 1901: 38; figure possibly wearing *hihikwispis* hanging down his back appears in Figure 46 *d*). Stephen writes to a similar effect in noting that, while the prescribed feathers for the Flute ceremony are those of the yellow warbler, two men used duck "because they had no yellow bird in their boxes" (Stephen 1936: 782). In another connection he says that the Snake priests at Shipaulovi in 1892 wore on their heads warrior bundles composed of differing combinations of feathers, some having turkey-tail, hawk-wing, and parakeet feathers, and others eagle, parakeet, and blue-bird (Stephen 1936: 753). And the various personators of the Hümis kachina at the Niman ceremony in Walpi in 1893 varied a good deal in the feathers used on their arm bands: some had eagle-wing, others hawk, dyed-pigeon, or hen (Stephen 1936: 531).

At Acoma it is said that "Nowadays just 'pretty' feathers are used" (Stirling 1942: 32). It thus becomes apparent that a good deal of latitude is permitted in the use of different kinds of feathers, and that a particular kind may not always be employed in a given association. If we may assume that a comparable state of affairs obtained when our

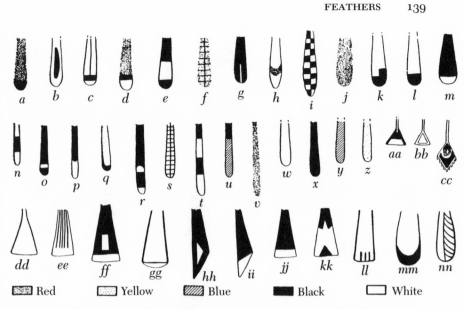

Fig. 7.1. A selection of feather conventions as used in the Jeddito mural paintings. Compare with Figures 7.2 through 7.5.

murals were painted, we must conclude that specific identifications from them will very likely be difficult or at best uncertain.

Let us look, nevertheless, at those devices in the murals that suggest feather portrayals for one reason or another. Where they are realistically portrayed, there should be no question as to their identification, but difficulties will arise in cases in which the portrayals are abstract or highly conventionalized. In such cases identification can be made, if at all, only on the basis of similarity to known modern conventionalism or to association with some other identifiable object with which the feather in question always is used in a fixed relationship. Since we are attempting to use the feathers as criteria diagnostic of other objects, ceremonies, or impersonations, this latter approach rather begs the question through the specious process of identifying the diagnostic feature by means of the thing of which it is thought to be the indicator.

In Figures 7.1 to 7.5 there appear reproductions of all the feather [and bird] types that occur in the murals. A few of these are fairly obvious in any case, and the identity of some others can be corroborated by comparison with modern Pueblo artistic conventions, although parallels between the two categories are less frequent and convincing than might be expected.

Red   Yellow   Black   White

EAGLE-TAIL FEATHERS

The feather most widely illustrated and identified in the reports of Pueblo ethnology and archaeology is that from the tail of the eagle. This is a large and very distinctive feather, whose most striking characteristic is the white body and black tip, the latter being longer on one side of the shaft than on the other. Its representation occurs frequently in the murals in the form indicated in Figure 7.1 *k*, either singly in radial relationship to "sun shields" (as for example in Test 5, Room 4, Right Wall Design 3, Smith 1952b, Fig. 72 *a*; Test 14, Room 3, Right Wall Design 9, Smith 1952b, Fig. 73 *a*); or around a mask (Room 788, Right Wall Design 4, Smith 1952b, Fig. 79 *a*); or in a series in the form of the tail of some monster (Room 788, Left Wall Design 5, Smith 1952b, Fig. 71 *a*); the pseudo-tail of a quadruped (Test 5, Room 4, Right Wall Design 10, Smith 1952b, Fig. 56 *b*; Test 14, Room 3, Front Wall B Design 11, Smith 1952b, Fig. 49 *a*); or as a part of some of the highly conventionalized geometric patterns of Layout Group III (Test 14, Room 3, Front Wall B Design 9 and Right Wall Design 16, Smith 1952b, Fig. 59 *a*, *b*).

Kenneth M. Chapman has thoroughly and lucidly considered the history of the use of this convention in Pueblo art and has pointed out the rather striking fact that it "had its origin and development in a rather brief period of Pueblo culture; a period known to be comparatively late in pre-Spanish times. It is never found in the decoration of the most archaic 'black on white' pottery which had so wide a distribution throughout the Southwest, nor is it used by the Pueblo Indians of today," except for those on First Mesa who have consciously imitated the old Sikyatki style (Chapman 1927: 539, 1938: 144, Pl. 8 *b*, *f*). Chapman implements this statement with illustrations of the device as used on pottery from Hawikuh, Kawaika-a, Frijoles, Tyuonyi, San Cristóbal, Amoxiumqua, Gran Quivira, and Pecos, all of shortly pre-Spanish date. It also occurs rarely in the mural paintings at Kuaua.

That the device really did represent an eagle-tail feather seems to be reasonably certain, both because of its graphic similarity to the real thing as well its representational use by modern Pueblo artists

Fig. 7.2. A selection of feather and bird motifs painted on Jeddito pottery contemporary with mural paintings containing similar devices. Compare Figures 7.1, 7.3 through 7.5. a-e, h-n, p-r, Sikyatki Polychrome; f, g, Jeddito Black-on-yellow; o, San Bernardo Polychrome. See Smith 1952b, Figure 10 for proveniences and Peabody Museum catalogue numbers. See Smith 1952b, Figures 48 a, b, 49 a, 59 a, b for examples of Sikyatki style in the paintings.

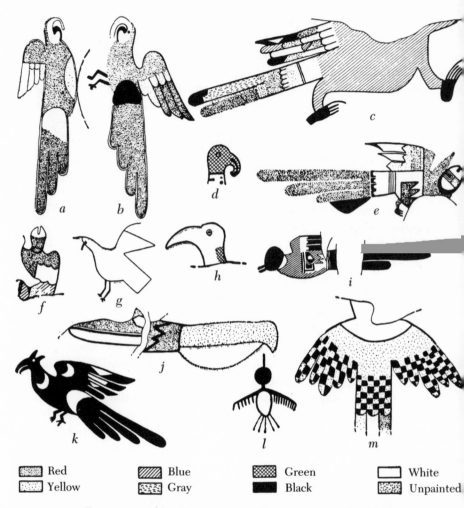

Red   Blue   Green   White
Yellow   Gray   Black   Unpainted

Fig. 7.3. Illustrations of birds portrayed in the Jeddito mural paintings. Others are shown in Figure 7.4. Compare with the similar birds painted on contemporary Jeddito pottery in Figure 7.2 and with the various styles used in the mural paintings to depict feathers shown in Figures 7.1 and 7.5. See Smith 1952b: 183-189 for full discussion of birds in the mural paintings. a, b, e, f, j, almost certainly parrots; c, g, h, resemble a jay; k, probably a roadrunner; l, suggestive of the Thunder Bird; m, probably some form of falcon. See Smith 1952b, Figure 11 for proveniences.

(Smith 1952b: 175, Note 72). This usage does not really contradict Chapman's statement just quoted, however, for it still remains true that although the convention is now used representationally by Pueblo artists in portrayals of costume or paraphernalia in which actual eagle-tail feathers occur, it is not now employed directly or independently as a symbol or decorative device on pottery, altars, masks, and the like.

Despite the certainty of its identification as an eagle-tail feather, however, it was used in the Jeddito murals as a tail; between body and wing of a stylized bird; depending from the body of a bird; in a plumed headdress; on the head of a human being; on the heads of animals; and several times without direct association (Chapman 1927: 537, Figs. 7–20). Its discovery in a variety of uses in the Jeddito murals is consistent with its distribution through the Hopi, Zuñi, and Rio Grande areas during Pueblo IV as outlined by Chapman, but the questions of its sudden and unexplained origin and abandonment are still unanswered. The device apparently survived into the Spanish period, at least in modified form, as evidenced by three bowls illustrated in Mera (1939, Pls. 16, 32, 52), although the execution of these cases is not exactly like that of the older examples. It has not been used in recent times on pottery, nor so far as known on masks, altars, or wall paintings, although in drawings by native artists it is frequently approximated (Smith 1952b: 175, note 72).

Dr. Fewkes failed to recognize the device as an eagle-tail feather when he found it on a Sikyatki bowl (Fewkes 1898a: 684, Pl. 133 1898b: 11–12, Figs. 8, 9), and called it instead a "breath feather," apparently because it occurred at the junction of what he regarded as the body and wing of a highly schematized "bird." He emphasized the mistake by adding that the breath feather's "ancient symbolism is very clearly indicated. . . and is markedly different from that of either the wing or tail feathers. . . . "

A possible variation of the eagle-tail convention occurring in our murals is that shown in Figure 7.1 l. This is a long white feather with its rounded tip painted solid black, and is found in the three large radial patterns of Group IV in Room 218, Front Wall Designs 11, 12, and 14 (Smith 1952b, Fig. 42 a, b, c), and also, but in a slightly different form, at the termini of the two long pendent lines at the left end of Test 14, Room 3, Front Wall B Design 2 (Fig. 7.1 mm; Smith 1952b, Fig. 52 a). This device is identified as an eagle feather by the Hopi artist, Fred Kabotie (1949, No. 11).

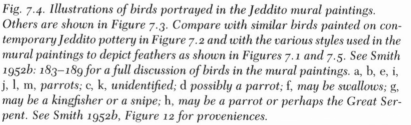

▨ Red	⬚ Blue	■ Black	▨ Unpainted
⬚ Yellow	▨ Gray	☐ White	

Fig. 7.4. *Illustrations of birds portrayed in the Jeddito mural paintings. Others are shown in Figure 7.3. Compare with similar birds painted on contemporary Jeddito pottery in Figure 7.2 and with the various styles used in the mural paintings to depict feathers as shown in Figures 7.1 and 7.5. See Smith 1952b: 183–189 for a full discussion of birds in the mural paintings. a, b, e, i, j, l, m, parrots; c, k, unidentified; d possibly a parrot; f, may be swallows; g, may be a kingfisher or a snipe; h, may be a parrot or perhaps the Great Serpent. See Smith 1952b, Figure 12 for proveniences.*

The abandonment of this conventional symbol in Pueblo ceremonial does not, however, imply the non-use of the actual eagle-tail feather, its wide usage in modern times being indicated by the following incomplete list of altars on which it is employed:

VILLAGE	CEREMONY	AUTHORITY
Sia	Querräna	Stevenson 1894, Pls. 27, 29
Santa Ana	Cikame	White 1942: 332, Fig. 41
Santa Ana	Hunter's society	White 1942: 338–339, Fig. 47
Jemez	Eagle society	Parsons 1925b, Pl. 5 b
Acoma	Antelope clan	Stirling 1942, Pl. 3 (1)
Acoma	Fire society	Stirling 1942, Pl. 8 (2)
Acoma	Cacique's	White 1942, Pl. I a
Zuñi	Né wekwe society	Stevenson 1904, Pl. 104
Zuñi	Há lokwe society	Stevenson 1904, Pl. 122
Zuñi	Shúmaakwe society	Stevenson 1904, Pl. 125
Zuñi	Cimex society	Stevenson 1904, Pl. 126
Zuñi	Great Fire society	Stevenson 1904: 507
Walpi	Flute society	Stephen 1936: 791, Fig. 427
Oraibi	Soyal	Dorsey and Voth 1901, Pl. 28
Oraibi	Powamu	Voth 1901: 38, 76–77, Pl. 43
Oraibi	Snake	Fewkes 1897b, Pl. 73
Hano	Soyal	Parsons 1939: 919
Hano	Soyal	Parsons 1925a, Fig. 11
Hano	Soyal	Fewkes 1899: 268, Pls. 18–19
Hano	Soyal	Stephen 1936: 40, Fig. 24

From the data thus adduced, both with regard to the conventional symbol and the feather itself, indicative of its use in a wide variety of associations, there seems practically no possibility of endowing it with any virtue as a criterion of specific cultural affiliation or of ceremonial identification. As we have already seen, the representational stereotype occurred in Pueblo art pretty well throughout the area and in many differing associations during Pueblo IV and perhaps early Pueblo V, and the feather itself is so widely used in Pueblo ritual today that its presence can hardly be indicative of a particular ceremony, a particular cult society, or a particular impersonation.

Mrs. Parsons (1925b: 112) says that at Jemez eagle-tail feathers are "by far the commonest used on masks." At Zuñi they are worn "by many different kachinas" (Bunzel 1932: 863), and among the Hopi they are "used on masks, standards, altars, arrow shafts and for many

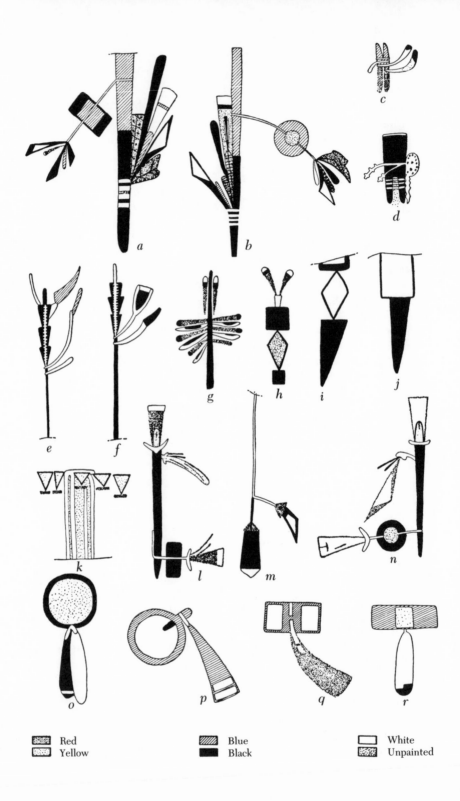

a

b

c

d

e

f

g

h

i

j

k

l

m

n

o

p

q

r

Red
Yellow

Blue
Black

White
Unpainted

other purposes" (Voth 1912a: 109). Their extensive use in costume embellishment is well illustrated in Dr. Fewkes' collection of drawings of Hopi kachinas, in which at least fifty different supernaturals are shown wearing them (Fewkes 1903; other instances of their widespread use: Stevenson 1904, Parsons 1925a, White 1932, 1942, Stephen 1936).

Eagle-tail feathers are also used in some curing ceremonies to drive away evil (Dumarest 1919: 156; Parsons 1920a: 125, 1920b: 62), and in the Hopi Snake dance they are used to stroke or "whip" the snakes (Stephen 1936: 585, but sometimes turkey-tail feathers are used, Fig. 358).

What symbolism if any, can be attached to eagle-tail feathers is also somewhat variable, although in many instances they appear to represent the rays of the sun, especially among the Hopi, when arranged radially around a central disk (Voth 1901: 76, 1912a: 109; Dorsey and Voth 1901, Pl. 28; Fewkes 1896: 244, note 1, 1898b: 11, 1903: 110), and in one case at Oraibi, they carried prayers for warm weather (Voth 1901: 76–77). In an instance at Jemez, however, they are shown radiating from the moon (Parsons 1925b: Pl. 3 b), and at Zuñi they are said to be "for the clouds" (Bunzel 1932: 1065), and the wearing of eagle-tail feathers by the kachinas there is explained by the legend of the little boy who was once saved and returned to his home by an eagle, who gave him some of his tail feathers. When the boy reached his home he gave the feathers to his father, who forthwith proclaimed that the kachinas would thereafter wear such feathers, "because the eagle is strong and wise and kind. He travels far in all directions and so he will surely bring us the rains" (Bunzel 1932: 864–867). Fred Kabotie (1949: No. 11) says they are associated with fierce animals and are symbols of boldness and power.

I have no idea of the significance of the pseudo-tails of eagle feathers that protrude from the ani of some quadrupeds in the Jeddito

Fig. 7.5. Prayer-sticks or pahos portrayed in the Jeddito mural paintings. The feather conventions used on these pahos should be compared with those shown in Figures 7.1., 7.3, and 7.4, as well as with those painted on contemporary pottery shown in Figure 7.2. See Smith 1952b: 189-198 for a full discussion of prayer-sticks in the mural paintings. c, d, examples of double pahos; k, unidentifiable object that may be some form of paho; o, p, annular pahos; q, r, probably cylindrical pahos; rest, standard pahos. See Smith 1952b, Figure 13 for proveniences.

murals, such as those in Test 5, Room 4, Right Wall Design 10 (Smith 1952b, Fig 56 *b*) and Test 14, Room 3, Front Wall B Design 11 (Smith 1952b, Fig. 49 *a*). An amusing though ribald parallel is provided by Stephen, however, in an anecdote of the treatment accorded a group of clowns by a burlesque Navajo medicine man during the public part of a spring kachina dance at Hano. The unfortunate clowns, pretending illness, were made to lie flat on their bellies, whereupon the medicine man removed their breech cloths, and slapped on the anus of each a quantity of grass pulp into which he stuck an eagle tail feather (Stephen 1936: 384).

TURKEY–TAIL FEATHERS

Here again is a feather of distinctive character, and one fairly easy to recognize from even a crude attempt at representation. Its principal features are its elongated isosceles triangular shape, with a whitish tip set off by a black stripe from the reddish-brown area of the shaft, across which delicate herringbone lines are sometimes apparent. In the Jeddito murals there is no detail that closely simulates such a feather, but there are several instances of long triangular feathers with white tips that probably are intended as such (Fig. 7.1 *ff*, *ii*, *jj*).

The modern convention of depicting these feathers is usually by a long triangle, colored black with a white tip, or with a white stripe or spot just short of the tip (Fewkes 1903, Pls. 9, 38; Bunzel 1932 Pls. 29 *b*, 38 *b*, 40 *b*; White 1942, Fig. 13; Stephen 1936, Fig. 454), although they are sometimes more realistically rendered (Fewkes 1903, Pl. 46). A very realistic turkey tail occurs on a classic Mimbres black-on-white bowl (Cosgrove and Cosgrove 1932, Pl. 216 *d*). On the other hand, there are examples of long solid-black triangles (Fewkes 1903, Pl. 21), and others that are white with orange tips (Fewkes 1903, Pl. 28) or black tips (White 1932, Fig 7, 1935, Figs 44, 46, 47; Kabotie 1949, no. 11). This variety would suggest that the only constant criterion is the elongated triangular outline, but even this is not used in one drawing from Zuñi, which has almost parallel edges and a sharply rounded tip, colored entirely black except for a white transverse stripe at about its mid-point (Bunzel 1932: 958, Pl. 25 *a*). It will not be very convincing, then, to attempt identifications of turkey-tail feathers in the Jeddito murals, although there are several examples that approximate them (see Fig. 7.1 *ff*, *ii*, *jj* for examples of the triangular type, Fig. 7.1 *o* for examples like that cited above from Zuñi).

The use of turkey-tail feathers in modern Pueblo ritual is fairly general, though less widespread than that of eagle-tail feathers. Dr. Parsons (1925b: 112) says that on Jemez masks "turkey feathers, particularly tail feathers, are also used," but she does not suggest that they are limited to any particular kind of mask or other usage. At Zuñi "feathers from the breast and tail of the turkey. . . are worn by many different kachinas. . . " (Bunzel 1932: 863) and Fewkes illustrates at least six Hopi kachinas that wear them (Fewkes 1903, Pls. 7, 9, 21, 28, 38, 46). They are used at Cochiti (Dumarest 1919: 156), Santo Domingo (White 1935, Figs. 44, 46, 47), and elsewhere fairly extensively.

The symbolism attaching to the turkey-tail feather, like that of the eagle-tail feather, is varied. At Cochiti they seem to be tokens of the dead (Dumarest 1919: 156), and a similar usage obtains at Zuñi (Bunzel 1932: 677, note 19). Among the Hopi they have a sun symbolism when used radially about a shield (Stephen 1936: 126–127) or on sun prayer-sticks at Powamu (Stephen 1936, Fig. 97), as a prayer for water on the long water prayer-stick (Stephen 1936: 834, Fig. 452), or in the common Hopi prayer-plumes (*nakwakwoshi*; Nequatewa 1946: 16). Fred Kabotie (1949, No. 11) says they are associated with fish as symbols of gentleness.

PARROT FEATHERS

There seems to be no recognizable convention for depicting parrot feathers, beyond the elementary one of showing them simply as long, narrow strips of red, yellow, blue, or green. In the native drawings shown by Fewkes of Hopi kachinas, many are so embellished although in only seven cases are they actually identified in the accompanying text (Fewkes 1903, Pls. 20, 31, 34, 38, 63, where no importance seems to be given to color).

In the drawings of Santa Ana kachinas (White 1942, Figs. 13–21), as well as in those of San Felipe (White 1932, Figs. 3–10), a similar method is used. There are in our mural paintings numerous examples of long, rounded feathers in red, yellow, and blue, though none in green (Fig. 7.1 *j*, *v*, *y*, *z*). There are some others of only slightly different character: red with black tip (Fig. 7.1 *a*); blue with black shaft (Fig. 7.1 *u*); yellow with black tip (Fig. 7.1 *q*). These are used in a variety of ways, the long red ones being especially frequent radiating from the periphery of white disks or "shields" usually in alternation with eagle-tail feathers. They also appear in what seem to be prayer-sticks of various sorts, and frequently in headdresses of anthropomorphic figures. In a few cases they depend from the lower edge of basebands.

Parrot feathers are used today in a variety of ways by all Pueblo groups, although their frequency is limited by the small supply available (Stephen 1936: 166). One of the most highly valued gifts that a white visitor can bestow upon a Pueblo Indian is a collection of parrot feathers, since the birds are not native in the Southwest except for one species (*Rhynchopsitta pachyrhyncha*), a rather small green bird that occurs in the mountains of southern Arizona and New Mexico (Hargrave 1933a: 59). It is known, however, that parrots or macaws were possessed by the Pueblos in pre-Spanish times, and they could only have been obtained by trade from Mexico, a traffic now legally prohibited (Smith 1952b: 180, note 115 [see Hargrave 1970]).

At most of the modern villages parrot feathers are used on a variety of masks, costumes, and prayer-sticks (Smith 1952b: 180, Note 116). As with other feathers, their symbolism seems to be the general one of carrying prayers to the supernaturals, but they also possess several specific powers, "to make the clouds come" (Bunzel 1932: 1012, Pl. 35a, Zuñi), to represent the nadir, the region of all colors (Stephen 1936: 216), etc. It is unsafe to assume unreservedly, however, that the red, blue, and yellow feathers in the murals are those of the parrot or the macaw, since they may equally well represent feathers of like colors from other birds native to the area.

Thus, the yellow feathers could come from the yellow warbler, yellow-winged blackbird, oriole, canary, or perhaps other birds native in the area, which are known to be used today (Hopi: Nequatewa 1946: 16; Stephen 1936: 144, 64, 776, 781; Fewkes 1895: 437; Isleta: Parsons 1932: 274). The wild canary feather is used by the Hopi on the tassels of wedding robes, because they "carry prayers for brightness and joy in life" (Nequatewa and Colton 1933, Fig. 4). Stephen (1936: 782) says that the color of the yellow warbler indicates that it scatters pollen and that "when there is plenty of rain there are plenty of grass seeds and multitudes of yellow birds are seen eating the seeds and scattering the life-giving pollen over the land."

Likewise, the red feathers could have belonged to cardinal, woodpecker (Stephen 1936: 7, 140, 800, 960, etc.), or redwing, or they could be simply any feathers stained red, as is sometimes done nowadays (Fewkes 1903: 63; Bourke 1884: 125). During our seasons of work in the Hopi country, we saw many instances of the use of chicken feathers, dyed red and green, on ceremonial costumes.

The blue feathers also could have come from the bluebird, jay, blue grosbeak, or king-fisher at Hopi (Fewkes 1895: 437; Stephen 1936: 753, 791, 885, 962, etc.); Zuñi (Bunzel 1932: 660), and Isleta (Parsons 1932: 274). Four Hopi informants at Awatovi agreed that they were bluebird. The bluebird is the rain bird, "his cry is heard when the rain comes" (Stephen 1936: 791).

OTHER FEATHERS

In the Jeddito murals there appear also some examples of feathers that are painted in a variety of checkerboard or lattice patterns. They are represented in Figure 7.1 *f, i, s*, and all of them are drawn with a longitudinal midrib in black crossed at right angles by short transverse black lines. They have either a white or red background, and in two examples the alternate squares are filled with black to form a true checkerboard. These devices do not very accurately depict any natural feather, but they suggest those of several birds that are used today in Pueblo ceremonials. Of these, the most common is probably the turkey-wing feather, which is long and narrow with thick black chevrons on a brownish or yellowish ground, and they are so represented in modern native drawings at Hopi (Earle and Kennard 1938, Pl. 25), at Santa Ana (White 1942, Pls. 13–21), and at Zuñi (Bunzel 1932, Pl. 33 *d*). Another possible identification would be the pheasant (Earle and Kennard 1938, Pl. 28), the flicker, several of the woodpeckers, or the hawks (Bunzel 1932: 1065, "for the rain" at Zuñi; Earle and Kennard 1938, Pl. 14; White 1942, Figs. 13–21). Four Hopi informants at Awatovi identified the feather in Figure 7.1 *s*, as that of a sparrow hawk, and another one closely similar as that of a rock wren.

There remain among the murals a wide variety of black and black-and-white feathers that could be tentatively identified with any of several native birds. Some must almost certainly represent either the magpie or the roadrunner, whose wing feathers strongly suggest those shown in Figure 7.1 *hh*, or perhaps the crow, raven, blackbird, or phainopepla (silky flycatcher), most of which are used today by the Hopi and other Pueblo peoples. Stephen (1936) recorded the magpie and the blackbird on Flute *tiponi* (p. 801), the magpie on an altar at the Wuwuchim (p. 962), the raven in death exorcism (p. 826), on a war standard (p. 95), and on a kachina mask (Fig. 156), and the crow on a

kachina mask (p. 257) and on a Niman altar (p. 529). Four Hopi informants at Awatovi identified the feathers in Figure 7.1 *hh* as that of a
roadrunner and Figure 7.1 *x* as that of the magpie. Bandelier (1890:
296) says that in the Rio Grande plumes of owl, crow, and woodpecker
are dreaded implements of evil magic.

The roadrunner is regarded by the Hopi as an exemplar of
speed, and his feathers are believed to produce fleetness in any one to
whom they are attached (Stephen 1936: 950). The raven evidently
connotes death, for in the Hopi War dance, its presence is said to imply that it will feed upon enemies to be slain by the warriors, and
those persons who carry out a burial are later exorcised with the
feather of a raven (Stephen 1936: 95, 826).

The long plain-white feather shown in Figure 7.1 *w* was identified by four Hopi informants as that of a white duck. Duck feathers are
used by the Hopi in many ways and in different ceremonies (Stephen
1936): on a prayer-stick for the spring kachina dance (p. 397), on
Snake-Antelope prayer-sticks (pp. 625, 673, 685), on a Flute prayer-
stick (p. 782), on a circlet used at the Niman (p. 536), on a circlet for
the Summer Flute ceremony (p. 802), and on an Antelope altar (p.
607). Parsons (1939) records the use of duck feathers at Zuñi (pp. 276,
954), Isleta (pp. 373, 586, 728), Laguna (pp. 276, 954), and most other
villages (p. 275).

As usual, the significance of the duck feathers has to do with rain,
and it is said to be used by the Hopi "because ducks swim in ponds of
water... after rain" (Stephen 1936: 782), and at Zuñi (Parsons 1939:
174, 201–202), and Santo Domingo (White 1935: 175) the kachinas
turn into ducks and fly away following their appearance at a ceremony.
It is of interest to note, however, that duck feathers appear not to be
worn by the Duck Kachina himself in the Hopi villages—at least no
mention is made of them in the principal descriptions as published
(Stephen 1936: 220–221, 469–481, Figs. 135, 136, 260, 261, 263,
265, 266; Fewkes 1897a: 299–300, Figs. 43–46, 1903: 78, Pl. 15).

Other small white feathers may be the downy feathers from a
wide variety of birds, and are used in many ways and with divergent
symbolism. For example, the downy eagle feather on the Agave society helmet at the Hopi Wuwuchim represents snow (Stephen 1936:
975); hawk down is used at Zuñi on the faces of warriors as symbolic of
the clouds (Stephen 1940: 212), and downy feathers are used at other
villages for similar purposes (Parsons 1939: 832, 840, Buffalo dance at
Tesuque and Taos).

There still remain a number of feathers that pretty well defy identification, such as those shown in Figure 7.1 *c, g, n, r, t, bb, cc, dd, ee,* and others. Some of these may have been meant to represent specific feathers or they may only be schematized designs suggestive of feathers in general. In either case they are of no evidentiary value to this inquiry, since they are not identifiable with any particular ceremony of any recognizable ritual symbolism.

In several instances a device appears whose identity at first glance is not obvious. This is exemplified by what appear to be bifurcated tassels at the extreme left end of the painting in Room 788, Left Wall Design 5 (Smith 1952b, Fig. 71 *a*) and at the extreme right end of the painting in Test 14, Room 3, Front Wall B Design 2 (Smith 1952b, Fig. 52 *a*). These are probably intended to be feathers split along the shaft, a practice that is often followed by the Hopi.

We cannot abandon the subject of feathers, however, without some attention to the matter of certain other Pueblo decorative devices, both ancient and modern, that have been interpreted as feathers. As might be suspected, Dr. Fewkes leads the field in this pursuit, and he has found many supposed feather symbols, especially on Sikyatki pottery. While it would be supererogatory to repeat or summarize Dr. Fewkes' writings on the subject, it may be useful to point out certain features in the murals that are closely similar to what he has elsewhere identified as feathers. A series of black triangles arising from the circumference of a circle or a disk are said by Fewkes to be feathers, for example, and are illustrated by the central circular device in Test 14, Room 3, Front Wall B Design 11 (Smith 1952b, Fig. 49 *a*), Right Wall Designs 12 and 16 (Smith 1952b, Figs. 48 *a*, 59 *b*). The former of these occurrences is almost exactly like that painted around the orifice of a Sikyatki bowl illustrated by Fewkes (1898a: 690, Fig. 274, Pl. 143 *b*, 1898b: 9). Another device, in the form of a rectangular fret or involute, the terminal member of which is embellished with three or four elongated triangles extending inward to the center of the involute (Smith 1952b, Fig. 48 *b*), is designated as the symbol of wing feathers (Fewkes 1898a, Pls. 145 *b*, 147 *a*, 150 *f*, 1898b: 9). An example occurs in Test 14, Room 3, Front Wall A Design 4 (Smith 1952b, Fig. 48 *b*). Instances of other conventions identified by Fewkes as feathers, or wings or tails of birds may be recognized in the mural paintings of Layout Group III (2), and compared with the illustrations of Sikyatki pottery (Smith 1952b, Figs. 48 *a, b*, 49 *a*, 59 *a, b*; Fewkes 1898a, Pls. 132–158, 1898b: 5–8).

Finally, the series of triangles with parallel lines extending from their bases, that occur in semi-circular arrangement in the paintings in Room 218, Front Wall Designs 11, 12, and 14 (Smith 1952b, Figs. 42 b, c, a), and singly on Front Wall Design 8 (Smith 1952b, Fig. 44 c), are almost exactly like devices illustrated by Fewkes and designated as feathers (Fewkes 1898a: 697, Pl. 153 a).

Admittedly, the preceding discussion is an inadequate treatment of the subject. It would be possible to construct a tabulation of all the feathers used in all the ritual paraphernalia and costume in all the Pueblo villages, but I believe that such research would be only an egregious foray into obscurantism, and further that it would serve at best only as ponderous emphasis of the points that I have attempted to make by the relatively eclectic discussion above. These points are that virtually all types of available feathers are used today in Pueblo ritual in a wide range of associations, that there is no strictly observed limitation of particular feathers to particular ceremonies, that with only a few exceptions there are no absolutely prescriptive feather requirements for most masks, prayer-sticks, altars, or impersonations, and furthermore that the artistic conventions for the graphic depiction of feathers are very elastic. As to the symbolism of feathers, here again it mostly comes down to association with prayers and clouds, perhaps because, in terms of sympathetic magic, a feather resembles a cloud; it is the distinguishing feature that gives a bird the power to soar into the clouds; and it floats gently on the wind, and so can carry messages to those Powers that control the clouds and the rain. Bandelier (1890: 297–298) says: "The feather, plume, or down floats in the air, even in a still atmosphere, and is therefore to the Indian the emblem of thought. A prayer is a thought, and often a suppressed sigh only, consequently the plume is above all the emblem of prayer." All this is fairly evident in modern Pueblo ritual, and I think that on analogy we can ascribe the same meaning to the use of feathers in the Jeddito murals, without however being able to use them by themselves in associating particular mural designs with specific ceremonies.

8. Pots on the Kiva Walls

The Awatovi expedition recorded more than a half a million potsherds representing several thousand vessels (Smith 1971: 14). By far the most unusual "pots" recovered, however, were the twenty-nine vessels that the ancient Hopi had painted on the walls of their kivas (Smith 1952b: 134). Those two-dimensional pots, which are interesting both as examples of Hopi artistic endeavors and as evidence of the ceremonial use of pottery vessels, offer certain advantages to the sherd-weary archaeologist that no other collection of Southwestern pottery can match. They can be studied without worrying about paste and temper. No tedious measurements of thickness are even possible. And since only one surface is visible, their description and analysis need not be overly long. Watson Smith certainly understood these advantages. He was able to describe and discuss these twenty-nine representations of pots in a baker's dozen pages (Smith 1952b: 249-261), but he needed almost six hundred pages to cope with the thirty thousand pieces of decorated pottery from the Western Mound at Awatovi (Smith 1971).

The twenty-nine unique pots are also attractive to the museum curator charged with storing and caring for the huge collections of ceramic artifacts from archaeological excavations in the Southwest. Watson Smith was also able to appreciate this characteristic of the vessels painted on the kiva walls, for he had been involved in several efforts to improve storage conditions at the Peabody Museum. Shortly after World War II, he and Philip Phillips were intrigued by the rapid recording capabilities of the then new Polaroid camera. With the assistance of Robert Greengo they developed a system for recording and discarding certain materials

in storage, such as the natural cobbles and chipped shale that had
been gathered from the "Trenton gravels" during the concerted,
but unsuccessful, late nineteenth-century search for a Palaeolithic
occupation in the Americas (Abbott 1872).

Smith played a creative role in the consideration of another attempt to address the storage problems of the Peabody Museum. It
began with a memo written on 17 January 1957 by Brew, as Director of the Museum, to Philip Phillips, Curator of Southeastern Archaeology and unofficial chairman of a shadow "storage committee"
(Smith 1987: 139). Brew sought the help of Phillips, Smith, Fred
Orchard, the Preparator and resident memory bank for the location
of the collections, and Helen Whiting, the Cataloguer. He wanted
them to explore the possibility of returning some collections to the
attic, a sixth floor under the eaves that served then as now as a
storage area for many of the museum's collections. According to
Smith (1987: 137) the attic was "a horrendous shambles, dusty, ill-
lighted, unventilated, unsafe, stuffed with assorted 'stuff,' and an
obvious fire hazard." In other words, it was, unfortunately, not unlike the storage areas of many museums at that time.

Although Smith was then living in Tucson where he had established the Peabody Museum West of the Pecos, he assured
Brew in a memo dated 15 February 1957 of his willingness to assist
in the effort to find room in the attic for more material (Smith 1987:
140). As was often his wont, he recorded his thoughts in poetic
form. Inspired by the famous "Ode on a Grecian Urn," written in
1819 by John Keats, he presented his views in a piece that contains
several name puns referring to his co-conspirators (Smith 1984a:
245, 1987: 140):

SECOND THOUGHTS ON AN ATTIC SPACE

Thou still unravish'd bride of quietness,
Thou fusty child of silence and slow time!
O Attic Space! Fair Altitude! What breed
Of men or Gods pierce thy inviolate womb?
What pipes and timbrels? What wild ecstasy?
What Orchard strews its blossoms on thy breast?
What witch's Brew imparts its Fillip to thy dust?
What Whiting'd sepulchre shall catalogue thy bones?

Thou, silent void, dost tease us out of thought
As does Eternity; dim storage vault,
When old age shall this generation waste,
Thou shalt remain, obscured by brighter lights
On other floors, a friend to dust and shades,
And from thy cavernous heights shall speak a voice:
"Beauty is dust, dust beauty!" – That is all
Ye know on earth, and all ye need to know.

He continued his memo to Brew with what he called "a plea on behalf of the ideal of the inviolability of things as they used to be" (Smith 1987: 140):

John Keats was born a century and a half too soon. He squandered his poetic genius on an isolated ancient artifact; had he lived to know the peace and tranquillity of Divinity Avenue he might have written somewhat as indicated above, in shocked horror at the thought of profanation of the sanctuary of ten thousand sherds of Harvard in Attic chastity.

Nevertheless, Smith could not resist the challenge presented by the storage problems of the attic, of which he had been aware ever since his service as a civil defense warden early in World War II (Smith 1984a: 243-245). He confessed to Brew that the "prospects, however dreadful, of an archaeological ascent to that sanctuary, cabined, binned, and shelved as it may be, fills me with only the utmost lust" (Smith 1987: 140).

Nothing came of Brew's plans to deal with the storage problem in the attic until the late 1970s when Harvard University finally recognized that although the Peabody Museum was admired and envied for the size and quality of its collections, it was severely criticized for the inadequate way that it cared for them. The attic was completely renovated and converted into a state-of-the-art collection storage area (Lamberg-Karlovsky 1982) that Smith (1987: 138) has described as "resplendent with brightly painted partitions, refulgent with fluorescent lighting, protected by sprinklers, dustless from air-conditioning, relieved of its former burden of disorganized 'stuff,' and occupied by happy personnel, who probably know nothing of the horror of its Mediaeval darkness."

Watson Smith was never able to satisfy his "utmost lust" concerning that attic space. Nor did he have to find storage space for the twenty-nine "pots." However, he was able to illustrate how valuable ceramic artifacts can be to the archaeologist by his careful study of those twenty-nine pots that long ago had been painted on the walls of Hopi kivas (Smith 1952b: 249–261).

R.H.T.

Ceremonial Bowls

In many, if not all, Pueblo kiva ceremonies a medicine bowl, so-called, plays an important part, and is variously placed before the upright altar, on the sand painting, or carried in the hands of one of the celebrants. These bowls contain such things as prayer-sticks, stone fetishes, yucca suds, water, "medicine" made of plants and herbs, corn, meal, pollen, pebbles, feathers, etc. To attempt any detailed analysis of their various usages and contents in all the villages would serve no useful purpose, but one feature is provocative of special inquiry.

CRENELLATE BOWLS

Generally speaking, the term "medicine bowl" is applied nowadays to a vessel of specialized purpose and peculiar form, distinguished from other bowls that may also be used in esoteric ceremonies. The former are rectangular or circular in horizontal section and nearly always have a crenellate rim, above which there extends a series of stepped terraces, rising like mountains from the rim itself. Frequently, a strap handle in the form of an arch extends across the top of the bowl. These bowls are usually decorated on their exteriors with life forms, clouds, lightning, and other ritualistic devices differing notably from the more stylized geometric patterns that embellish the ordinary food bowls used contemporaneously in the same villages. Food bowls, however, are also used in ceremonies, to contain corn meal and the like, but their role is less important than that of the

Reprinted with the permission of the Peabody Museum from "Kiva Mural Decorations at Awatovi and Kawaika-a," by Watson Smith, pages 249-261, *Papers of the Peabody Museum of American Archaeology and Ethnology*, Volume 37, Harvard University, 1952.

medicine bowl, which is never used for any secular purpose and frequently is very old.

As I have said, the crenellate form is in modern times used at most villages (Smith 1952b: 250, Note 668), although not to the exclusion of the plain sub-spherical food-bowl form, which also appears as altar paraphernalia in many cases, sometimes together with the crenellate form, sometimes alone. The presence or absence of the food-bowl form, however, is not for our purposes important, but that of the crenellate bowl is, since its origin and the history of its distribution are not clear. With the situation as it exists today, in which this form seems to be generally in use throughout the area, we may contrast that of Pueblo III and earlier, during which such bowls apparently were not in use anywhere, if we may accept as evidence therefor the failure of archaeologists to find them in excavating ruins of early date. When they were introduced and from what source we do not know, but our murals suggest that they were not in use in the Jeddito up to the end of Pueblo IV; this inference is based on the fact that in the murals there appear numerous representations of the usual sub-spherical food bowl, but not a single example of the crenellate form.

In his excavations at Sikyatki, Fewkes (1898a: 655) found no crenellate bowls, and was unable to account for their later introduction to the Hopi. At Pecos a few fragments of crenellate rims were found, of Glaze V and Plain Red types, assigned to the early and late seventeenth century by Kidder (Kidder and Shepard 1936: 274-275, 609, 620-621, Figs. 326 *a-c*, 283 *d-g*), who goes on to explain that "no surely identifiable example of rim-terrace has come to light in earlier strata, while there are terraced fragments which almost certainly belong to Glaze V or subsequent periods" (Kidder and Shepard 1936: 275). No mention of crenellate bowls is made in the La Plata area from Basket Maker III through Pueblo III (Morris 1939, Fig. 76).

In the Jeddito excavations only one fragment that might have been from the rim of a crenellate bowl was found, and its identification as such is not certain (Peabody Museum Cat. No. 37-111-10/10885). Moreover, it was found on the surface of the southwest slope below the ruin, and is consequently undatable. Typologically, it appears to belong to the Jeddito yellow wares, but whether pre- or post-Spanish cannot be determined. This fragment is flat on both surfaces, about 8 mm in thickness, and has the outer edge formed into a double terrace of four steps. The inner edge is concavely semi-circular, producing a shape resembling a yoke, with a neck at each of the lower corners by which it was originally attached to the vessel. It could have been one of several terraces rising from the rim of a rectangular bowl, with a cut-out semi-circle beneath it; on the other hand, it might have been a vertical handle extending from the orifice of a small bowl or jug, or the flat horizontal tail of a "duck bowl" so-called, examples of which were found at Awatovi as well as elsewhere in the Southwest. These are all, however, entirely hypothetical identifications.

POSSIBLE EVOLUTION OF THE CRENELLATE BOWL

What may be the prototype of the crenellate bowl is exemplified by a rectangular vessel from Kiva C at Awatovi which was occupied during Pueblo IV, prior to the Spanish occupation. This specimen has a plain rim, but on its vertical side is painted a double-terraced figure surmounting a semi-circle and flanked by dragonflies and bird(?) symbols (Peabody Museum Cat. No. 35-126-10/5513, Smith 1952b, Fig. 17 o). A closely similar design was painted on a circular dish with flat bottom and almost vertical sides from Sikyatki (Fewkes 1898a, Pl. 120 f); and on another vessel from Sikyatki there was painted a terrace surmounting a semi-circle, in outline almost exactly like the pottery fragment from Awatovi (Fewkes 1919, Pl. 78, v). This terrace is a decorative feature not found on ordinary domestic pottery of the period. If these vessels were for ceremonial use, as is suggested by their unusual shape as well as by their decoration, it can easily be imagined that at some later date the idea of the terrace should have been extended and applied in such a way as to produce a style having terraces actually superimposed above the rim instead of merely painted on the surface—a development that apparently did not occur until later.

It has often been said that throughout the Pueblo area the decorations applied to ceremonial bowls, whether or not crenellate in shape, are different from those painted on domestic pottery, the former bearing clouds, lightning, animal and plant forms, and the like, whereas ordinary bowls have almost always been decorated in a style either purely geometric or highly conventionalized. Mrs. Parsons (1940: 541-542) makes this distinction in discussing a bowl found by Hough "either at Kawaika or Kokopnyama," which had anthropomorphs, snakes, and what Mrs. Parsons regarded as a "locust"—why I do not know, certainly not on morphological grounds. She goes on to express the opinion that this bowl was ceremonial because of its naturalistic designs. I cannot agree with this reasoning, however, for in the light of the large number of vessels with naturalistic designs that were found by Fewkes at Sikyatki and by the Peabody Museum Expedition in the Jeddito ruins, to say nothing of those from the classic Mimbres horizon and various Pueblo III and IV sites in the Little Colorado area, it seems impossible to believe that they were all ceremonial or that they constituted a ceramic class separable in any fundamental way from the bulk of contemporary pottery, and, on the other hand, there are examples in modern times of the use of ordinary utilitarian bowls in ceremonial association at Zuñi (Stevenson 1904, Pls. 125, 127), and at Hopi (Fewkes 1903, Pl. 49; Stephen 1936, Fig. 24). Examples of non-crenellate medicine bowls bearing, however, specialized decorations have been noted at Santo Domingo (White 1935, Figs. 30, 45).

With respect to the Jeddito mural bowls, then, we may draw the tentative conclusion that, during the period of their painting, crenellate bowls were not in use and that bowls of the standard sub-spherical form were used ceremonially. Were they, however, of a special decorative style different from that applied to utility bowls of the same period? And if so, were they made locally for the express purpose of ritual use, were they preserved from an earlier time as valuable antiques, or were they imported from an exotic source? These questions can be answered by a comparative study of ceramic design in the Jeddito ruins and other areas of contemporary habitation, and their solution will perhaps shed some light on the habits and customs of the Jeddito people, as well as upon their foreign-exchange associations. As a basis for such a comparison, we shall first examine and analyze the character of the designs on the mural bowls themselves.

DESIGNS ON MURAL BOWL REPRESENTATIONS

Disregarding the matter of color, which is variable and has no relationship to that of any actual Pueblo ceramic product, the designs on bowls painted on the walls of Jeddito kivas are very homogeneous and simple. All are applied in a horizontal band extending in width from the rim of the bowl about half way to the bottom, and every one is based either on the terrace or the interlocking rectangular fret. The simplest is that on the bowl at the right end of Room 529, Right Wall Design 4 (Fig. 8.1 j; Smith 1952b, Fig. 49 b), in which a series of rather badly drawn three-step terraces, all facing in the same direction, rise on stems from a horizontal base. This is an elementary pattern, of rather general distribution though not very frequent occurrence in the Southwest, and certainly not of sufficient distinctiveness to be regarded as peculiarly ceremonial in character. Its distinguish-

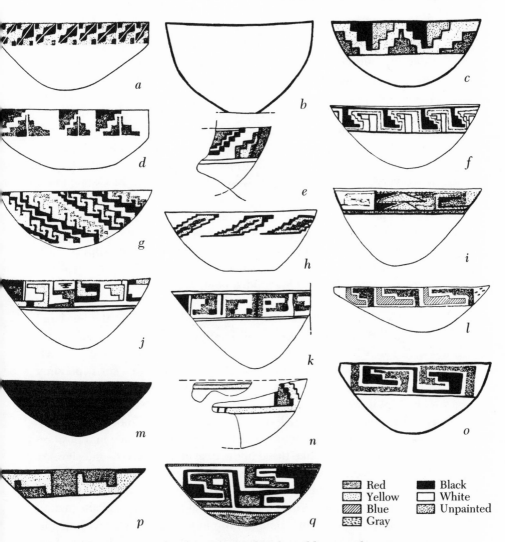

Fig. 8.1. Decorations on bowls represented in the Jeddito mural paintings; not to scale. Compare with designs found on actual contemporary ceramics shown in Figures 8.2 and 8.3 and with designs on kilts worn by human figures in the mural paintings shown on Figure 8.4. See Smith 1952b, Figure 20 for proveniences.

ing feature is the fact that its painted elements all are oriented in the same direction and are not balanced by corresponding elements of the same or another color facing in the opposite direction. It thus lacks any form of symmetry, unless the background areas can be regarded as balancing the more prominently painted alternate ones. In other parts of the Pueblo area this manner of repeating an asymmetrical element without balancing it against an homologous one is found prior to and during early Pueblo III but seems almost if not quite to have disappeared after that date (Smith 1952b: 252, Note 680). Examples like it are very rare in the Jeddito, although one Jeddito Black-on-yellow olla (Peabody Museum Cat. No. 36-131-10/7458) was found at Awatovi on the upper surface of which a row of similar terraces was painted around the rim. Each of them was embellished with a hooked or key figure extending from the upper corner. It thus appears possible that this pattern was archaic during Pueblo IV at Awatovi, but there is no doubt that it was indigenous, if rare, on vessels of a non-ceremonial character.

A variation of the design just discussed appears on the left-hand bowl in Test 5, Room 2, Left Wall Design 4 (Fig. 8.1 d; Smith 1952b, Fig. 88 a) where a similar row of repeated but asymmetrical half-terraces is painted along the upper border, although a corresponding series of symmetrical double terraces is applied along the lower edge. This combination produces the curious result that each upper terrace is balanced in birotational symmetry by the contiguous half of the lower terrace, leaving the other half of the lower terrace in a position of imbalance, exactly like those in the case of the preceding design. As a matter of fact, however, this design has the appearance of being incomplete; if the upper row of half-terraces were completed to form double terraces, the resulting pattern would be a series of alternating double terraces, each one being in birotational symmetry with its immediate neighbor, as is the case on the bowl in Test 5, Room 2, Left Wall Design 6 (Fig. 8.1 c; Smith 1952b, Fig. 67 d), discussed in the second paragraph below.

The third pattern used on Jeddito mural bowls is the familiar one of opposed and balanced half-terraces of contrasting colors, as evidenced by the left-hand bowl in Room 788, Left Wall Design 4 (Fig. 8.1 l; Smith 1952b, Fig. 79 b), and probably by that in Test 5, Room 4, Right Wall Design 5 (Smith 1952b, Fig. 86 b), although the latter is too badly weathered to make the design clearly discernible. This scheme occurs widely over the Pueblo area throughout all periods

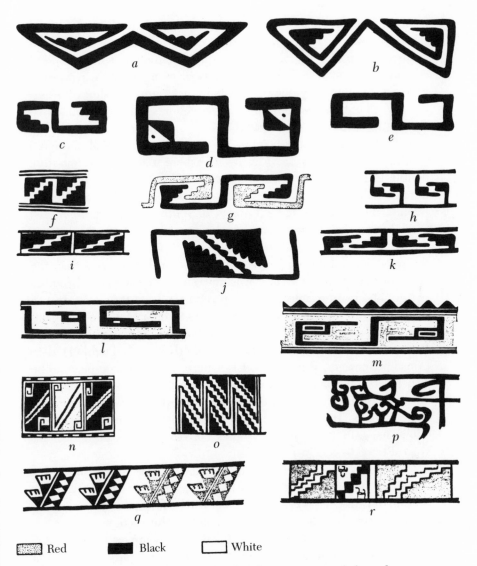

Red   Black   White

Fig. 8.2. A selection of borders and isolated geometric motifs from the exteriors of Jeddito bowls and jars contemporary with the mural paintings.
Others are shown in Figure 8.3. Compare with the designs painted on the
bowls portrayed in the murals shown in Figure 8.1 and those applied to kilts
worn by human figures in the mural paintings shown in Figure 8.4. See Smith
1952b, Figure 21 for proveniences and Peabody Museum catalogue numbers.

from at least Pueblo I onwards, and was common in the Jeddito and the Hopi country during the time of occupation of Awatovi, so that its occurrence in the mural bowls is quite consistent with the local ceramic tradition of the time. Characteristic examples of the pattern as used on contemporary bowl exteriors from Awatovi are shown in Figure 8.2, all of them on Jeddito Black-on-yellow vessels.

A design closely related to the latter, but differing in certain features, is that used on the bowl in Test 5, Room 2, Left Wall Design 6 (Fig. 8.1 c; Smith 1952b, Fig. 67 d), where a series of alternating double terraces occurs, each one being in birotational symmetry to the next. This is actually the completed version of the design in Test 5, Room 2, Left Wall Design 4 (Fig. 8.1 d; Smith 1952b, Fig. 88 a), discussed above, and at first glance, appears to be essentially the same as that of the alternating half-terraces. While it undoubtedly belongs to the same general decorative tradition, it is much more rare than the latter in Pueblo ceramics and it is not represented on actual Jeddito pottery at all. An example has been reported from the northern San Juan area (Martin and Willis 1940, Pl. 60 4, on a McElmo Black-on-white mug from near Lowry Ruin, Colorado), and it was found at Pecos on Black-on-white vessels of Pueblo III or early Pueblo IV date (Amsden 1931: 17, Fig. 8 h, j). Elsewhere, the pattern appears to be either very rare or wholly absent except in the Little Colorado area, where it is fairly common in a variety of rather elaborate forms on some Pueblo III types, such as Wingate Black-on-red (Martin and Willis 1940, Pl. 91 3) and St. John's Polychrome (Martin and Willis 1940, Pls. 98 6, 99 1, 100 1, 101 4).

It would appear possible, therefore, that the bowl bearing this design might represent an archaic or exotic style not indigenous to the Jeddito during Pueblo IV. This subject will be further discussed under Inferences of Specialized Styles at the end of this section.

An elaboration of the opposed half-terraces appears in the interlocking S-pattern, in which alternate terraces form embellishments at the extremities of a line drawn in the form of an angular S, each terrace being balanced by a corresponding one of a different color forming the terminal embellishment of a similar angular S-figure, each S being thus interlocked with the ones on either end of it. Examples appear in Room 788, Right Wall Design 4 (Smith 1952b, Fig. 79 a), the right-hand bowl on Left Wall Design 4 (Fig. 8.1 q; Smith 1952b, Fig. 79 b), Left Wall Design 5 (Fig. 8.1 o; Smith 1952b, Fig. 71 a), and at the extreme right of the bowl in Test 4, Room 7, Right Wall Design 2

(Fig. 8.1 *i*; Smith 1952b, Fig. 88 *c*). In Room 529, Right Wall Design 4 (Fig. 8.1 *k*; Smith 1952b, Fig. 49 *b*), the bowl at the left displays one complete and one incomplete S-figure, but the opposing or interlocking one is omitted. Basically, however, this example is not different from the more usual form of the completed pattern, and can be considered as belonging to the same category. Examples of this design were frequently found on the exteriors of bowls or on the upper surfaces of jars at Awatovi, contemporary with the mural representations thereof, so that it seems pretty certain that what we see in the murals are merely reproductions of the current fashion in bowls. Characteristic examples of this design on pottery from Awatovi are shown in Figure 8.2, belonging to a variety of local types contemporary with or later than the murals. Some of these are completely interlocking and in others the S-figures stand alone. The feature of rectangular open areas or boxes within the basal portions of the terrace elements, like those appearing on the right-hand bowl in Room 788, Left Wall Design 4 (Fig. 8.1 *q*; Smith 1952b, Fig. 79 *b*), provides a further bit of evidence for the inference that the pottery then in ordinary use was also employed in kiva ceremonials, since two polychrome jars from Awatovi displayed the same feature (Fig. 8.2 *l*, *m*). At the right extremity of the decorative band on this same bowl appears a small star symbol composed of four black rectangles, continuous at their inner corners, around an open rectangle in the center. This, too, is a very common element on contemporary local pottery, but it occurs nowhere else in the kiva wall paintings.

On two of the mural bowls an additional element is introduced into the pattern of opposed half-terraces, by the insertion between their stepped faces of a stepped line. In one case the half-terraces are attached to the border lines of the decorative band along their bases, as in Test 14, Room 4, Front Wall Design 1 (Fig. 8.1 *e*; Smith 1952b, Fig. 73 *b*), whereas in the other case the half-terraces are attached alternately to the upper and lower border lines by their stems, and the stepped lines form the terminal segments of a continuous fret of successive S-curves that run continuously between and around the half-terraces as in Test 4, Room 4, Right Wall Design 8 (Fig. 8.1 *f*; Smith 1952b, Fig. 60 *a*). Variations of this pattern are common on contemporary Jeddito pottery. Characteristic examples on contemporary Jeddito bowls are shown in Figure 8.2.

What may be regarded as a peculiar variant of the design described in the last paragraph occurs on two of the bowls in Test 4,

Red   Black   White

Room 4, Right Wall Design 8 (Fig. 8.1 *h*; Smith 1952b, Fig. 60 *a*, *b*), where a stepped line occupies the central area of a diagonal panel the sides of which are enclosed by stepped lines. If horizontal and vertical straight lines are drawn from the upper and lower ends, respectively, of these stepped lines until they intersect, a series of alternate half-terraces will result, having between their opposing diagonal faces the stepped line exactly as in the usual form previously discussed. The incompleteness of the implied half-terraces does not change the basic character of the design insofar as its classification at this point is concerned. I have seen nothing exactly like this on actual pottery, either in the Jeddito or elsewhere, but its homogeneity with the general "school" under consideration is evident.

A different decorative scheme appears on the other two bowls in Test 4, Room 4, Right Wall Design 8 (Fig. 8.1 *g*; Smith 1952b, Fig. 60 *a*, *b*), composed of a series of parallel stepped lines, from the external angles of which extend small key-shaped devices. The latter occur along only one side of each stepped line, and are arranged so that they interlock with those of the next line. Thus, only the alternate interlinear areas are filled with keys, the other areas being left blank, so that we have in effect a series of pairs of interlocking diagonal stepped lines. I have seen nothing exactly like this in the Jeddito or elsewhere, but the use of series of keyed or spurred triangles or squares, either in single rows or in interlocking rows, is a very widely diffused Puebloan character from Basket Maker III times onward. To find it here, although in an unusual arrangement, is not surprising. Other examples of similar character are found in lower border decorations on some of the ceremonial kilts painted on Jeddito murals. These are fully discussed elsewhere (Smith 1952b: 277-279), together with the probable origin of the pattern in the ceramic series culminating in Fourmile Polychrome (Figs. 8.2, 8.3, 8.4).

The bowl depicted in Test 4, Room 7, Right Wall Design 2 (Fig. 8.1 *i*; Smith 1952b, Fig. 88 *c*) is decorated in part with the interlocking terrace motive and in part with a pattern that is not duplicated elsewhere among the mural bowls, nor in the actual ceramic remains from

Fig. 8.3. A selection of border motifs from Jeddito pottery contemporary with the mural paintings. Others are shown in Figure 8.2. Compare with the decorations on bowls represented in the mural paintings shown in Figure 8.1 and with similar designs applied to the borders of kilts worn by human figures in the mural paintings shown in Figure 8.4. See Smith 1952b, Figure 1a for the identification of the pottery types and for other details.

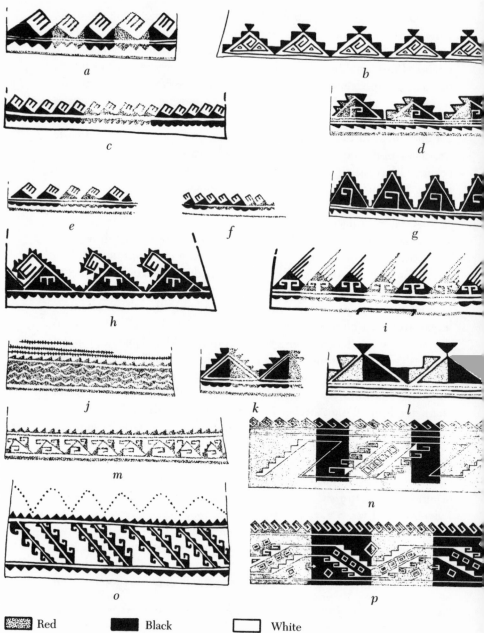

a

b

c

d

e

f

g

h

i

j

k

l

m

n

o

p

Red   Black   White

the Jeddito villages. For that matter, I have not seen anything exactly like it on any Pueblo vessel, modern or ancient. This is not to say, however, that it is beyond the range of the local decorative tradition, but merely that it is an unusual variant on a fairly common pattern. In detail, this decoration forms an elongated rectangular panel within the usual horizontal band that encircles the bowl, and this panel is in turn subdivided into two equal sections, one above the other, by a horizontal line midway between the upper and lower borders. Within each of these two portions, the area is further subdivided by diagonal lines extending from the lower corners to the mid-point of the upper edge, producing a broad isosceles triangular area in the center, its base extending the full length of the main panel, the upper right and left portions of which thus remain to form elongated right triangular areas, the short legs of which coincide with the ends of the main panel. Within the right triangles are solid black fillers, the one at the left being also a right triangle similar to but smaller than the area in which it is painted, that at the right being an attenuated terrace not quite filling the triangular area.

Considering the entire panel in comparison with contemporary local pottery, it will be seen that each of the two rectangular subdivisions is very closely similar to a design element that occurred fairly frequently at both Sikyatki and Awatovi in Pueblo IV. This feature was ordinarily not painted within an enclosed rectangular panel or band, but instead on the unrestricted exterior surface of a bowl, where it took the form of two diagonal lines sloping outward and downward from a point of intersection or origin, and corresponding to the sides of the isosceles triangle in the mural example. From the outer and lower ends of these lines arose more or less elaborate embellishments in the form of frets, triangles, terraced figures, and the like, filling the triangular areas above the sloping lines, the entire figure being roughly in the form of an expanded letter W. Usually, but not always, the isosceles area in the lower center was left undecorated. Examples on

Fig. 8.4. Lower border decorations on kilts worn by human figures in the Jeddito mural paintings, with comparative modern examples. Although there is no certain means of determining the decorative techniques actually applied to contemporary Jeddito kilts, the designs strongly suggest embroidery (Smith 1952b: 270-276, 289-291). Compare with designs on Jeddito pottery shown in Figure 8.2 and 8.3 and with those on pottery portrayed in the mural paintings shown in Figure 8.1. a-m, Awatovi; o, Kawaika-a; n, p, modern examples from Acoma. See Smith 1952b, Figure 25 for details of provenience.

bowls from Sikyatki are illustrated in Fewkes (1898a, Figs. 319, 320, 321, 323, 324) and some similar examples from the Jeddito are shown in Figure 8.2 *a, b*. Thus, we see that the only substantial divergence by which the mural bowl differs from its ceramic contemporaries is in the application of two such W-figures, one above the other, and even this characteristic is suggested in the case of a jar of Sikyatki Polychrome from Sikyatki, in which a rectangular panel is, in effect, but without the execution of an actual dividing line, subdivided into two horizontal panels one above the other. Each of these areas contains two attenuated, horizontally disposed terraces, one based on each end and birotationally symmetrical. No actual sloping lines are present, but the over-all visual effect is not unlike that provided by the mural bowl (Fewkes 1898a, Pl. 136 *b*).

The rather simple but pleasing decoration applied to the right-hand bowl in Test 5, Room 2, Left Wall Design 4 (Fig. 8.1 *a*; Smith 1952b, Fig. 88 *a*), presents a version of an almost universally distributed pattern, but one that very strangely seems to be rare on pottery in the Jeddito. The basic analysis of this design will show a horizontal band containing a series of square or rectangular panels, separated by vertical bars, and each bisected by a diagonal line extending from one lower corner to the opposite upper corner, the distinguishing feature being that throughout the row of panels the diagonal lines all slope in the same direction. Each right triangle formed by the subdivision of the panels is itself subdivided into a diagonal row of small solidly painted right triangles, whose hypotenuses coincide with the main diagonal, leaving an open area, square or stepped, in the opposite corner of the large triangular panel, that is either entirely unpainted or is filled with some simple embellishment such as a fret, a small solid figure, or the like.

In the case of the bowl in Test 5, as indeed in the majority of cases elsewhere in the Southwest, the enclosing triangles contain only two smaller solid triangles leaving a simple square at the apex of the enclosing triangle. This square is partly filled by a smaller square of solid color, not concentric with the enclosing square but coincident with its outer corner. About the only example from Awatovi is a sherd of Sikyatki Polychrome, illustrated in Figure 8.2 *r*. A Jeddito Black-on-orange mug, found at Kawaika-a, bears a design rather remotely resembling the same pattern (Peabody Museum Field No. 4464; Fig. 8.2 *n*).

A review of Pueblo pottery design from Pueblo I to modern times will show this basic pattern with a multitude of variations, distributed over much of the Pueblo area in all periods. Its apparent rarity in the Jeddito in Pueblo IV is puzzling and unexplained, especially since examples of it occur in Little Colorado and other villages of only slightly earlier or even of contemporary date (Smith 1952b: 259, Note 692).

Just possibly, I have devoted unwarranted attention to this special design pattern, for from a larger point of view it is closely akin to the alternate interlocking half-terraces that have already been discussed and that are found copiously on pottery in the Jeddito ruins. These two patterns are essentially similar in being constructed on a scheme of triangular areas filled with solid elements and separated by a form of angular meander composed of alternate diagonal and vertical segments and forming a sort of continuous series of letter N's. The basic layout of both is thus the same; the distinction exists in the relative emphasis placed upon the components in each. In the opposed-terrace pattern the main interest is directed toward the terraces themselves, permitting the meandering separation band to take care of itself as a secondary background feature. In the other form of the arrangement, however, the meander is itself the determining feature and the embellishments inside the resultant triangles are less strongly emphasized. Both variants of this pattern of alternate diagonal and vertical lines differ from the opposed double-terrace pattern in that the separation meander in the latter is composed of segments sloping in alternate directions and forming a sort of continuous W.

Two other bowls in the Jeddito murals bear decorative bands, but that in Test 5, Room 2, Left Wall Design 2 (Smith 1952b, Fig. 66 c), is indecipherable, and the one in the layer immediately beneath it on the same wall (Smith 1952b, Fig. 66 d) shows only a small fragment containing a terraced element of indeterminate character.

In Room 788, Left Wall Design 3 (Fig. 8.1 m; Smith 1952b, Fig. 80 b), are two bowls painted completely black, another similar one appearing in Room 528, Left Wall Design 1 (Smith 1952b, Fig. 69 a), while in Test 5, Room 4, Right Wall Design 1 (Fig. 8.1 b; Smith 1952b, Fig. 68 b), there are two others painted completely white. The latter, of course, are not unusual, since bowls without external decoration existed all over the Pueblo area in all periods, although they were less frequent in the Jeddito during Pueblo IV than in earlier times. But solid black bowls were more unusual, although they did occur fairly widely in the Pueblo area in prehistoric horizons. Some pure black vessels were found at Pecos in the historic part of the ruin, probably late seventeenth century in date (Kidder and Shepard 1936: 287, 610, Fig. 249 *a-g*).

All bowls portrayed in the murals occur in designs belonging to Layout Group I and with three exceptions all rest upon the baseband. Those exceptions are the one in Test 5, Room 2, Left Wall Design 6 (Smith 1952b, Fig. 67 *d*), which is carried on the head of an anthropomorphic figure, and the two in Room 788, Left Wall Design 3 (Smith 1952b, Fig. 80 *b*), each of which is held in the hands of two seated human figures.

POSSIBLE INFERENCES FROM THE MURAL BOWLS

Chronological Inferences

It is difficult to formulate any very convincing conclusions from the study of bowls in the murals. I do not know what significance, if any, can be attached to the fact of their occurrence only in Group I; if our chronology is correct (Smith 1952b: 315-319), this would indicate that they were represented on the kiva walls during only a relatively late period, but their absence from mural paintings of early date does not negate the use of actual pottery bowls in ceremonials of those times, since the mural style was not then addressed to a representation of altars or ceremonial paraphernalia, as later became the practice. Doubtless, bowls were ceremonially used in the earlier times, but we have no graphic proof of such a custom.

Inferences of Specialized Styles

In amplification of what has been said in the preceding paragraphs relative to similarities between the decorations on mural bowls and those on actual bowls found in the ruins, some further discussion of contemporary local ceramic design will be helpful. Throughout the Southwest it has always been customary for Pueblo potters, in the painting of bowls, to apply the principal decoration to the interior surfaces. In fact, prior to Pueblo IV the exteriors were hardly ever decorated at all. During Pueblo IV, however, the practice of placing relatively inconspicuous designs on the exteriors arose, and has continued to evolve since that time, until today bowl exteriors are treated as a major decorative field.

Jeddito Black-on-yellow and Sikyatki Polychrome were made at a period when outside bowl decoration was present but definitely secondary, and also when the style of interior design was undergoing a vigorous evolution from the older geometric patterns to a new and more naturalistic style involving scrolls, feathers, zoomorphic, and even human forms. So striking are these interior features that most archaeologists have been prone to ignore or pass over with little notice the simpler exterior details, which were not usually within the spirit of the interior "Sikyatki" style, but tended to preserve the older and more traditional geometric elements of an earlier period. Such underemphasis on the exteriors of Pueblo IV bowls influenced all of us at Awatovi, and led us at first to the belief that the conventionally decorated bowls depicted in mural paintings were not of the same artistic school as the flamboyant ones represented in the contemporary ceramic collections.

As a matter of fact, this hypothesis was quite erroneous, and arose from the failure to realize that the bowls with gay Sikyatki interiors also possessed exterior decorations closely comparable to those painted on the kiva walls. Thus the two styles, though different, were not mutually exclusive, and actually did co-exist on most of the local pottery of the era. The geometric exterior designs were archaic in a sense, but they persisted throughout, and their presence on the mural bowls does not therefore mark most of the latter either as antiques or as outside the contemporary decorative tradition.

If we may accept the decoration on the mural bowls as reasonably faithful to that appearing on the actual bowls used contemporaneously, it seems highly probable that no distinctive style, either of shape or decoration, differentiated the bowls used ritually from the general utilitarian class. This inference seems to follow from the fact that, while every design used on the mural bowls cannot be exactly duplicated among the ceramic remains found in the Jeddito, still their general stylistic similarity is sufficiently close to warrant the conclusion that the differences are mere minor variations of style, due perhaps to the use of the plane wall surface instead of the convex surface of an actual bowl, perhaps to the probable fact that the actual pottery bowls were painted by women, and the mural bowls by men. In such case it would not be surprising to find the men unfamiliar with the detail of standard ceramic decoration, and consequently producing somewhat aberrant patterns. Representative decorations from the outsides of contemporary bowls found in the Jeddito ruins are illustrated in Figures 8.2 and 8.3.

In a few cases, however, it must be recognized that the almost complete local absence of pottery remains bearing certain of the design features used on some of the mural bowls, taken together with the occurrence of those features at other locations or at an earlier period, suggests the possibility that at least a few ceremonial bowls may have been hand-me-downs from earlier times or imports from other villages. I am not convinced of this hypothesis, however, for even if the unusual mural bowls were simulations of antique or exotic vessels, remains of such prototypes should have been found in the extensive excavations at Awatovi, had they been there. On the whole, I am inclined to believe that the seeming oddities in the mural bowls are significant only of a degree of carelessness on the part of the painters in their adherence to the strict canons of the local ceramic school, which produced relatively slight variants within the broader framework of the decorative tradition.

9. *The Potsherd Paradigm*

In the second decade of this century a handful of the first professional anthropologists in this country significantly changed the
direction of Southwestern archaeology by what archaeologists in the
ninth decade call a paradigm shift. They accomplished this shift
without any of the bombast, pretension, and truculence that seem
to have characterized subsequent paradigm shifters. Nels Nelson
(1914, 1916) in the Galisteo Basin, A. V. Kidder (1914, 1915, Kidder and Kidder 1917) on the Pajarito Plateau and at Pecos, and
Leslie Spier (1917) and A. L. Kroeber (1916) at Zuñi all made their
very considerable contributions by paying attention to potsherds
rather than to "whole vessels for museum display and symbolic
analysis" (Taylor 1954: 563–564). They moved Southwestern archaeology away from its antiquarian beginnings toward the systematic discipline that it is today. Richard Woodbury (1973: 90) has
summarized this change as follows: "Potsherds had become a source
of historical information and not merely fragments of once hand-
some works of art."

Southwestern archaeologists have exploited that historic resource most successfully. By the beginning of the fourth decade of
this century, they were able, with the aid of the absolute dating of
dendrochronology, to establish a measure of time control that made
them the envy of their colleagues in the rest of the New World.
They were able to use that chronological control to maximum ad-
vantage because they had developed a solid taxonomic approach to
the study of those potsherds that had been at the center of that first
paradigm shift. By the fourth decade, the progress of ceramic
studies made it possible for the Museum of Northern Arizona to

publish its remarkable "Handbook of Northern Arizona Pottery Wares." Watson Smith played an important role in the preparation of that unique work (Cotton and Hargrave 1937), as Woodbury has pointed out.

In fact, Smith was one of the Southwest's acknowledged experts in the systematic description and sensible interpretation of broken prehistoric pottery. He and other Southwestern archaeologists perfected the systematic study of pottery to such an extent that one latter-day paradigm shifter (Taylor 1954: 569) strongly criticized what he considered an over emphasis on ceramic analysis: "There can be no doubt that pots and potsherds have carried a big stick in the Southwest, although it cannot be said that they have spoken very softly."

Much of the criticism that Taylor and others have directed toward Southwestern ceramic studies was valid. Interpretations of a higher order were badly needed. It is interesting to note, however, that many successful efforts to progress beyond the traditional kinds of interpretation have been carried out in the Southwest precisely because the taxonomic and chronological controls so essential to such studies were already solidly in place. The following analysis by Watson Smith of one common class of decorative devices used on prehistoric Southwestern pottery is an excellent example of the thorough, no-nonsense approach to ceramic studies for which Southwestern archaeology is renowned (Smith 1971: 85–97).

R.H.T.

Analysis of the Use of Hooks, Scrolls, and Keys

A characteristic feature of the painted pottery of many areas in the prehistoric Southwest, including the Western Mound at Awatovi, was a basically simple device composed of a line bent into the shape of a simple angle, hook, or angular scroll, or into a curved scroll or involute. These were often further embellished by the elaboration of their distal ends into stepped terraces or keyed figures.

Hooks, scrolls, or keys occurred sometimes as isolated figures on vessel surfaces, but usually they were attached to some other and larger element of the design, usually a line or solid figure, the latter nearly always a triangle. Where hooks, scrolls, or keys were attached directly to a line they were usually arranged in a repetitive row and the line formed either an endless longitudinal circuit of the vessel or was one of the boundaries of a circumscribed panel that constituted a major subdivision of the entire decorated area.

Where hooks, scrolls, or keys were appended to solid triangles they were formed by the prolongation of one leg of the triangle, usually its longer one if the triangle was not isosceles, so that each rose from the apex of its triangle as a kind of crest. The triangles themselves were usually arranged in rows with the hypotenuse serving as the base, along circumferential or panel-bordering lines, in exactly the same manner that characterized the free-standing hooks, scrolls, and keys described above. Sometimes these devices were arranged in a single row along one side of a line, but much more often they were set

Reprinted with the permission of the Peabody Museum from "Painted Ceramics of the Western Mound at Awatovi," by Watson Smith, pages 85-97, *Papers of the Peabody Museum of American Archaeology and Ethnology*, Volume 38, Harvard University, 1971.

in two opposing rows along the facing sides of two parallel lines in a relationship of bifold rotational symmetry (Brainerd 1942, Fig 12; Shepard 1956, Fig. 37). They constituted, thus, the fillers within an elongated band or panel in such a manner that the prolongations extended parallel to and toward each other. Spacing between the repeated units varied but was always approximately uniform on any one specimen. In the triangles, these might be contiguous at their basal corners or they might be separated by an appreciable interval.

An important factor contributing to the arrangement of the elements and the degree of complexity of the pattern created by them lay in the distance between the two bordering parallel lines relative to the height of the triangles or of the hooks, scrolls, or keys. If the bases of the opposing rows were sufficiently far apart relative to the height of the constituent elements, the extremities of the latter might not extend beyond an imaginary line parallel to and midway between the two baselines, so that the opposing rows were completely separated from each other.

But much more often the elements were sufficiently high for the hooked portions of one row to penetrate the interspaces between those of the other row. In this alignment it was possible for the outer or dorsal contours of the hooks, keys, or scrolls of one row to be arranged back-to-back (or addorsed) with those of the other row. A more frequent relationship however, was one in which the hooks, keys or scrolls of one row interlocked with their counterparts. Usually the elements remained separate, but often they were tied together by a diagonal line from the tip of one to the tip of its fellow, or by a right line connecting the two parallel stalks inboard of the terminal members. Each of the variations of angular hooks or keys exhibited these connective forms, but curved scrolls were connected, if at all, only by a reverse curve that prolonged the spiral of one scroll into that of its opposite. Each of the several varieties of angular hooks occurred with terminal terraces or keys, but curved scrolls were never so embellished.

In rare instances opposed rows of triangles with non-interlocking hooks or keys were separated by a continuous zig-zag meander running between them. This meander might be a simple continuous line or it might itself be embellished with terraces, keys, or hooks that in turn were interlocked with corresponding devices rising from the triangles themselves, an arrangement that on occasion became very complex and that could be elaborated into an expanding overall pattern in which the two baselines disappeared altogether. This latter form is discussed elsewhere (Smith 1952b: 129, Fig. 80 *y, z, aa*).

Simpler arrangements of hooks, scrolls, and keys, both free and attached to triangles, sometimes occurred as patterns superimposed on a trellis underframe, but in themselves these examples did not differ essentially from the standard forms. They are discussed in connection with other applications of the trellis motif (Smith 1952b: 109–110, Fig. 63).

Another and different application of hooks, scrolls, and keys was found in their use as fillers for small areas left open and unpainted within large solid triangles. Such areas were usually at the corner formed by the right angle of a right triangle, within which was inscribed a hook, scroll, or key, usually arising from one of the legs of the triangle. Sometimes the open space was a disc-shaped area at the midpoint of the base of an isosceles triangle, and in such instances a curved scroll was used as the filler. Triangles with open areas were always relatively large and were not used in interlocking series. They usually occurred singly and often as the principal element in a triangular panel, which was in turn a major subdivision of the design layout. Structurally and functionally these large, open-corner triangles were not closely related to the rows of smaller hooked triangles, but they will be considered here for convenience.

What has been said heretofore is of general application to much of the painted pottery of the Anasazi area, but our further and more detailed discussion will be concerned specifically with the manifestations of hooks and hooked triangles in the Western Mound at Awatovi. For purposes of analysis we have broken down the total number of examples, of which about 700 were used in the design study, into eight groups. It should be borne in mind, however, that this classification is purely pragmatic and that many other equally logical ones could be made. Furthermore, while no two examples were identical, some degree of generalization is essential to any comprehensible presentation. We have recognized about 120 variations on the basic theme, most of which are illustrated herein (Figs. 9.1 to 9.7). This is in itself a rather frightening array, and further consolidation and generalization could, of course, be made, but we shall grant that privilege to the reader. The illustrations that appear on the following pages, incident to the discussion and description, are to a considerable degree stylized. They have been drawn without reference to any standard scale and without reproducing the innumerable minor variations of artistic skill exhibited by different potters. Such details are important and may in some contexts be significant of temporal, areal, or cultural factors. They will be more broadly discussed elsewhere, but our purpose at this point is the more restricted one of exploring the manner in which the artistic concept of the hook and the hooked triangle was exploited by the people who produced the output of the Jeddito Ceramic School. Illustrations elsewhere (Smith 1952b) showing specific vessels, or major portions thereof, may be consulted for an elucidation of these minor features and for an understanding of the use of hooks, scrolls, and keys in combination with other elements and motifs in the total decorative scheme.

Before entering upon a detailed consideration of the formal variations that characterized hooks, scrolls, and keys, it will be of interest to investigate both their stratigraphic occurrences and their distribution in terms of various types and color classes. These devices occurred in one form or another throughout the five stratigraphic groups and in each of the four principal color classes. They are individually illustrated in Figures 9.1 to 9.7, and the distribution of their major groupings is shown in Figure 9.9, Parts 1 to 3.

The relative frequencies of their stratigraphic distribution are summarized in Figure 9.10, which shows plainly the comparative complacency in the ratio of frequencies for this feature throughout the chronology of the Western Mound. For hooks, scrolls, and keys attached to triangles there is a slightly lower frequency in Ceramic Groups C, D, and E than in the two uppermost Groups, A and B.

Figure 9.11 presents the same data in a different form, showing the relative frequencies of major groups of this feature as they occurred on all specimens of the four principal color classes. This table deals with a larger number of specimens than does Figure 9.10 because it includes all specimens from the entire excavation, not merely those used in the stratigraphic analysis. Figure 9.11 indicates that the frequency of hooks, scrolls, and keys attached to triangles was greater on Tusayan Black-on-white specimens than on any other type, especially with relation to the orange-polychrome types, where it was only about one-half as high. The case with these features when not attached to triangles was not quite the same, however, for the highest proportion in the entire collection was borne by Awatovi Black-on-yellow, especially in the Group B levels. Comparing the two tables, it becomes apparent that on the whole the feature under consideration occurred with appreciable frequency on all color classes and at all levels;

that hooks, scrolls, and keys not attached to triangles were throughout the Mound about half again as frequent as they were when attached to triangles; that the frequencies were slightly lower in the bottom levels, highest on Tusayan Black-on-white, and lowest on the orange-polychromes.

The real meaning of all this is that this feature had significance only in comparatively limited statistical terms and cannot be meaningfully used either as a type diagnostic or as a time marker. We shall see, however, by a more detailed analysis, that certain minor variations are perhaps useful for one or the other of these purposes.

HOOKS, SCROLLS, AND KEYS NOT ATTACHED TO TRIANGLES

As stated above, the simplest forms of hooks, scrolls, and keys were found on specimens on which they were used either as isolated elements or as embellishments of a line or a pair of parallel lines. Examples of the several forms thus used are shown in Figure 9.1, and a consolidated summary of their distribution among the stratigraphic groups and the major color classes appears in Figures 9.9–9.11.

The use of simple lines to form right-angled hooks or scrolls is shown in Figure 9.1 *a–d*. In each form the stalk of the element rose vertically from a baseline, and its distal end was embellished by one (*a*) or two (*b*) short lines extending like flags at right angles to the stalk; when single, this flag might itself be elaborated by recurving to form a sort of shepherd's crook or rectangular scroll (*c, d*), or it might bear a terraced triangle or key, as in *e, f, g, h*. In almost all instances, these devices were set in series at short intervals along a line or in bifold rotational symmetry along two parallel lines. Sometimes, however, they were isolated, usually on exterior surfaces of bowls. Example *i* was one such, on a bowl that also exhibited an open-corner triangle containing a bull's eye. In one case a broad hatched hook was used, as shown in *j*.

The second degree of complexity was achieved by arranging two opposing rows of hooks or keys so that their extremities interlocked. This was done with each of the single forms, as shown in Figure 9.1 *k* to *r*. In only one case was there an example of a joining of the interlocking hooks (*n*) and only one instance of a series of unattached keys between the usual parallel border lines, as show in *s*. Curved scrolls were rare and were always disjunctive, occurring as isolated figures unattached to baselines, either single (*t*) or interlocking (*u*).

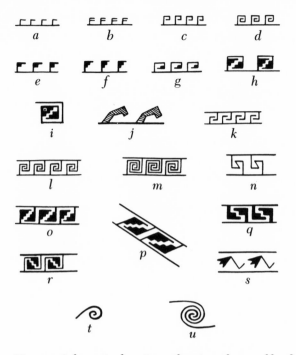

Fig. 9.1. Schematic drawings of various forms of hooks, keys, and scrolls not attached to triangles. Distributional data are shown in Figures 9.9, Part 1, 9.10, and 9.11.

An inspection of the distribution according to color classes of the various forms shown in Figure 9.1 does not lead us to any very meaningful conclusions, except that in most cases in which a particular form appeared with sufficient frequency to be more than a casual or sportive occurrence, it was found on all or nearly all of the color classes with the exception of the orange-polychromes, where there were only six occurrences altogether. Thus, forms *c, d, e, f, k, l, m,* and *o* occurred on all the three other color classes in fairly constant relationships, although one rather striking disparity did appear in the fact that *l* and *m* occurred on Jeddito Black-on-orange much more numerously than on any other type, and much more numerously than any other form on this type. Even so, it cannot be regarded as a type-diagnostic because it did appear fairly frequently on all other types. We can only conclude, then, that these forms of hooks, scrolls, and keys belonged to the common heritage of the Jeddito Ceramic School, available for use by all potters on all ceramic types throughout the period of occupation of Awatovi.

HOOKS, SCROLLS, AND KEYS ATTACHED TO TRIANGLES OR USED IN RELATION TO TRIANGLES

It was an easy step from the arrangement of these elements along a line or lines, as discussed above, to their use in combination with another simple element, the triangle, and this in turn led to an almost endless proliferation of increasingly elaborate and involved combinations of the same few basic elements already seen in the simple devices shown in Figure 9.1. Literally scores of variants were constructed on essentially the same theme, and a consolidated summary of them appears in Figure 9.9, Parts 1 to 3, which indicates their distribution both stratigraphically and in terms of occurrence on the principal ceramic types and color classes.

It will be necessary, however, for an adequate explication of the subject to consider the many examples through a more intimate analysis than that shown in Figure 9.9, Parts 1 to 3. Such an analysis is presented graphically in Figures 9.2 to 9.7 and is discussed in the following pages. For a better understanding of the anatomy of the many variants they will be considered in groups based on certain distinctive characteristics, in sequence from the simpler to the increasingly complex, but it must be made clear that this procedure is one for analytical convenience only and has no implication of a chronological nature. There is no convincing evidence for an inference that decorational intricacy increased with time during the period of occupation of the Western Mound, and in general both simple and complex devices appeared in all levels, on all pottery types, and often on the same vessel.

SIMPLE, NON-INTERLOCKING HOOKED TRIANGLES

The simplest form in which a hook, scroll, or key could be used in combination with a triangle was one in which the flexed element was formed at the apex of the triangle by the prolongation of one of its legs. In theory any kind of triangle might have been employed, but in practice it was nearly always a right triangle with legs of unequal length, placed so that the hypotenuse served as the base and the right angle as the apex. Usually the prolonged leg was the longer one. Sometimes the triangle was isosceles or equilateral, but instances of these forms were comparatively infrequent. While there was no uniformity in the orientation of the triangles, the prolonged and flexed elements usually extended toward the right.

Rarely were these elaborated triangles placed singly or in isolation. In the vast majority of cases they were arranged serially along a

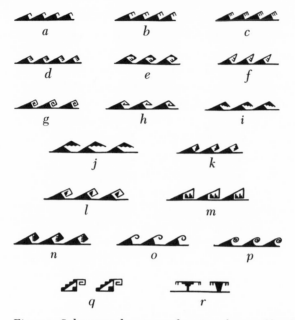

Fig. 9.2. *Schematic drawings of various forms of hooks, keys, and scrolls attached to triangles in single rows. Distributional data are shown in Figures 9.9, Part 1, 9.10, and 9.11.*

line, each one identical with all the others. There was no case (except very rarely, as the result of apparent carelessness) in which more than one form was used in a single series. The baselines, like those used for the elements shown in Figure 9.1, were either continuous and latitudinal or formed the boundary of an enclosed panel. The flexed elements themselves were essentially identical with those used independently.

The simple angle or flag occurred in single, double, or triple form as shown in Figure 9.2 *a*, *b*, and *c*, and together they were the most frequent, accounting for about two-fifths of all occurrences in this group. The fringe lines might extend backwards, as in *d*, *e*, and *f*, and the hook might be elaborated into an angular scroll, as in *g* and *h*.

A stepped terrace or key was frequently added to the hook or scroll, as in *i*, *j*, *k*, *l*, and *m*, and occasionally a fringed triangle was used instead of a terrace or key (*n*). Curved scrolls were less common than angular ones, but they also occurred (*o*, *p*). All forms of the triangles in this group were found in single rows along a baseline and in opposed rows in bifold rotational symmetry along the inner sides of two parallel lines, each row completely on one side of an imaginary median, without penetration into the interspaces of the opposing row.

Sometimes the leg of the triangle from which arose the hook, scroll, or key was itself stepped or serrated, but not all examples of this feature have been systematically isolated in the analysis. One unusual example is shown in Figure 9.2 *q*, which was peculiar in several features: not only was one side terraced but the interior was not solidly filled, and the angular scroll was not a prolongation of the leg but lay at an angle to it.

Two instances of unusual devices that may be considered here are shown in Figure 9.2 *r*. These were almost alike, although one was a simple triangle and the other a terrace. The peculiar feature was that each stood on its apex, while double hooks extended from each end of its inverted base. It should be noted that the unusual figures shown in *n* and *o* all were found on specimens of Awatovi Black-on-yellow, which was a relatively late type occupying a position transitional to Jeddito Black-on-yellow. As will be remarked in other contexts, it often exhibited features that were different in detail from the normal standards of the other color classes, although similar to them in general character.

Like the flexed elements without triangles, most of these forms occurred on all or several of the types and color classes and were not generally diagnostic of any particular color class or any stratigraphic level, although their occurrence was rare on the orange-polychromes. The simple hooks (Fig. 9.2 *a*, *b*, *c*), angular scrolls (*g*, *h*), and simple keys (*i*, *j*, *k*) were by far the most frequent.

ADDORSED AND INTERLOCKING BUT NON-CONNECTED HOOKED TRIANGLES

Any one of the forms displayed in the preceding group could have been modified for use in an addorsed or back-to-back relationship along two parallel baselines, but in practice only a few of them actually occurred, and these are shown in Figure 9.3. Here were the single and double flag (*a*, *b*), the recurved flag (*c*), and a single example of addorsed keys (*d*). The unusual pair (*e*) were not properly in addorsed relationship but were closely similar to a bifold rotational arrangement of the one shown in Figure 9.2 *q*. It is notable, however, that whereas the latter occurred on Awatovi Black-on-yellow the former was found on a specimen of orange-polychrome. As with the non-

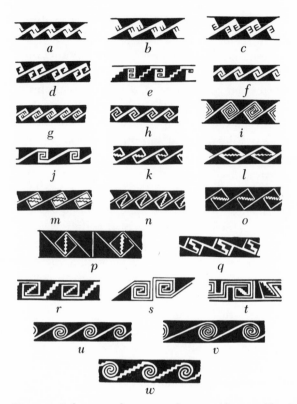

Fig. 9.3. Schematic drawings of various forms of hooks, keys, and scrolls attached to triangles in double rows, either addorsed or interlocking. Distributional data are shown in Figures 9.9, Part 1, 9.10, and 9.11.

addorsed forms, the most common were the single and double flags (Fig. 9.3 *a, b*).

By slightly altering the relative positions of the triangles in the two opposed series relative to each other, an arrangement was sometimes created in which the hooks, scrolls, or keys were interlocked rather than addorsed. Instances of this style were much more numerous than those of any other group. Examples of the several forms used are shown in Figure 9.3. As before, there were the direct hook, with both single and double bars (*f, g*), and recurved hook (*h*), and the rectangular scroll (*i*). A variant of the latter appears in *j* which is similar to those in Figures 9.2 *q*, and 9.3 *e*.

The simple terrace or key occurred frequently (Fig. 9.3 *k, l*) with a rare variant in which the triangle was not solidly filled in (*m*). The examples illustrated by *n* and *p* represent cases of recurved keys, and q was a variant of the latter in which the stalk of the key was at an angle to the leg of the triangle, as with *j*, *r*, and *s*. In *r* the free standing side of the base triangle was also stepped. Example *o* was unusual in that the triangle forming the key was not stepped but ticked; and in *p* the pairs of interlocking keyed triangles alternated with large plain triangles extending completely across the band. In *q* the keys arose from the basal corners rather than from the apices of the triangles. Two unusual forms are shown in *s* and *t*. The first was incomplete in that one of the interlocking keys arose directly from its baseline and not from a triangle. In the second one interlocking key arose from its baseline, while the other was attached to the end of a simple rectilinear meander.

Curved interlocking scrolls were the most numerous form in this group. Specimens occurred with scrolls of varying length, of which extreme examples are shown in *u* and *v*. A few instances were found on which the long sides of the triangles were stepped (*w*), as was also the case with *r*.

Within this group the several forms were for the most part used on all types and color classes, but with very few occurrences on the orange-polychromes. As usual, the direct and recurved keys were especially numerous. But it is noteworthy that curved scrolls were very much more frequent here than in any other group, and although they occurred on all color classes they were especially common on Tusayan Black-on-white. In most cases these examples were from specimens belonging to Kayenta Variety, characterized by a negative design style and usually by a relatively high degree of excellence in execution, resembling though never quite equalling the virtuosity of corresponding examples from sites north of Black Mesa. It may thus be remarked that this feature was a characteristic of Tusayan Black-on-white, but it was not diagnostic for that type, since it also occurred fairly frequently on Jeddito Black-on-orange and to a smaller extent on Awatovi Black-on-yellow.

INTERLOCKING CONNECTED TRIANGLES WITH HOOKS

A relatively small number of examples that closely resembled those in the preceding group but in which the hooks, scrolls, or keys were not only interlocked but actually connected by a short line, are shown in Figure 9.4. The simplest form was the single direct hook, in which the ends of opposing hooks were merely prolongations of each

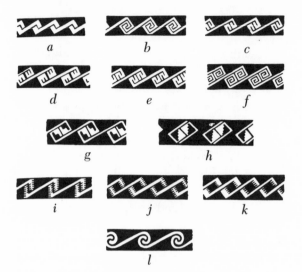

Fig. 9.4. Schematic drawings of various forms of hooks, keys, and scrolls attached to triangles in double, interconnecting rows. Distributional data are shown in Figures 9.9, Part 2, 9.10, and 9.11.

other (*a*). A reverse angular scroll appears in *b*. Examples *c* to *h* introduce a new feature, in which the extremities of the hooks or keys were left unmodified, but in which their parallel stalks were connected by a right line. Several variants occurred, from single direct hooks (*d*), bifurcated double hooks (*e*), rectangular scrolls that were, however, not actually interlocking but rather abutting (*f*), and direct keys (*g*).

The arrangement of Figure 9.4 *h* was unusual and similar to that in Figure 9.3 *q*, in which the keys arose from the basal corner of the triangle rather than from its apex. The three occurrences shown in Figure 9.4 *i*, *j*, and *k* were essentially like that in *a* except for the added embellishment of ticks on the triangles and across the connecting line, which in some instances was thickened to form a solid rectangle. A few cases of reversed connected curved scrolls occurred (*l*), mostly on Tusayan Black-on-white specimens.

Although the quantities within this group were small, and although they occurred on all color classes, examples on orange-polychromes and Awatovi Black-on-yellow were extremely rare. Connected direct hooks were the most frequent and occurred in a much higher proportion on Tusayan Black-on-white than on Jeddito Black-on-orange.

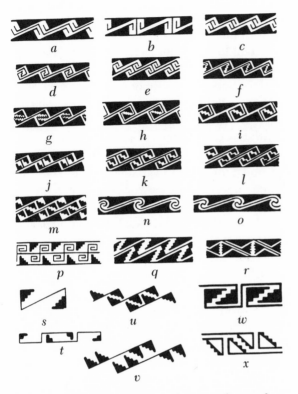

Fig. 9.5. Schematic drawings of various forms of opposed rows of triangles separated by meanders and involving hooks, keys, or scrolls. Distributional data are shown in Figures 9.9, Part 2, 9.10, and 9.11.

OPPOSED TRIANGLES SEPARATED BY MEANDERS

The forms included in this group varied widely in their details but they had in common an additional element not found elsewhere. This was a meander, either continuous or broken, running in a zig-zag course between the opposed rows of triangles but not physically connected to them. The triangles themselves were either plain and unembellished or had attached hooks, scrolls, or keys, and the meanders also varied similarly. Numerous examples are shown in Figure 9.5. The simplest form that appeared was composed of abutted direct hooked triangles, with a continuous plain meander between the rows (*a*); a variant of this occurred in *b*, where the meander itself was lacking and was replaced by a vertical line between pairs of abutting triangles.

In *c* the meander was composed of basically independent segments, each interlocked with the next by a single hook at its end, the
two segments joined by a right line anterior to the hooks, in the manner applied to the examples shown in Figures 9.4 *c*. A variant occurred in Figure 9.5 *d*, where the meanders interlocked with
recurved hooks directly connected by a stepped line; *e* resembled *c*
except that in the former there were hooks on the triangles themselves that interlocked with those of the meander.

Terminal keys were used in an interlocking relationship on the
segmented meander in *f*; and *g* presented a variant of this by the addition of a cross-ticked line connecting the ends of the keys. A slight
elaboration occurred in *h*, in which the keys were attached to interlocking angular scrolls, and *j* resembled *c* but with the addition of keys
at the ends of the segmented meanders. A somewhat irregular form
occurred in *i*, where interlocking keys arose from the baseline at
points between unembellished triangles.

A more complex arrangement is shown by Figure 9.5 *k*, *l*, and *m*,
in all of which the triangles as well as the segmented meanders were
equipped with keys that interlocked. In *k* and *l* the keys on the
meanders interlocked with keys arising from the triangles, but the two
examples differed in that the meanders in *k* were connected as in *e*
and *j*, whereas in *l* the meanders were not cconnected. The variation in
m lay in the fact that the keys of adjacent meanders interlocked with
each other but abutted the keys attached to the triangles. A few instances of curved meanders were found, each between plain triangles.
Terminal scrolls on the meanders interlocked in *n* and were connected
by a reverse curve in *o*.

Three abnormal arrangements were represented by *p*, *q*, and *r*.
The first was formed of opposed stepped triangles in offset mirror
symmetry alternating with angular S-shaped scrolls or meanders at
right angles to a median line between the baselines. Example *q* somewhat resembled *c* or *e*, but the triangles had stepped sides and the
meanders were embellished with alternate stepped triangles that interlocked with the stepped sides of the basal triangles. Example *r* employed saw-tooth triangles in face-to-face relationship on diagonal
lines running between plain triangles. These diagonals did not form a
meander, however, but arose individually from the baselines, as did
those in *i*. Two instances of this form, varying slightly, were found,
one on a Tusayan Black-on-white and another on an Awatovi Black-on-
yellow vessel.

Occurrences of specimens in this group, taken as a whole, were almost entirely on Tusayan Black-on-white and Jeddito Black-on-orange, in somewhat greater frequencies on the latter type. There was only one occurrence among the orange-polychromes and only two on Awatovi Black-on-yellow specimens. One instance of balanced solid-and-hatched elements occurred with a specimen of Figure 9.5 *h* on a Jeddito Black-on-orange vessel—the only occurrence in the entire collection of this style of triangles bearing hooks, scrolls, or keys.

The use of keyed meanders without associated triangles was not frequent but a few instances did occur, as shown in Figure 9.5 *s* to *x*. The form illustrated in *s* was identical with the meander that was used between plain triangles in *f*, but in this case it occurred as an isolated device on bowl exteriors. The meander shown in *t* was almost identical with those in *l* and *m*; but *u* and *v* were rather more elaborate, with their double interlocking terraces, than any other examples, although in general effect they closely resembled *l* and *m*. Specimen *w* was only a slightly elaborated form of *t*; the precise nature of *x* was not clear because the sherd did not contain the complete pattern, but it was unusual in having open keys. The few instances of keyed meanders without triangles occurred almost exclusively on Jeddito Black-on-orange and Awatovi Black-on-yellow.

TRIANGLES WITH OPEN CORNERS CONTAINING HOOKS, SCROLLS, OR KEYS

A device that was not in itself very much like the others considered in this section, but that may conveniently be included here, was a large solid triangle with an open square at one corner, almost always the right-angled one, in which was inserted some form of hook, key, or scroll. Examples are illustrated in Figure 9.6. The triangles were used in two ways, either singly as fillers for triangular panels that formed parts of a larger pattern, or in opposed pairs as fillers for rectangular panels that were in turn either segments of a broad continuous band or parts of a more complex pattern, often in association with the triangular panels just referred to. At present we shall not concern ourselves with the broader questions of layout, but only with the detailed characteristics of the triangles themselves.

Most of these triangles were straight-sided, but a few were stepped. Most had bases longer than their altitudes, but some were isosceles. In the examples illustrated in Figure 9.6 only single units are shown, but several of the examples actually occurred in opposed

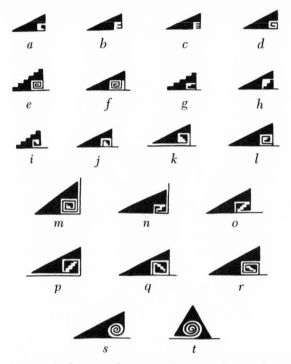

Fig. 9.6. Schematic drawings of various forms of triangles containing
hooks, keys, or scrolls in open corners. Distributional data are shown in
Figures 9.9, Part 2, 9.10, and 9.11.

pairs as fillers for rectangular panels, and some similar ones are shown
as such in Figure 9.7.

The simplest form of corner insert was a direct hook, of which
single, double, and triple examples were found (Fig. 9.6 a, b, c).
Recurved hooks and rectangular scrolls occurred also (d, e, f). Single
keys occurred in a variety of relationships to the legs of the triangle
and were either without stalks (g, h), with stalks (i, j, k), or at the ends
of rectangular scrolls (l, m). Interlocking keys occurred in several
forms, one of which was composed of a key rising from one leg of the
triangle interlocking with another key rising from a line outside the
triangle (n); another form involved two keys, each of which arose from
one of the legs of the triangle (o); and still a third form was made with
both keys attached to the stalk of a single scroll (p, q, r).

The most numerous instances of corner-insert triangles were

those containing curved non-interlocking scrolls. One example was a right triangle like those discussed above (*s*), but the others were all isosceles or equilateral and the open area occurred at the midpoint of the base, the scroll being a prolongation of one portion of the base (*t*).

Most forms of corner-insert triangles were found on all color classes except orange-polychrome, where only one instance was recorded. The greatest number occurred on Jeddito Black-on-orange, but it is noteworthy that those containing curved scrolls were, with only one exception, confined to Tusayan Black-on-white.

INTERLOCKING HOOKS AND KEYS WITHIN ANGULAR
SCROLLS OR PANELS

An application of the keyed hook, quite different in decorative function and effect from their use in the continuous bands or zonal arrangements already discussed, was the elaboration of this basically simple element into a relatively intricate angular scroll, either single or interlocking. Examples of this usage occurred either as isolated figures or as fillers for rectangular or triangular panels that in turn were parts of a larger design, examples of which are illustrated in Figure 9.7. These panels sometimes constituted subdivisions of larger patterns, as in the intricate "Y-frame" layout characteristic of many of the larger Tusayan Black-on-white jars (Smith 1952b: 164–166, Fig. 109), but more often they served as repetitive but not interlocking segments of a circumferential paneled zone on both bowls and jars.

In only a few cases were these scrolls of a single or non-interlocking form. Examples are shown in Figure 9.7 *a*, *b*, and *c*, all of which were evolved from the simple hooks and keys illustrated in Figure 9.1 *a*, *c*, *d*, and *e*, through the extension of the stalk into a complete scroll with as many as three or four circuits.

Interlocking examples, a wide variety of which are illustrated in Figure 9.7 *d* to *l*, were much more common. The common characteristics of all these were: that each member arose from a baseline; that each scroll completed at least one full circuit; that each carried a key or terrace at its distal end; and that they interlocked in bifold rotational symmetry. Morphologically these units were not essentially different from those shown in Figure 9.1 *k*, except that they formed full scrolls rather than merely recurved hooks. They were also functionally different in that they were larger and were used in discrete panels rather than as merely repetitive elements along a line or within a nar-

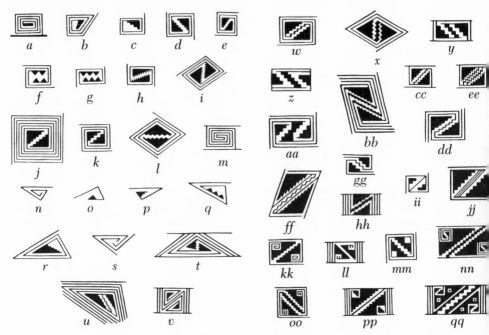

Fig. 9.7. Schematic drawings of various forms of interlocking hooks or keys within angular scrolls or panels. Distributional data are shown in Figures 9.9, Part 3, 9.10, and 9.11.

row zone. Example Figure 9.7 *m* differed from the others in that the ends of the interlocking scrolls were connected to form a meander and keys were omitted.

A fair number of triangular scrolls occurred, as shown in Figure 9.7 *n* to *v*. These varied from the single, unembellished form without a key (*n*) to progressively more elaborate forms (*o* to *r*). Only a few occurrences of interlocking triangular scrolls were found (*s* to *u*). These devices rarely appeared as fillers in a continuous zone, although pairs were sometimes used as fillers in the rectangular panels of such a zone, as shown in *v*, and the sawtoothed keys of *t* were fillers in a triangular panel in a zonal layout. Example *u* was within a set of nested lines and was not truly a scroll, but its effect and application closely allied it with the others in this group. These forms were most often used either as isolated figures on bowl exteriors or as fillers for small, secondary panels in triangular areas of larger and more elaborate layouts.

There frequently occurred modifications of interlocking keyed scrolls in which the opposed stepped triangles or keys were separated by a stepped, corbeled, or zig-zag line or pair of lines running between them and connected at their ends to the stalks of the scrolls just below or anterior to the triangles or keys. Examples appear in Figure 9.7 *w* to *ff*. Slight variations in this scheme are shown in illustrations *gg* to *jj*. In *gg* the stepped line itself was a meander and became in effect a part of the scroll; and in *ii* and *jj* the connecting lines were straight rather than stepped. Example *hh* was unlike any of the others in this group in that its triangles were attached solidly on their baselines and the dividing zig-zag also arose from the baselines. It was not dissimilar to the one shown in Figure 9.5 *q*.

The examples shown in Figure 9.7 *kk* to *qq*, were structurally similar to those shown in *w* to *jj*, except that they contained an open corner within which were inscribed hooks, keys, or scrolls like those illustrated in Figure 9.6. There was considerable variation in detail among these units, each of which was usually unique. The majority were in the form of rectangular scrolls like most of the others in this group, but a few (Fig. 9.7 *ll*, *nn*, *pp*, *qq*) were actually merely interlocking keyed hooks, essentially like those shown in Figure 9.1 *o* to *r*, with which they might logically be classified. They are included here because of their larger size and their functional character as fillers for discrete panels in a broad circumferential zone, each panel set off from its neighbor by one or several vertical or diagonal dividing lines. The examples in Figure 9.1 were smaller and usually constituted repetitive elements in a non-paneled zone. The specimen shown in Figure 9.7 *mm* was unusual because no hooks or keys were inscribed in its open corners.

Usually the panels containing the units considered in this group were separated from one another by from one to three vertical lines completely transecting the zone and quite independent of the scrolls that filled the panels. This arrangement was fairly common at Awatovi on both Tusayan Black-on-white and Jeddito Black-on-orange vessels but it appears to have had little or no counterpart on Pueblo III types to the north and northwest. In that region there was a precedent for it, however, on Kana-a Black-on-white during Pueblo I and on Black Mesa Black-on-white during Pueblo II. Its closest affiliations seem to have been toward the southeast in the Upper Little Colorado area. Some examples of closely similar panels from black-on-white vessels found at Awatovi but classified on technological grounds as belonging to types other than Tusayan Black-on-white, are illustrated in Figure

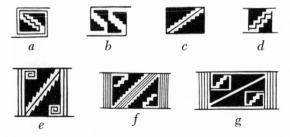

Fig. 9.8. Schematic drawings of selected examples of triangles, hooks, and keys in panels from exotic examples of black-on-white types.

9.8 for comparison (also Smith 1952b: 269, 275–277, 282 Figs. 130 *b*, 147 *a*, 148 *a*, 152 *d*, *j*).

The panel fillers discussed in this section were found about equally on Tusayan Black-on-white and Jeddito Black-on-orange, with very rare occurrences on the orange-polychromes and with only moderate frequency on Awatovi Black-on-yellow. Many of the specimens illustrated were unique or nearly so, but almost two-fifths of the entire collection were examples of the one shown in Figure 9.7 *d*, the simplest form of interlocking keyed scroll, which occurred on all types.

We may note here that a fairly large number of specimens of the orange-polychromes exhibited a manifestation of interlocking keys that were used as fillers in large lunette-shaped panels occupying about one-third of the interior area of many bowls. Although these were morphologically similar to some examples we have been considering and might logically be included in this context, they were so different functionally in the decorative scheme that they will be discussed elsewhere in connection with layout analysis. Vessels of this character (Smith 1952b, Fig. 282 *b*) were very rare at Awatovi though fairly common in the Kayenta-Marsh Pass area during Pueblo III (Beals, Brainerd, and Smith 1945, Figs. 62 C, 63 A, 65 A).

SUMMARY

In review of the data presented in this section a few generalizations may be made with a bearing on the problems of stratigraphy and typology in the Western Mound [Figs. 9.9–9.11].

First, it appears that with very few exceptions most of the basic forms of hooks, scrolls, and keys, with or without attachment to triangles, were an important feature of the decorative style on pottery of

Decorative Features — Painted sherds in each Ceramic Group	Tusayan B-W 1036 C 325	D 218	E 448	Orange Polys. 223 C 89	D 69	E 55	Jeddito B-O 1303 A 78	B 60	C 895	D 242	Awatovi B-Y 269 A 105	B 107	C 52	Tusayan Black-on-White 1500	Orange Poly-chromes 314	Jeddito Black-on-Orange 1969	Awatovi Black-on-Yellow 625
Compare Figure 44																	
a-d	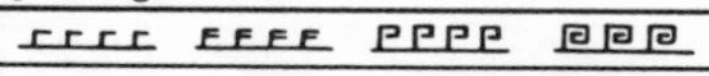 5	2	5	3			1	1	11	1	3		1	42	4	37	10
e-i	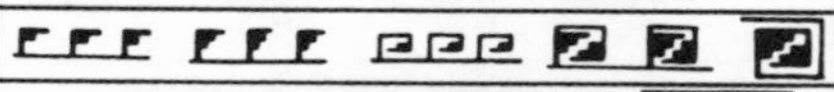 3		1	1					6	3	1	2	2	12	1	26	14
k-n	 3	3	10				1				1			40	2	6	3
o-s			 1	1			1	1	1	2		1	1	4	4	24	8
t-u	 5	4	5	3	1				4			1		39	4	11	3
Compare Figure 45																	
a-h	 4	3	4			1	3	3	16	10	5	5	1	24	1	72	16
i-n	 2	3	2						2		4			12	3	6	8
o-p				 1				2	3					10	3	11	1
Compare Figure 46																	
a-e	 3	4	3				1		9	2	2	2		21	1	16	4
f-k	 4	6	8	3				1	3	1	2			29	5	12	3
l-t	 10	5	10	5	1	1	4	4	36	4	2	2	7	48	15	98	21
u-w	 5		13	1	1		1	1	1	1	1	1		33	2	10	5
Totals carried forward and cumulated in Part 3	44	30	62	18	3	3	11	13	92	24	21	14	12	344	45	329	96

Fig. 9.9, Part 1. Distribution according to major pottery types and ceramic groups of decorative details illustrated in Figures 9.1, 9.2, and 9.3 (44, 45, and 46 in left-hand column above). See Smith 1952b: 81-85 for a detailed explanation of this type of chart.

Decorative Features (Painted sherds in each Ceramic Group)	Tusayan B-W 1036 C 325	D 218	E 448	Orange Polys. 223 C 89	D 69	E 55	Jeddito B-O 1303 A 78	B 60	C 895	D 242	Awatovi B-Y 269 A 105	B 107	C 52	Tusayan Black-on-White 1500	Orange Polychromes 314	Jeddito Black-on-Orange 1969	Awatovi Black-on-Yellow 625
Compare Figure 47																	
a–f	 2	3	6					1	10	2				15	1	22	1
g–k				 1				1	2	1				5	1	7	1
l	 1		1			1			1					4		1	
Compare Figure 48																	
a–e	 1	2	3					1	4	1				6		8	
f–m	 3		3					1	8	1			1	6	1	17	2
n–o					1				 1					3		1	
s–x	 1		1		1			1	5	1	3	3		2	1	7	6
Compare Figure 49																	
a–f	4	4	4		1			1	3			2		13	1	10	5
g–m	 2		4						5	1				7		11	3
n–r	 4	1	1						3	1			1	8		4	3
s–t	 3	3	12											18		1	
Totals carried forward and cumulated in Part 3	21	13	35	2		1	5	5	42	8	3	6	1	87	5	89	21

Fig. 9.9, Part 2. Distribution according to major pottery types and ceramic groups of decorational details illus-

Fig. 50	Painted sherds in each Ceramic Group	1000			225			166				205			Black-on-White 1500	Polychromes 314	Black-on-Orange 1969	Black-on-Yellow 625
		C 325	D 218	E 448	C 89	D 69	E 55	A 78	B 60	C 895	D 242	A 105	B 107	C 52				
a-c			1	2						1					4		1	
d-m		4	5	11		1		5	1	10	3	2	3		36	1	28	13
n-r		2	4	1		1		1		14	1				8	5	15	
s-u		1													2		2	
v-jj	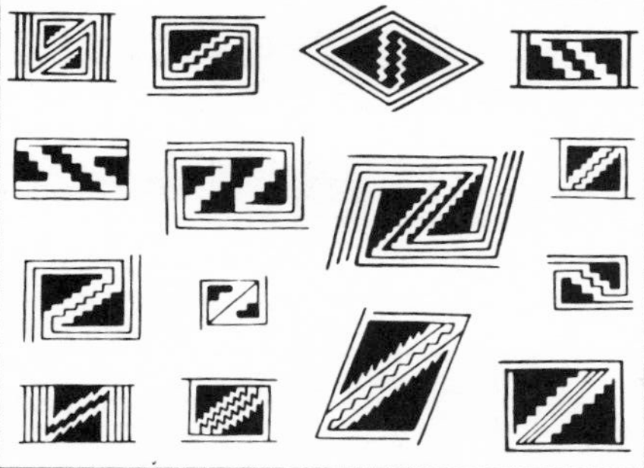	5	2	7				1		13	1	1	1		14		15	17
kk-qq		2		2				1		5			2	16	4		7	5
Totals including quantities from Parts 1 & 2		79	57	120	20	6	3	19	19	176	37	25	25	16	499	56	486	152
Percentages including quantities from Parts 1 & 2		24.3	26.1	26.8	22.4	8.7	5.4	24.3	31.6	19.9	15.2	23.7	23.3	30.7	33.3	17.8	24.6	24.3

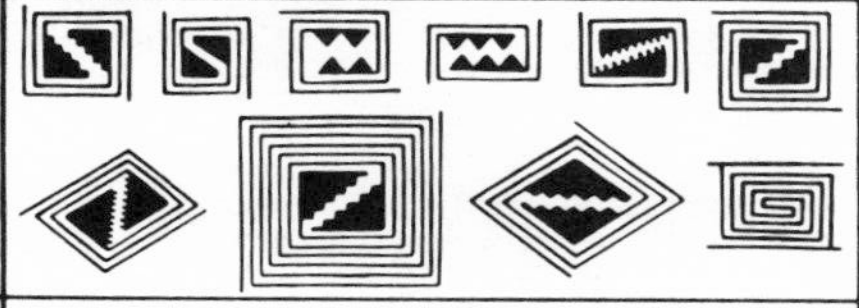

Fig. 9.9, Part 3. Distribution according to major pottery types and ceramic groups of decorational details illustrated in Figure 9.7 (50 in left-hand column above).

Ceramic Group	Total Number of Specimens in Sample	Column 1 Hooks, Keys, and Scrolls attached to Triangles		Column 2 Hooks, Keys, and Scrolls free or pendent from Lines		Column 3 Sum of Columns 1 & 2	
		Quantities	Per Cent	Quantities	Per Cent	Quantities	Per Cent
A	183	17	9.2	14	7.8	31	17.0
B	167	14	8.3	22	13.1	36	21.4
C	1361	92	6.8	133	9.8	225	16.6
D	528	29	5.5	38	7.2	67	12.7
E	671	42	6.2	74	11.0	116	17.2
Totals	2910	194	6.7	281	9.7	475[a]	16.4

a. This quantity slightly exceeds that shown on the distribution charts, because a few specimens exhibit both characteristics and are counted twice here.

Color Classes	Total Number of Specimens in Sample	Column 1 Hooks, Keys, and Scrolls attached to Triangles		Column 2 Hooks, Keys, and Scrolls free or pendent from Lines		Column 3 Sum of Columns 1 & 2	
		Quantities	Per Cent	Quantities	Per Cent	Quantities	Per Cent
Tusayan B-W	1500	159	10.6	176	11.7	335	22.3
Orange Polychs.	314	15	4.7	19	6.0	34	10.7
Jeddito B-O	1969	142	7.2	164	8.3	306	15.5
Awatovi B-Y	625	43	6.8	92	14.7	135	21.5
Totals	4408	359	8.2	451	10.2	810[a]	18.4

a. This quantity slightly exceeds that shown on the distribution charts, because a few specimens exhibit both characteristics and are counted twice here.

Fig. 9.10. (Left) Quantities and frequencies (expressed in percentages of the total number of painted sherds of all kinds used in the design study from each ceramic group) of hooks, keys, and scrolls used with and without triangles, as illustrated in Figures 9.1 to 9.7. See Smith 1952b: 81-85 for a detailed explanation of this type of chart. a, this quantity slightly exceeds that shown on the distribution charts, because a few specimens exhibit both characteristics and are counted twice here.

Fig. 9.11. (Right) Quantities and frequencies (expressed in percentages of the total number of painted sherds of all kinds used in the design study from all excavated levels for each major pottery type) of hooks, keys, and scrolls, used with and without triangles, as illustrated in Figures 9.1 to 9.7. a, this quantity slightly exceeds that shown on the distribution charts, because a few specimens exhibit both characteristics and are counted twice here.

all types and at all stratigraphic levels. Taken collectively their frequencies were not markedly different as between either the several stratigraphic groups or the principal pottery types or color classes.

Secondly, the simpler forms in every classification tended to be more frequent, for example, Figures 9.1 *c, d, e, f, l, m;* 9.2 *a, b, c, g, h;* 9.3 *f, j, l;* 9.4 *c;* 9.7 *d.* Many of the more complex forms were unique or nearly so.

Thirdly, within the orange-polychromes a marked difference in frequencies appeared between Ceramic Group C, where the proportion was 27 percent of all analyzed specimens, and the combined Groups D and E, where it was only 6.4 percent. This is a puzzling circumstance, the significance of which is not clear, but since the absolute quantities involved were small, the divergence may be more illusory than real.

Fourthly, curved scrolls, though never very common, were much more frequent on Tusayan Black-on-white than on all other types and color classes combined. The ratio of black-on-white occurrences to all painted black-on-white specimens was 4.7 percent, whereas the ratio of occurrences on all other classes to the total number of painted specimens of those classes was only 0.8 of 1 percent.

10. A School for Cracked Pots

Watson Smith received his college education at Brown University, which, having been founded in the pre-Revolutionary days of 1764, is one of the oldest educational institutions in the country. Brown awarded him the degree of Bachelor of Philosophy (Ph.B.) in 1919. His undergraduate studies, which were interrupted by a period of active duty during the First World War, included many courses in history and literature and a brief flirtation with geology. Smith attended Brown too early to have taken a course with Professor Josiah Stinckney Carberry, because that famous eccentric did not make an appearance on the Brown campus until ten years later. In fact, no Brown student ever had the benefit of a course from Professor Carberry (Clough 1954: 9), for he is an entirely mythical figure in the Brown pantheon of the great and famous.

Professor Carberry seems to have been brought to the venerable institution in Providence in 1929 through the imaginative genius of several faculty members in the Classics Department, notably Benjamin Crocker Clough. The wide-ranging research interests of Professor Carberry, his indefatigable travels, and his many non-lectures have been chronicled by Brown faculty and alumni ever since. It must be emphasized, however, that Professor Carberry is in no way a hoax. He is the incarnation, maybe even the apotheosis, of the erudite faculty eccentric whose spirit, in popular belief, haunts the halls of American institutions of higher learning.

Professor Carberry's scholarly interests are eclectic in the extreme, but his favorite subject is psychoceramics, which in some cases has meant the study of crack-pots (Clough 1963: 12; Dickenson 1960: 11), and in others, the effort to derive deeper meaning from the study of ancient pottery (Smith 1966: 928, 1971: 75). Carberry's lecture titles on this subject range from "Aboriginal Pottery: Its Cause and Cure" to "Pot Shards of the Amazon Delta." However, his lectures have not been properly appreciated because according to his biographer (Clough 1963: 12), "failing to deliver an announced lecture was in fact Professor Carberry's specialty." He often sent postcards explaining his absences, such as the one in which he reported that he could not deliver a lecture on "Positive Negativism" because he was "unavoidably detained in Chichen-Itza hatching out a job lot of Middle High Mexican Potsherds" (Clough 1963: 12). One does not need to have any further insight into the persona of Professor Carberry to realize that it was inevitable, indeed preordained, that his path would one day cross that of Watson Smith.

In fact Smith, who had earned a law degree from Harvard in 1924, was practicing law in the firm of Hinckley, Allen, Tillinghast, and Phillips in Providence when Professor Carberry first appeared on the Brunonian scene. He became an enthusiastic follower of the Carberry myth and some years later developed a professional appreciation for the potential of the study of psychoceramics. Smith contributed to the growing store of Carberriana in many ways, including the writing of an etymological exegesis of the great professor's name (Smith 1960).

It took some time for official Brown University to appreciate Professor Carberry, but it finally did accord its most famous and most traveled faculty member his rightful place in the life of the university. An example of the official acceptance of the great psychoceramist is the reference to him in the citation for the honorary degree of Doctor of Laws that Brown conferred on Watson Smith on the first of June in 1964. Smith, ever a loyal son of his alma mater, had already served two terms as a Trustee and had just been selected as a Fellow. Brown, however, was honoring him not only for his considerable service to his alma mater, but also for his scholarly contributions to archaeology. The citation that President Barnaby C. Keeney read at the ceremony recognized both of these facets of Smith's career:

> Watson Smith, you are known to the world of science and scholarship as a curator and archaeologist whose delvings into

the material remains of the Indians of the Southwest have
added greatly to our knowledge of the American past. We
alone know you here as a wise and generous trustee, as a sage
advisor on anthropology, as wit, wag, good friend, and deflator
of inflated balloons. We honor you for your work and for your-
self, and as a leading member of a class that has been the
envy of those before and an example to those after in its service to Brown.

President Keeney, following a long-standing Brunonian tradition,
continued in Latin:

Quae cum ita sint et quia sub omni olla cerrita Carberry
videas, auctoritate mihi commissa te ad gradum in Legibus
Doctoris admitto, omniaque jura atque privilegia ad hunc
gradum pertinentia tibi concedo. In huius testimonium hoc
diploma tibi solemniter trado.

The Latin portion may be translated as follows:

These things being so, and because you see under every
cracked pot a Carberry, I confer upon you the degree of Doctor of Laws and all of the rights and privileges pertaining
thereto. In testimony thereof and according to custom, I give
you this diploma.

In fact, of course, Smith saw more than Carberry under every
cracked pot. He is probably the only scholar to make effective use
of Professor Carberry's ideas about psychoceramics. For example,
Smith (1966: 928) commented in a review of "Ceramics and Man"
(Matson 1965) published in *Science*:

This volume contains at least five essays which deal with the
little-explored but potentially illuminating field that Carberry
has called psychoceramics. The range of these studies extends
from inferences of social organization, divisions of labor, social
status, and occupational conservatism, to psychological facets
of individual personality as evidenced by the product.

Smith (1971) again addressed the more serious side of
psychoceramics in his study of the painted pottery at Awatovi. Both
Carberry (one entry) and psychoceramics (four entries) are listed in
the index. Smith obviously enjoyed finding places where he could

use psychoceramics legitimately. He described the broken life-line motif as a "psychoceramic ascription of a purpose" in the mind of the potter (p. 144), discussed the "psychoceramic dynamics" of the potter's mind (p. 157), referred to "similar psychoceramic aesthetic manifestations" (p. 563), and invoked "factors of psychoceramics which we do not understand" (p. 592). In a section explaining his methods of ceramic analysis, Smith (1971: 75) made some important observations on the need to understand the mental processes of the makers of prehistoric pottery:

> From still another point of view, both the technological and aesthetic features of an artifact or an assemblage of artifacts may be applied toward an understanding and an interpretation of the mental processes of their makers. Why did certain peoples, or even specific individuals among those peoples, produce ceramic objects with forms and decorative character-istics that distinguish them from the products of other peoples and individuals? The rewarding possibilities of research in this direction, that is, in the field of what Carberry has called "psychoceramics," have heretofore been only tentatively approached, but its potential usefulness for providing us with a broader understanding of human culture and "human nature" seems very considerable, and while this field is not within the normal scope of competence of the archaeologist, he can and should seek to present his fossils in a context from which others may exploit their usefulness for social and indi-vidual psychology.
>
> Having adumbrated these somewhat idealized concepts, which may appear egregiously flamboyant to many readers, we must return to the immediacy of the more earthy level with which, as dirt archaeologists, we are primarily concerned... to present the ceramics in as comprehensive and as lucid a form as is consistent with the inherent limitations of the writ-ten word and the graphic illustration. It is our hope that in doing so we may provide a basis and suggest a stimulus for the subsequent pursuit of the objectives just adverted to.

Smith went on to say:

> Having said as much by way of *apologia*, we shall proceed to a detailed and systematic (hopefully a rationally systematic)

presentation and discussion of the pots and potsherds that constitute the focus of our attention.

Smith's considerable reputation as a student of prehistoric Southwestern pottery is, in fact, largely based on his "detailed and systematic" presentations, as the previous selection on the "Analysis of the Use of Hooks, Scrolls, and Keys" demonstrates. In addition, he has provided some of the most insightful statements about the use of pottery in archaeological analysis and interpretation. Perhaps the best example of his contributions in this area is the essay, "Schools, Pots, and Potters," which was published in the *American Anthropologist* (Smith 1962). By the early 1960s, Smith was already deeply involved in the analysis of the huge quantity of pottery recovered by the Awatovi Expedition. In the process of seeking new and productive ways of looking at large samples of painted pottery, he developed the concept of a "ceramic school."

Smith set forth the theoretical basis for his "ceramic school" in a manuscript that he submitted for publication in *American Antiquity*, the journal of the Society for American Archaeology. I was about halfway through my term as editor of that journal and had been urging Smith to formalize his ideas about ceramic schools. As it happened, my colleague, Ned Spicer, had just taken over the editorship of the *American Anthropologist*, the journal of the American Anthropological Association. Spicer and I had many discussions on editorial matters. I bemoaned the lack of articles on archaeological topics in the *Anthropologist*, and he countered that archaeologists submitted very little material for his consideration. Under these circumstances, it was not long before the three of us agreed that "Schools, Pots, and Potters" was an appropriate archaeological paper for the more general readership of the *American Anthropologist*. Smith successfully made a case in that paper for the idea that there were ways of looking at pottery that transcended the increasingly narrow taxonomic approaches then popular in American archaeology.

Unlike many of the theoretical or methodological essays in the archaeological literature, Smith's paper on "Schools, Pots, and Potters" does not exist in isolation. It stands at the mid-point of the two decades during which Smith was concerned with the idea of "schools." He anticipated the concept in 1952 in his monograph on the kiva murals at Awatovi (Smith 1952b: 148-150) and he demon-

strated the utility of the concept in an extended discussion of the
Jeddito School in 1971 in his study of the painted pottery from
Awatovi (Smith 1971: 606-612).

In the brief discussion in the kiva mural volume that adumbrated the concept of a school, Smith (1952b: 149) offered a "few
remarks suggestive of some of the more immediate artistic influences through which the 'Jeddito School' was evolved" and concluded (p. 150) that "although this discussion in no way purports to
be a thorough treatment of the subject, enough has been said, I
believe, to establish the argument for suspecting the ancestral
source of a great deal of the spirit of the Jeddito wall paintings in
the decorative school of Four Mile Polychrome."

Fortunately for Southwestern archaeology, Smith maintained
an interest in capturing something of the "spirit of decorative
schools" and two decades later presented a full description and interpretation of the Jeddito School. Both the theoretical paper on
"Schools, Pots, and Potters" (Smith 1962: 1165–1178) and the discussion of the "Jeddito School" (Smith 1971: 606–612) are offered
on the following pages not only as examples of vintage Watson
Smith on pottery, but also as outstanding contributions to Professor
Carberry's favorite subject, psychoceramics.

R.H.T.

Schools, Pots, and Potters

The eminent professor was fulfilling his role as Autocrat of the Luncheon Table at the Faculty Club. "But Philosophy never built a bridge," he was saying. "It is too imprecise. Exactness, mensuration, statistics, order—these are the elements of Science, and only Science can make a World."

Some of his listeners were in agreement, but the discussion festered in the minds of several of the archaeologists present, who remembered many similar and, as it seemed, fruitless discussions among their own fellows as to the most productive procedures for manipulating archaeological data. At the time, I was involved in an interesting but inconclusive controversy over those eternal verities of archaeology—potsherds—and the problem of their taxonomy. It seemed to me that, despite the acrimonious belaborings that raged around types, modes, varieties, systems, classes, groups, families, foci, horizon styles, and so on, there was implicit in the thought processes of the protagonists at least one basic assumption that remained usually unquestioned. This was the mathematical axiom that the whole is equivalent to the sum of its parts. Well, this was sound Euclidean geometry, and undoubtedly the Eminent Professor thought of it as a foundation stone of his scientific Bill of Rights, like that other axiom that a straight line is the shortest distance, etc.

But, on second thought, wasn't that last one already obsolete in modern non-Euclidean terms? And in a "philosophical" sense, perhaps the former might not be quite eternal either.

Reprinted with the permission of the American Anthropological Association from the *American Anthropologist,* Volume 64, Number 6, pages 1165–1178, 1962.

It seemed to me that some of my fellow taxonomists might have been stricturing themselves unnecessarily by a sort of auto-Procrustean procedure through their determined effort to apply to their sacred potsherds the analogy of Euclidean geometry in a situation that could more helpfully be elucidated in non-Euclidean terms, using the analogy of an Expanding Universe, in which, for purposes of minute analysis, the traditional concepts of finite categories and limited wholes could usefully be employed, but which at the same time was a kind of open-ended affair like the arms of the great spiral nebula in the constellation of Andromeda, coherently unified but diverging forever without limit.

Was it really necessary or even desirable for the productive study of archaeological objects and their implications to reduce every last one of them to taxonomic precision? Not so long ago James Ford made some relevant and revealing observations about that curious but instructive folk, the Gamma-Gamma (Ford 1954). Ford's study confined itself to house types, and he may not have known that the Gamma-Gamma were in fact also ceramists of great virtuosity. The center of the Gamma-Gamma pottery industry lies on the far side of the island near the Bong Tree Forest on the Cerro Buho y Gatillo at the base of La Gran Sierra Roca de Dulce. The potters there can procure with their runcible digging implements a great abundance of ceramic ingredients: clays of many kinds, sand and rock for tempering, wood, coal, and dung for firing. That they use all these in a bewildering variety of combinations is evident from their product, individual specimens of which vary greatly from each other, though all bear a strong stamp of family resemblance that marks them clearly of the Gamma-Gamma School.

Subsequent to Ford's investigations, I made some careful studies of Gamma-Gamma pottery by the usual taxonomic methods and was able to arrive at a list of several dozen types (with appropriate varieties), and went on to integrate them into clusters, systems, or groups, and to cross-breed them into styles of design, horizon markers, and even traditions. All this would have worked out beautifully, except that somehow there were always a few sherds or pots that didn't fit. This, of course, could have been due to a failure to construct appropriate definitions for the categories, and so these were finally adjusted to meet every need. But there was still something else that was much more disquieting. Even when every sherd had been neatly put to bed and all the categories were closed, there seemed to be no structural significance in the summation of the categories: the parts had not managed to make a whole. Other students had felt this incompleteness in the uses of taxonomic systems, but usually they had not stepped out into the empyrean where taxonomy suffocates from the absence of precision and the impact of the illimitable. As an experiment I put down my statistics and took a tentative step toward meta-taxonomy, and, along the way, I got to thinking about the determinants that underlie and condition the products, tangible or intangible, of a people—for example, the Gamma-Gamma. For experimental purposes and in order to prevent the problem from getting out of hand, I felt that it would be helpful to address my speculations to the matter of primitive ceramics, although any other class of objects would have done as well.

I remembered Rouse's work in Haiti (Rouse 1939), and it occurred to me that I might effectively apply his approach to other and similar situations. It was quite evident that the most positive factor conditioning a ceramic industry is the availability to a folk of materials suitable for potential pots. Simply stated these are clay, water, pigment, and tempering materials. But by themselves these cannot make a pot. There must be tools to work the materials; there must be fire, and fuel to kindle it; and even more importantly, though very elusively, there must be mental processes to direct the gathering, the working, the forming, and the firing. In almost any environment there will occur clay beds of varying character—from those free or almost free of iron to others with a heavy ferric content, some almost without sand, other with an admixture thereof. Nearby there will very likely be river or lake beds of pure sand, some of it perhaps containing micaceous particles; and sometimes there will also be volcanic cones of fine black cinders, some of which will have washed down into the river beds. The ambitious potter already has a considerable latitude of choice in possible combinations between the various clays and the several tempering materials. She also has at hand several sources of pigment for decorative purposes—minerals providing perhaps iron, manganese, copper, lead, and organic products containing carbon. And she has a selection of tools for application of these pigments— brushes of yucca fibre or animal hair, as well as her own good forefinger. She has other tools for manipulating the plastic materials—a smooth pebble for polishing, a pointed stick for incising, and her thumb nail for indenting.

She has a choice (though not so many) of several firing methods—with free or limited access of oxygen, with complete exclusion of oxygen, and at least a limited range in ultimate temperatures and duration of firings. These will in part depend on the fuels available, for example, wood, coal, or dung. It thus appears that our Happy Potter has at her disposal an extremely large number of combinations, which can easily be calculated with an electronic computer, by multiplication of clay times temper times pigment times manipulation times firing. But the sky is still her limit. She has also at her disposal an alarmingly ramified set of intellectual complexes that act to control her ultimate output. Some of these are restrictive, some are expansive. We call them Tradition and Imagination, Conservatism and Invention, Timidity and Boldness, and these intellectual characteristics themselves are qualified by personal attributes of skill, dexterity, and experience.

It begins to look at this point as if our Happy Potter is in a position in which she can at will concoct almost unlimited combinations from the factors that we have listed and thus manufacture all the pottery in the world, achieving infinite variety from combinations of finite elements. This is not actually a mathematical paradox, as we shall see, but in point of fact she cannot really go so far. Her cultural heritage will operate as an intangible coercive force on her ideal potential and will limit severely the number of combinations that she may achieve. If she is a Gamma-Gamma, for instance, she cannot possibly produce a Celadon vase (although Gamma-Gamma does provide the material ingredients necessary) primarily because she has never learned to speak Chinese. For similar reasons neither can she produce a Wedgwood plate nor a Greek amphora. But within the limitations of her experience she can, and will, effect very nearly all the theoretically possible combinations available from her materials and her cultural tradition.

Time was limited at Gamma-Gamma, and the potters there were reluctant to disclose their craft secrets, but I left the island with a desire to apply to a collection of prehistoric ceramics some of the ideas that had made Ford's analysis of house types so enlightening. The opportunity to move from an ethnographic to an archaeological context and from the ivory tower of speculation to the immediacy of a particular mass of ancient pottery was provided by the vast collection of more than a million sherds recovered during the Peabody Museum's excavation of the famous Hopi site of Awatovi in the Jeddito area of Northeastern Arizona. Awatovi had been a large pueblo covering some 25 acres and building up to maximum depth of about 8 meters. There had been an uninterrupted occupation of about 300 years before the arrival of Spanish missionaries in the early 17th century, who remained for another 70 years before the village was finally abandoned. Although the Awatovians were part of the wide-spread Anasazi tradition, they seem to have been a fairly self-sufficient group, with adequate opportunities for autonomous viability. The population of at least several hundred at any one time was large enough to provide individual variety and innovating impulse. They seemed to have had two main occupations—making pottery and breaking it—and the remains of their ceramic industry provided an unusually fine mass of material for study.

To begin the study, this pottery was segregated into groups according to the conventional method of Southwestern ceramic analysis, first according to color class (white or gray, orange, red slipped, yellow, polychrome, etc.) and next in terms of already described types. Up to a point this procedure worked out reasonably well, but as further subdivisions were attempted, difficulties arose. It became readily apparent that much of the pottery in the lower levels of the Western Mound at Awatovi bore a close resemblance to that made at about the same date a few miles to the North in the Marsh Pass–Kayenta area. Examples of similarities are found in such types as Tusayan, Kayenta, and Kiet Siel Polychromes, Tusayan, Betatakin, and Kayenta Black-on-whites, and Tusayan Corrugated. These similarities have of course long been recognized, and indeed several series of types have been named and described from the Jeddito region on analogy with the better known types from Marsh Pass and Kayenta. It seems an inescapable inference that the first settlers at Awatovi came from the North and brought with them their ceramic techniques and decorative concepts.

As the study continued, however, certain unconformities became apparent. Although large components of the pottery from Awatovi were practically indistinguishable from examples excavated in the North, other components showed increasing degrees of variation, which displayed themselves by a greater flexibility in the use and arrangement of colors in the painted decoration, by the introduction of new elements and motifs of design, and by variabilities of clay and temper. Some of the novel decorative features immediately suggested similar though not identical features characteristic of the pottery of the Upper Little Colorado River area to the south and southeast. Among such features are the use of white or black-and-white decoration on the exteriors of orange or red bowls (unknown in the Marsh Pass–Kayenta region), and a variety of details, including cribbed lines, balanced hatched and solid motifs, conventionalized bird forms, rows of corbelled or staggered lines, and many others.

All this is not in itself surprising and exhibits simply an expectable recombination of decorative traditions meeting at a point midway between their places of origin. But it does begin to raise a small cloud in the bright sky of the taxonomic idealist, who is faced with the problem of distinguishing the local examples from those indigenous to north and south. This challenge was met at Awatovi by describing and naming several new types and varieties that incorporated the newly observed complexes. But then there appeared still further disquieting features. By megascopic observation, later confirmed by petrographic analysis, it was found that each of the shiny new types embraced examples that displayed a whole gamut of variation in tempering materials, ranging from sand to crushed rock to "sherd" particles, with varying combinations thereof, some being without any visible temper at all. Extensive petrographic and chemical analyses were done by Miss Anna O. Shepard and Dr. Herbert W. Dick. Miss Shepard distinguished among examples of single "types" six categories based on temper content: sand, sherd, sand and sherd in about equal quantities, more sand than sherd, more sherd than sand, and no visible temper. Clearly a further subdivision in terms of temper proportions could be achieved, but hardly with helpful results.

The taxonomist's cloud is now becoming larger and blacker. Shall he create six varieties of each type to reflect these variabilities in temper? For laboratory purposes he does so and goes on to the next phase of his study. This turns out to be an investigation of the clay used in the paste of his sherds. At first glance it seems likely that several clays were used with differing mineral content: one, for example, with little or no iron, producing, when fired in the presence of oxygen, a light gray or creamy pottery; another, containing a medium quantity of iron, producing a yellow or buff pottery; and perhaps a third, with a heavy iron content, producing an orange or brown pottery. At Awatovi clays with these characteristics do indeed occur, and the actual spots where some of them had been mined by the ancient potters were discovered, as were examples of pots made from them, formed and painted but not fired. Miss Shepard tested numerous samples of raw clay, and also samples of already fired sherds, in an electric furnace and demonstrated their variabilities in behavior under controlled conditions of firing. Her results have been confirmed and expanded by further tests at the Peabody Museum West of the Pecos.

The taxonomist now suspects that his basic categories founded on color class are beginning to disintegrate. He observes, first, not only that the original types, which were based on particular combinations of color of paste with definable decorative features of paint and design, are becoming fuzzed at the edges. He has met this situation by further subdivision into varieties based on temper (six of them) and on clay (at least three). But his travail is only well begun. Up to this point he has assumed the presence of a consistent correspondence between basic color class and over-all decorative character. This is a reasonable hypothesis, justified by the observation that often in Southwestern ceramics a particular inventory of decorative features was applied to only a single color class, say white, whereas other characteristic decorative features were usually applied to a different color class, say orange.

But this is apparently not uniformly or inevitably the case. At Awatovi there are numerous examples in which design features that have been categorically ascribed to a particular color class appear also on other classes. For example, there are numerous features that in the Kayenta–Marsh Pass area were used, so far as we yet know, only on white pottery. Other features are equally distinctive of white pottery in the Upper Little Colorado River area. But at Awatovi these characteristically "white" features occur frequently on orange, polychrome, red, and yellow vessels. Miscegenation is obviously at work.

Paint was almost equally varied in the ceramics of Awatovi. Although qualitative analyses have been limited, investigations indicate that organic as well as metallic substances were used. Carbon, iron, copper, and manganese have been identified, and it appears quite possible that all of them, and perhaps combinations of them, were applied in conjunction with the several clays and in the different decorative traditions used at Awatovi. A great deal of meticulous study would be required to elucidate this oubliette, but it is at least clear from visual observation that a wide variation in appearance does characterize the paint on local pottery of all color classes. What is sometimes euphemistically called "black" ranges from genuine black through innumerable shades of brown and reddish, and may be dense, matte, glazed, or pale to the point of ghostliness. White pigment, probably iron-free kaolin, is indeed invariable, but the reds exhibit a range from deep maroon to brownish (either dense or very thin), and in some instances tend to approach the rusty end of the "black" spectrum.

In addition to her choices of paste, temper, paint, and design, our Happy Potter was free to apply or to withhold a slip from her pots. She had at hand the several clays already discussed; she could use any of them as a slip on paste made from any one of them. Supposing a minimum of three distinguishable clays, her potential combinations would be nine, and since she had a choice to slip or not to slip, the ultimate potential would be twelve. As a matter of fact, examples of at least seven or eight of these theoretical possibilities have been recognized in the material from Awatovi.

Further contemplation of the subject matter, combined with a reappraisal of firing techniques and their effects, leads to a new plateau of confusion. Given the several clays available, it was possible for an Awatovian potter to produce by means of a single firing technique a series of colors ranging from cream or buff through yellow to orange to red. Not only was it possible—she did it! But she was not finished. She had available another firing technique by which the circulation of oxygen could be curtailed, whereby the same clays could be baked into vessels ranging in color from almost white to very dark gray. She did this, too. But her diabolique was still not at an end. Uniquely in the prehistoric Southwest, the Awatovian potter used coal as well as wood for fuel, and thereby she attained higher temperatures, with resulting differences in her product, involving deeper colors, increased hardness, and sometimes a partial glaze from paints that, under normal wood-firing procedures, would produce a matte appearance.

But despite the awesomeness of the potential (and actual) number of combinations in this material, and the taxonomic difficulties implicit in it, let us not despair. It may still be true that certain of these combinations, regarded as modes or attributes, can prove useful as time markers in establishing a chronology throughout the 8-meter depth of the Western Mound at Awatovi. In this hope we shall not be entirely disappointed, although even here we shall have to readjust our thinking to some extent in terms slightly different from those imposed by conventional concepts. In the first place, the stratigraphy itself of the Western Mound is complex. As Robert F. Burgh has effectively demonstrated, the deposit involves inversions and interruptions that render its chronological interpretation difficult. The evidence submitted by Burgh (1960) of the numerous instances of sherds of single vessels widely distributed both horizontally and vertically throughout the Mound indicates convincingly that fine chronological sequences cannot be safely inferred from any single part of the profile, and that in general the entire deposit must be taken as a relatively coherent mass.

Yet, in broad terms, certain evolutionary features do reveal themselves. Color classes do wax and wane with the growth of the Mound, as do a few other relatively minor characteristics. At the lower levels black-on-white and orange polychromes of the Marsh Pass-Kayenta style are dominant, gradually giving way to a distinctive black-on-orange, which in turn is supplanted by a form of black-on-yellow characterized by great variability in texture, temper, and color, this in turn giving way to a different yellow, more mature, lighter in tone, more stable in technology, and bearing a novel and more flamboyant style of decoration—the well-known Jeddito Black-on-yellow and Sikyatki Polychrome.

Another example is the proportional decrease of sherd relative to sand temper, from lower to higher levels—but this is essentially a statistical factor and indicates only a changing ratio in the "popularity" of the respective materials. At no point is either material completely supplanted by the other, and vessels occur in all color classes with almost all possible combinations of tempering, being in other respects generally similar.

Conversely, it becomes apparent that certain other features frequently used in taxonomic diagnosis are of little value here. Clay, slip, paint, even many features of design, are, as it were, interchangeable parts adaptable in almost any combination and to a bewildering roster of conceivable types (or varieties) which themselves merge into other conceivable types (or varieties) according to any one or more of several mutable characters.

Further confusions between "types" appear in the Western Mound, for it is virtually impossible in many cases to separate from each other examples within a particular color class that have elsewhere been described as discrete entities on the basis of decorative features. At Awatovi it is very difficult to classify into separate groupings sherds and vessels representative of Tusayan, Betatakin, Kayenta, Polacca, and Hoyapi Black-on-whites, for example. The characteristics of these five types are recognizable at Awatovi but not in consistently separable categories, with the result that here they would all appear to represent a single type, subdivisible if at all into varieties based on minor differences in detail or on variability of virtuosity in execution. Although the types just referred to have elsewhere been ranged chronologically in a Kayenta Series and a Polacca Series on the basis of temper and paste as well as decorative details, it seems to be impossible at Awatovi to separate them consistently on these criteria. Furthermore, many examples closely approximate one or more of the described types but display slight additional features apparently derived from the south or southeast and ascribable to such origins as Reserve, Tularosa, or Klageto Black-on-whites. In what has been described as Little Colorado White Ware (Colton 1955, Ware 9 B) the distinctive features are a heavy white slip on an iron-bearing clay that fires dark gray in the absence of oxygen, combined with a characteristic decorative style and an unusual, flaring rim. The Ware is said to be tempered with light-colored angular fragments (crushed sherds?), at least in the western parts of its range, but certain of its types are said to resemble closely other types of a different ware found to the eastward, made with quartz sand temper.

At Awatovi there occur an appreciable number of sherds that exhibit the technological features of Little Colorado White Ware, as well as examples that resemble the easterly affiliated types, and still others that can only be described as intermediate in terms of paste and temper. Most of the sherds of these wares were probably made elsewhere and imported into Awatovi, and if so they would not be regarded as a part of the local complex. But there also occur at Awatovi a few examples that display the same distinctive rims and painted decoration, but that are made with either a very thin slip or none at all, and with a light gray paste and temper particles of fine sand—features that characterize a certain named type (Flagstaff Black-on-white) ascribed to still a third ware (Tusayan White Ware), which is the same ware that embraces most of the white painted pottery at Awatovi.

Here, then, are at least four distinguishable types classified in three different wares, but each one having certain features that ally it with some of the others, although not with all. It is virtually impossible to indicate the interlocking features of these types by a strict taxonomic system, although it is clear that some sort of cultural affinity is present. A more cogent understanding of this affinity can be achieved by regarding the entire complex of specimens in terms of their broad similarities rather than merely of their detailed dissimilarities.

An analogous situation obtains, with perhaps even more insistence, among the Awatovi Polychromes. These are basically closely allied to Tusayan, Kayenta, and Kiet Siel Polychromes, but many examples display features of more than one of these types, and in addition variations unknown to any of them, and either indigenous to Awatovi or derived from such sources as St. Johns or Fourmile Polychromes. They also occur with orange paste or buff paste, with or without slips, and with variable tempering materials. Although the types defined in the Kayenta–Marsh Pass area have often been regarded as occurring in a chronological sequence, there is actually little evidence, even on the home grounds, flor this hypothesis in either vertical or areal stratigraphy. At Awatovi there seems even less justification for a time separation, because examples of all sorts occur without significant evidence of chronological change.

It may, however, still be true, although at this time it is not possible to report with finality, that certain decorative details or elements in themselves may prove to have chronological significance. It is suspected that they will, but if so, it will be not as markers of types or varieties but simply as modes or attributes, occurring on many types and cutting across color classes.

But we should not conclude that types, varieties, or other taxonomic categories are useless or inappropriate. On the contrary, their validity and value are not in the slightest degree called in question. A system of classification with careful and logical definitions and names is requisite for the adequate handling of data and the communication of information. In many circumstances we cannot go beyond it. For example, collections of sherds may be made under many different circumstances: they may be gathered thinly from a widespread surface survey, intensively from the excavation of a relatively small and short-lived site, or from a "test" excavation of a long-occupied site. In none of these instances is the material adequate for a definitive study. It is susceptible to the kind of precise (sometimes meretriciously precise) description afforded by its classification into finite categories, call them wares, types, series, varieties, or what not, but it is not susceptible to anything further. And in these cases we must be content with conventional taxonomic methods.

But these are very different situations, not only quantitatively but qualitatively, from the study of a vast and highly complex body of material excavated from a large number of rooms in a long-occupied site. Here we have a mass sufficient to display a range of variation and subtlety that are not evident in more limited collections, and they can be made to yield more significant results. In the instances of limited excavation suggested above, observable characters of the material stand as stage markers between fairly discrete and limited groups of examples and represent outstanding and easily recognizable modes (in the statistical sense) of selected variables. Thus the conventional taxonomic method is adequate for their analysis. But with a larger mass we must penetrate more deeply into an understanding of the mass as an entirety, and strict adherence to the limitations of conventional taxonomy will only restrict our view and obscure the forest by an unduly close focus on the trees.

Even in a ceramic syndrome collected from an extensive and intensive excavation at a single large site, the structuring of the material for analytical purposes can be intelligibly done only by the use of some consistent taxonomic system. Among the million potsherds exhumed at Awatovi there are indeed types and varieties and series and color classes. But these are not all, and, although probably a large majority of the multitude of specimens can be comprehended within a workable taxonomy of definable groups well below the astronomical in number, there will always remain a very considerable and very significant residue that cannot be successfully categorized without expanding the system to its own bursting point. Thus Chaos returns to Chaos. In this connection it is appropriate to recall that Gifford (1960: 432–443) defines a type as "the manifestation of regularities" or of an "esthetic ideal." It thus excludes by definition the imponderable deviations with which we are here concerned. It has been felt, I believe, by many systematists that any acceptable classification must be inherently capable of providing a place for every individual and of putting every individual in that place, ineluctably and eternally. This is the "It is or it isn't" attitude, which, doggedly pursued, can only continue to clutter the literature with a superficial semblance of certainty that may obscure the substance from the eyes of unwary students.

So, now we are back to the alleged inadequacy of the theorem that the whole is equivalent to the sum of its parts. To attempt grimly to classify every last specimen is to lose the pot for the potsherds, as Judd has said (Judd 1940: 430). To one who observes a collection in perspective, many large and distinctive vessels will stand out and will give character and scale to the whole, but the whole as such is a symbiosis, and it embraces within itself an infinitude of individuals that display almost endless minor variety. To name and describe certain groupings that cluster around outstanding individuals will provide useful markers, but the struggle for expansion or subdivision of these groups to care for the vagaries of every single specimen will only becloud the spectacle of the whole—and this is not necessary, if we will take the humanist view that the poem is not merely the listing of its component words, the symphony not merely the sounding of its musical notes.

Judd has expressed the idea very cogently (1940: 430):

> Despite craft conservatism, Pueblo potters are individualists; personal habits and preferences appear in their methods of shaping, decorating, and firing pottery. Their paste and paint are not always the same; they measure with cupped hands, judge consistency by taste or feel—as competent students of modern Pueblo art have repeatedly observed. Form, finish, and, most of all, decoration, are the diagnostic criteria that really distinguish the wares of one district or period from those of another. By magnifying minor variations in a few small fragments gleaned from the surface at one site we risk elevating the products of a single potter, or even parts of a single vessel, into one or more "types." We must not lose sight of the pot for the potsherds.

In the million potsherds from Awatovi, not in each one singly, not in any specific grouping of them, but in the entire mass, there are many things to be seen, most importantly, it seems to me, the revealing evidence that here, no matter how you slice it, is a basic coherence, a something that transcends taxonomy. Since potsherds are one tangible form of the artistic creativity of a people, we may borrow an established term from the vocabulary of the Fine Arts and refer to this manifestation as a "School," in the very sense in which such terms as Roman School, Florentine School, French Renaissance School, Impressionist School, are used to characterize not only the artists of a particular period and place, but also the common influences, inspirations, and products of those artists. To apply this concept to the sherds recovered from the Augean refuse of Awatovi is, I hope, to clarify the view and to purify the air. It is not to destroy or confuse a helpful taxonomy of types and varieties, but rather to sharpen the focus of these very entities by explicitly recognizing that they cannot be stretched or distorted to embrace every possible variation or combination of factors. The alternative is to attempt to create

finite categories for each of these almost literally innumerable variations, and that can lead to only one end—whom the Gods would destroy they first make mad.

If I may, then, speak of the Awatovi (perhaps better the Jeddito)
Ceramic School, we shall be prepared at once to recognize and to ap-
praise its innate coherence. The types remain, the undoubted Rem-
brandts and Goyas, the Nampeyos and Marias; but all the other works
of the students, the ateliers of the masters, the anonymous hacks, ex-
perimenters, and imitators, take their places and fill out the canvas. It
is a complex picture, but with a common genre that demands discussion but eludes definition, and that is sufficiently humane to account
for all its idiosyncrasies without losing its personality. Many problems
thus will disappear, or will be seen for the taxonomic quibbles that
they are: the presence of a white slip with "black-on-white" design on
an orange paste, the application of manganese instead of carbon paint,
the inclusion of more or less sand than usual in the temper, the use of
three colors instead of two, all these and many more will fall into place
as expectable manifestations of a basic genius, all part of the pattern of
the School, even though not readily susceptible to precise taxonomic
ascription.

Of course other schools can be recognized, as I hope they will
be. In fact, though not specifically called schools, they have been recognized implicitly as such by a number of Southwestern archaeologists. Already in the literature, awaiting only the label, are the following schools, among others: Mimbres, Mesa Verde, Chaco, Kayenta,
Little Colorado, Tularosa, Rio Grande, Chihuahua. Looked at in this
fashion, each of them fills a need not now adequately taken care of by
the mere summation of taxonomic categories, however valid and useful these categories may be in themselves.

It must be emphasized, however, that the School as here conceived is expressly not itself a taxonomic device. It is not, specifically,
a "ceramic group" as Colton defines that term (1953: 65), nor is it a
"ceramic system" as defined by Wheat, Gifford, and Wasley (1958:
41–42), nor a horizon marker, nor yet a co-tradition. If it were merely
another mountain to pile on Pelion, it would serve no useful purpose.
On the contrary, it operates outside and beyond the taxonomic framework. It is a loose and flexible entity, and, like that of the rainbow, its
end, however unattainable, delves in a pot of gold. Like the Expanding Universe it is more than everything within it.

Furthermore, a School is not synonymous with Kroeber's concept of style which he defines (1948: 329) as ". . . some specific method, technique, manner or plan of operations," or again (1957: 150) as ". . . a strand in a culture or civilization: a coherent, self-consistent way of expressing certain behavior or performing certain kinds of acts." Repeatedly throughout his lengthy discussion of the subject, Kroeber indicates that style is attributive rather than substantive. It is "characteristic; it is distinctive; it refers to manner and mode" (1957: 3), "to form as against substance, manner as against content" (1957: 4). It is ". . . concerned essentially with form" (1957: 26), and is to be distinguished from the subject matter which it characterizes.

Although Kroeber did not use the word "school" it may be appropriately applied, I think, to what he called "substance," "subject matter," or "product." A School, by its dictionary definition, comprises both the group of persons who create a class of products at a particular time and place, and derivatively those products themselves, taken collectively. It is with the second of these meanings that we are here concerned. A school is distinguished by style or perhaps by several styles, but it differs from its own style in the same way that a tangible object differs from the manner of its execution or from the esthetics that characterize it.

All this is not really anything new or frightening in this context. Classical and Oriental archaeologists have recognized "schools" in their study of ancient pottery, though they have usually employed the term in a somewhat more restrictive sense, with specialized pedagogical connotations, as referring mainly to the work of an identifiable master and his pupils and followers. I propose its use in a much broader and entirely impersonal or anonymous application, but even so the idea is implicit in what many taxonomists have already said, though some seem to have felt a sort of guilt complex in pandering to it. It is essentially what Michael Coe (1961: 47) called the "family effect" in a discussion of the pottery of La Victoria in Guatemala, in which he says that lines of demarcation between pottery there are difficult to draw, and that the ranges of variation within types overlap those of other types.

William H. Sears (1960: 326–327) felt that types are not "descriptive devices" and are "not adequate for the study of content and processes. . . description must supplement the typology which we use for work on skeletal chronicle." And he discussed the example of stamped pottery from Etowah, which he says can be divided into eight form varieties, eight temper varieties, eight decorative varieties, and a dozen design patterns, although it is all within a coherent tradition. He did not carry out the arithmetic, but it comes to 6,144 possible combinations. Surely there was a vigorous and seminal School at Etowah.

McKern (1939: 312) felt that "The lure of being methodical at all costs is a constant threat to the wholly profitable use of any method. . . . It is convenience and orderliness that is required of the classification, not a flawless, natural regimentation of the facts required by the classification."

Rouse (1960: 317–20) in discussing modes as type characteristics, pointed out that combinations of modes often will be found to cut across the taxonomic combinations on which types have been based and that types fall short of telling all that can be learned from a total assemblage of material.

John O. Brew (1946: 64) argued very forcefully for the use of varying systems of classification and for the changing of systems when needful: "In certain minds approval of such technique will be denied because it is not precise. Admittedly, it is not. And for that very reason it is practical and scientific. We are not able to treat precisely the material with which we are dealing." He added (1946: 66): "To present our results so that they will be useful to men at large we must, at times, leave our systematics with our test tubes in the laboratory." And he referred to what Alfred North Whitehead had called the "fallacy of misplaced concreteness."

This is quite "unscientific" in the narrow sense, and that is just the point. One of our gnawing troubles lies in our attempt to reduce all expression of thought to exclusively verbal and quantitative terms. This arises from the prejudices of a literate culture, which venerates words as the only (and almost sacred) medium of communication, and which also regards the ideal of mathematical precision with mystical awe. But we must always remember that imprecision is the condition of the world in which we live, that all definitions corrupt, and that absolute definitions tend to corrupt absolutely, that mathematics is the science not of the exact but of the incommensurable. And we may comfort ourselves with a dictum of Sir James Jeans that "Nature abhors accuracy and precision above all things."

It is not a sufficient answer to our problems, however, to meet them with an aphorism. All archaeologists are faced with the necessity of classification and interpretation in the study of artifacts, but it is my conviction that the concept of schools of ceramic (or other) crafts may help to exorcise what is really only a spectral conflict that appears to arise between those who would try to carry taxonomic precision to its ultimate extreme and those who would scorn the application of such detailed distinctions. We are dealing here with a problem that requires for an acceptable solution two methods of attack that are complementary and not mutually exclusive. They are, in truth, of quite different orders and are not merely successive degrees of the same thing. We cannot answer any of the questions of the world, material or speculative, in terms only of mathematical exactitude, or only of imprecise metaphysics. Both attitudes are required, and if we will accept this tenet we shall rescue ourselves from the sterile controversies that so often have led us into the cul-de-sac of taxonomic frustration.

The Jeddito School

The concept of the ceramic school, as a way of thought within which may be embraced an unstructured agglomeration of specific taxonomic categories, without itself becoming categorical, has been expounded elsewhere (Smith 1962). We shall not further elaborate upon its rationale, but it may perhaps be helpful to point out some features of the pottery from the Western Mound that seem to indicate the existence there of a ceramic concatenation that may well be called the Jeddito School.

A school, by its very nature, is not a taxonomic entity and possesses no explicit limits or clearly definable characteristics. It is, to use an ethnographic term, somehow analogous to the extended family, in which membership is recognized and accepted but never quite subject to precise definition, and which never becomes a closed system.

Within the ceramic school exists a roster of sharply defined types and other taxonomic entities, each differing from all the others, but sharing in common something that marks them as belonging together and that transcends the summation of the particularities of all. The whole is greater than the sum of its parts and in that element of excess lies the impalpable essence of the school itself. Although the word school has not been used by others with this exact connotation, its general meaning has influenced the thoughts of various authors. Brew (1946: 44–66) certainly had it in mind when he composed his classic discussion on the uses and abuses of taxonomy. Ford (1954), Kroeber

(1957), Judd (1940: 430), Sears (1960: 326–327), Coe (1961: 47), Shepard (1939: 249–287, 1956: 306–322) and many others have understood that no mere compilation of categories, however meticulously described, could "tell all" about a collection of material objects. Something a bit bigger than life is needed (Vanden Berghe 1965: 248).

In the lower levels of the Western Mound occurred a galaxy of pottery specimens that were essentially indistinguishable from examples of certain types, both black-on-white and orange-polychrome, originally named and described from the Kayenta–Marsh Pass area, and it seems an inescapable inference that the first settlers at Awatovi came from the north bearing with them their baggage of ceramic techniques and artistic ideas. This statement is subject to some exegesis, however. We do not mean to imply a belief that the actual individuals who laid the first stones at Awatovi themselves trekked across Black Mesa from the vicinity of Marsh Pass. But they were cousins of those who did. Certainly Antelope Mesa and its surrounding valleys had been for generations occupied by people of close cultural affinity with the habitants who lived farther to the north, on Black Mesa and beyond. The specific founders of Awatovi may have come directly from trans-montane Tusayan or they may have moved in from only a stone's throw away. In either case they carried the same cultural heritage, including Tusayan White Ware and Tsegi Orange Ware.

But these ideas seem soon to have suffered a series of modifications, evidenced by a greater flexibility in the use and arrangement of colors, by the introduction of new features of decoration, and by a wider eclecticism in temper, pigments, and clays. For example, the use of white paint on the exteriors of orange and polychrome bowls had been unknown in the north on the "classic" types of Tusayan, Kayenta, and Kiet Siel Polychromes, but it made its appearance at Awatovi, probably within the first generation there, in evident imitation of the established style of pottery made a little way to the southeast, in the Upper Little Colorado Valley, namely St. Johns Polychrome and similar types. Thus the inherited standards began to change, and modification (varieties, if you will) of the northern types evolved.

At about the same time or a little later, the use of red paint as an element in the decoration of orange pottery disappeared, and a change, but not a radical one, crept into the local ceramic habit. This change involved several factors: the use of a slightly different clay that produced a subtle change in paste color, an increasing use of black paint alone, and of white in combination with black on bowl interiors and jar exteriors, or white alone on bowl exteriors. The result was the production of Jeddito Black-on-orange and Jeddito Polychrome, both distinct from the older northern polychromes but still clearly affiliated with them. Other details of decoration changed also, not cataclysmically but by the gradual absorption into the basic tradition of elements from southern sources along the Little Colorado Valley.

Before further pursuit of this thread, however, we should retrace our steps to the north, where we shall find in the Kayenta–Marsh Pass homeland of the first Awatovians a complex of black-on-white pottery coexisting with the orange ware but quite different from it. This white ware had different technical properties as well as decorational standards. Its temper was composed mostly of sand with sometimes smaller quantities of crushed sherds, whereas the counterpart orange ware contained temper of predominantly crushed sherds, though it also contained some sand. More striking contrasts between the two color classes, however, were their very different layouts and decorative styles.

This white ware came to Awatovi, too, where it was not really alien, because in other villages roundabout were practically indistinguishable manifestations of the same ceramic complex. These northern and southern variants have been given a variety of taxonomic names, but in essence they were the same thing. As time went on, and as artistic influences from the southeast became manifest on the orange ware, so also the white ware underwent modifications in the form of adaptations of novel decorative features from the Upper Little Colorado River area. These were characteristic there of types known as Reserve, Tularosa, and Klageto Black-on-whites.

But a strange thing was happening at Awatovi. During the earlier years the potters there continued to make vessels of two color classes, white and orange, from clays with different mineral constituents, notably iron oxides. The clay used for white ware was low in iron content and was fired in a nonoxidizing manner; when oxidized it became a light pinkish yellow or straw color. The clay used for the orange ware was rich in iron and was fired with free access of oxygen, becoming various shades of red or brownish.

At first, in the tradition of the north, the designs and technologies of the two wares were distinctive. Now, however, as new motives and patterns infiltrated from the southeast, these were applied not only to the white ware but also to the orange. Strikingly characteristic motives from Tularosa Black-on-white became at Awatovi commonplace on Jeddito Black-on-orange, and as they did so, the old white ware declined in popularity and finally ceased to be made. For some years the scene was dominated by the evolving orange ware, exemplified by Jeddito Black-on-orange and its variant Jeddito Polychrome, with the mingled heritages from north and south, and incorporating some features that had earlier characterized only the white prototypes. At the same time the orange ware was evolving its own distinctive character, notably in terms of an increased intricacy of geometric design.

But the triumph was never complete, nor was it permanent. Just as the old white-ware tradition was dying out, a new manifestation appeared to replace it. This was a yellow ware, quite clearly made from the same clays used for the earlier white ware, but with three great differences. The vessels made from these clays were now oxidized to a variety of shades of light brown, pink, and yellow; they were decorated in a style very nearly that of Jeddito black-on-orange, but with certain innovations in the form of devices in black on bowl exteriors; they introduced some modifications in shape, notably squatter bowls with incurving rims; and they were tempered with comparatively small quantities of fine quartz sand. This pottery was called Awatovi Black-on-yellow.

After a while the orange ware disappeared entirely and simultaneously the yellow ware evolved gradually into something quite different, with lighter-colored paste, an almost complete absence of temper, and a striking flamboyance of decoration, involving for the first time a freewheeling eclecticism that permitted the use of life forms, asymmetrical layouts, and novel shapes, especially large, squat, neckless jars. This new dispensation expressed itself in Jeddito Black-on-yellow and eventually in Sikyatki Polychrome, and survived until the coming of the Spaniards, although some decline in the degree of excellence was evident before that cataclysmic event.

The tradition of Sikyatki Polychrome was, however, not overwhelmed even then, and the pottery that was made during the period of Franciscan dominance in the seventeenth century and in later years maintained the essential characteristics of Sikyatki Polychrome with modifications derived from Spanish sources. Exactly what happened to the ceramics of the Hopi country after the abandonment of the Jeddito area in 1700 is not clear, but it is extremely significant that when the old village of Sikyatki was excavated by Fewkes in 1895, the Tewa potter Nampeyo of the village of Hano on First Mesa was inspired by the beauty of the ancient vessels to adapt their designs to her own product. Thus was initiated a neoclassical school that has flourished to this day.

Nampeyo's example was followed by several First Mesa potters who periodically visited the Awatovi camp in the 1930s and systematically copied the designs on vessels of Sikyatki Polychrome from Awatovi as well as those illustrated in published volumes in our library. But perhaps the word "copied" is not quite apt. These women did not precisely reproduce the details of the original specimens; rather they referred to the latter for inspiration and guidance but adapted them to suit their own artistic predilections. Thus, whatever the genius of Sikyatki design, its continuing vigor remains unquenched.

What we have sketched is only the bare skeleton of the Jeddito School's history. Other less prominent factors were present to fill out its anatomy. We have referred to differences in the tempering formulae employed in the early white and orange-polychrome wares. These were not mutually exclusive, however, for both classes embraced specimens that contained temper in varying proportions, from all sand to all crushed sherd through varying combinations of the two.

Although there was no apparent chronological change in the tempering of the white ware before its disappearance, a progressive change did occur in the orange ware, with the relative abundance of sand increasing markedly in the later horizons but never becoming exclusive. A contrast in respect to temper came with the introduction of Awatovi Black-on-yellow, which contained mostly fine sand but often with admixtures of finely ground sherds. Even this was only a refinement of technique in the direction already established during the later life of Jeddito Black-on-orange, but it differed from the standards of the black-on-whites, even though the clay was evidently the same as had earlier been used for that ware, in which it had been heavily tempered with sand or sherds or both. Did this new technique, differing from those of both its orange and white predecessors, evince the incursion of an alien people with different cultural habits? We cannot be sure, but we remain skeptical, largely on the basis of the apparent continuation of a decorative style that carried over from Jeddito Black-on-orange to Awatovi Black-on-yellow.

Turning backward again for a moment, let us look at some of the less abundant ceramic products that accompanied the major types. It becomes apparent on closer scrutiny that the application of slip or its omission was apparently a selective choice on the part of the individual potter. Vessels of Tusayan Black-on-white seem usually to have carried a thin slip, but on a good many specimens it was either not present or was so thin as to be invisible. Among the early northern polychromes, both slipped and unslipped versions were made, the slipped examples distinguished as Kiet Siel Polychrome. Jeddito Black-on-orange and Jeddito Polychrome were normally unslipped, but a fair quantity of both bore a moderately thick slip of the same color as that of the paste and thus were often almost indistinguishable. These have been characterized as slipped varieties of the corresponding types. In both the white and orange wares no correlation was discernible among variations in slip, temper, and design.

Along with the development of Jeddito Black-on-orange and Jeddito Polychrome there was made also a similar product resembling those types in decoration and temper, but of a different clay that fired pink or straw. Examples occurred both with and without an orange slip, and they have been called respectively Antelope Black-on-straw, Antelope Polychrome, Kwaituki Black-on-orange, and Kwaituki Polychrome.

Perhaps a little later, when Awatovi Black-on-yellow was developing from Jeddito Black-on-orange, several variations also appeared. Huckovi Black-on-orange was made from the same iron-rich clays as Jeddito Black-on-orange, but it contained little or no fine sand temper, in this respect resembling Awatovi Black-on-yellow. Its decoration was coherent with that of both major types. But even this did not exhaust the inventory of variation, for a product was made from a clay similar to that of Awatovi Black-on-yellow but bearing a thin orange wash or slip. Most vessels were painted in black, but a few also had white outlines. These are called Kokop Black-on-orange and Kokop Polychrome.

Along with Awatovi Black-on-yellow two related but variant types were made, namely Bidahochi Black-on-white and Bidahochi Polychrome. Both were made from clays with a low content of iron identical with or similar to those used in Awatovi Black-on-yellow and, earlier, in Tusayan Black-on-white. Both contain little or no fine sand temper and were coherent in design character with Awatovi Black-on-yellow. But they were distinguished by the striking factor of differing firing techniques. Bidahochi Black-on-white was as nearly dead white in color as could be achieved and must have been fired without free access of oxygen. Bidahochi Polychrome, on the other hand, was oxidized to a range of colors closely corresponding to those of Awatovi Black-on-yellow, and in some cases approaching those of Huckovi Black-on-orange. It might be regarded as simply a variant of those two types distinguished by the addition of white outlines. It differed from Kokop Black-on-orange in not having a slip.

Although this is not the place for an exhaustive investigation or discussion of the ethnological or cultural implications suggested by the existence, side-by-side in a particular archaeological context, of ceramics exhibiting various different artistic traditions and technological processes, a few speculative observations may be useful. It is sometimes assumed, implicitly if not expressly, that a particular craftsman or a closely affiliated group of craftsmen always created a product that was standardized within very restricted limits of variation.

Granted the conservative character of most societies, especially the more "primitive" ones, the uncritical assumption of such rigidity seems hardly warranted. Undoubtedly there are standards of artistry and of technology that influence the work of craftsmen in any society, our own as well as the Anasazi, but it seems neither necessary nor reasonable to assume that these standards operated within the framework of only one specific pattern of procedure.

We know that throughout the Anasazi area pottery of widely different character was being used at particular villages at particular times, and that often the villages were small and comparatively isolated. It is possible to draw any of several inferences from the evidence: that each village contained several potters, each one of whom made vessels with a precisely limited set of material, technological, and artistic features different from those of all the others; that all vessels except those of one particular style were imported; that alien craftsmen had somehow found their way into the village as wives or husbands, slaves, or itinerant journeymen; or that individual craftsmen applied more than one set of standards to their product, were masters of a variety of techniques, and were sufficiently flexible to apply their techniques eclectically.

The final inference seems to us the most plausible. It is difficult to envisage any of the other postulated situations at a small two- or three-family settlement on the Pueblo II or early Pueblo III model, and yet there was universally present and simultaneously used in most such places a spectrum of at least three or four quite different classes of pottery: black-on-whites, orange or red polychromes, and plain or corrugated "utility" vessels. These classes differed from one another in the materials used (both clay and temper), in shape, in decoration, and in firing procedure. If examples of each had been discovered in isolation, the plausible inference would be that they represented cultural diversity, reflective of different "tribes" or eras or what not. But their repeated association in intimate context precludes any such conclusion. They must have been made by the same people.

Of course, there was unquestionably an active trade in ceramics in ancient times, and the evidence of it is usually fairly clear. To a large pueblo like Awatovi came artifacts from considerable distances, and traders and permanently settled immigrants must have been there constantly. Nevertheless, the indigenous potters certainly were the makers of the bulk of all ceramics used there, and the same individuals must have practiced more than one method of fabricating, decorating, and firing, with the resultant production in a single atelier of plain, corrugated, bichrome, and polychrome vessels in a variety of shapes. It is provocative here to contemplate a bowl from the Kayenta area that combined the characteristics of Tusayan Black-on-white and Tusayan Polychrome (Beals, Brainerd, and Smith 1945, Fig. 70 G). It is from this consideration that the concept of a ceramic "school" is basically derived.

We have thus far said little about paint in the Jeddito School, but both organic and mineral pigments were used there from the first. On vessels of Tusayan Black-on-white the pigment was probably always carbon, even on those specimens decorated in the Reserve-Tularosa style. But on the northern polychromes and on the later Jeddito Black-on-orange and Awatovi Black-on-yellow it was iron or iron-manganese. Bidahochi Black-on-white exhibited examples of both organic and mineral pigments.

The general evolutionary and interlocking nature of the ceramics of the Jeddito School has been demonstrated by the broad view provided in a consideration of its major categories. But it must also be emphasized that among virtually all the named and described "types" there were specimens that could have been classified with equal cogency with either of two or three of the others. It would be an invitation to chaos to attempt a definition for these, but it would also be egregious to ignore them. They were, in a sense, the mortar that bound together the bricks in a coherent structure. Such "transitional" pieces were, of course, mostly found among types of the same or

closely similar color classes, but a few crossed over the clay curtain between white and orange and exhibited a telling kinship between
them, evidenced, for example, by the application of white slip upon
an orange paste, and painted with a design in black-on-white style.

Perhaps our story of the Jeddito School has thus far been over-
simplified. While its basic affiliations were with the Kayenta–Marsh
Pass area, and its secondary influences came from the Upper Little
Colorado Valley, there was also some impingement from the Lower
and Middle Little Colorado Valley. These influences were evident on
some vessels of Tusayan Black-on-white in the form of certain decorative features that were diagnostic of what has been called Flagstaff
style, as well as in occasional outflaring bowl rims decorated in characteristic manner. At a later time there was clearly a close tie with
Homolovi, whence may have come the straw-colored pottery, and
perhaps some of the inspiration for Awatovi Black-on-yellow. Or was
the diffusion in the other direction? At this point we cannot say.

Another source of influence, though a modest one, came from
the general direction of Mesa Verde, probably indirectly via the
Chinle Valley or even the Chaco Canyon. This influence was never
really explicit in Jeddito ceramics, but it was almost certainly there,
even though it had very likely made its impact on the antecedents of
the Jeddito School in the Kayenta–Marsh Pass area, perhaps from
Alkali Ridge and other mesas and valleys in southern Utah (Lister
1964: 24–40).

Whether or not a significant influence on the culture and
ceramics of the Jeddito flowed westward from the Rio Puerco area still
remains a problem. Some archaeologists have seen in the florescence
of yellow pottery an actual influx of peoples from that direction. These
postulated immigrants have even been identified as Keresan speakers.
It is certainly true that a marked change in masonry technique took
place throughout the Western Mound coincidentally with the fairly
rapid transition from orange to yellow pottery, and this in itself may
argue strongly for a significant cultural change. It is provocative that
an almost identical change occurred at the old village of Hawikuh in
the Zuñi Valley at about the same time. It is also apparently true that
along with the changes in masonry and pottery the custom of painting
elaborate designs on the walls of kivas was first introduced at Awatovi.

These facts would be provocative in any case, but they are made
much sharper by the discovery of almost indistinguishable yellow pottery and very closely similar kiva mural paintings at Pottery Mound

and Kuaua, on the Rio Puerco and the Rio Grande respectively. That these mural paintings were contemporary with those at Awatovi seems to be established. While precise dating of the painted kivas at Awatovi was not possible, they all seem to have been occupied between the late fourteenth and early sixteenth centuries (Smith 1952b: 317–318). The painted kivas at Kuaua were dated in the late fifteenth and early sixteenth centuries (Dutton 1963: 22–25, 33, 39, 203–205), and those at Pottery Mound between 1300 and 1450 (Hibben 1960: 267–268). Certainly all were pre-Hispanic. That there was intimate interchange between the villages of the Jeddito and those far to the east is obvious. Whether it reflects an actual mass migration of peoples, of a parallelism of development within two similar but not consanguineous groups, we cannot say. We prefer, however, to err on the side of caution and to consider the story of Awatovi as autochthonous until an invasion may be proved beyond a reasonable doubt.

References Cited

ABBOTT, CHARLES CONRAD
1872 The Stone Age in New Jersey. *American Naturalist* 6: 144–160, 199–229. [Reprinted in *Annual Report of the Smithsonian Institution for the Year 1875*: 246–380, 1876].

ADAMS, ETHAN CHARLES
1989 Passive Resistance: Hopi Responses to Spanish Contact and Conquest. In *Columbian Consequences: Volume 1, Archaeological and Historical Perspectives on the Spanish Borderlands West*, edited by David Hurst Thomas, pp. 77–91. Washington: Smithsonian Institution Press.

AMSDEN, CHARLES AVERY
1931 Black-on-white Ware. In "The Pottery of Pecos, Volume I," by Alfred Vincent Kidder, pp. 17–72. *Papers of the Phillips Academy Southwestern Expedition* 5. New Haven: Yale University Press.
1949 *Prehistoric Southwesterners from Basketmaker to Pueblo.* Los Angeles: Southwest Museum.

BANDELIER, ADOLPH FRANCIS ALPHONSE
1890 Final Report of Investigations Among the Indians of the Southwestern United States, Carried on Mainly in the Years from 1880 to 1885, Part I. *Papers of the Archaeological Institute of America, American Series* 3. Cambridge: J. Wilson and Son.

BANNISTER, BRYANT, WILLIAM JAMES ROBINSON, AND
RICHARD LEE WARREN
1967 *Tree-ring Dates from Arizona J: Hopi Mesas Area.* Tucson: Laboratory of Tree-Ring Research.

BARRETT, SAMUEL ALFRED

1927   Reconnaissance of the Citadel Group of Ruins in Arizona. *Yearbook for 1926*, Vol. 6: 7–58. Milwaukee: Milwaukee Public Museum.

BASSO, ELLEN BECKER

1987   *In Favor of Deceit: A Study of Tricksters in Amazonian Society.* Tucson: University of Arizona Press.

BAUM, LYMAN FRANK

1900   *The Surprising Adventures of the Magical Monarch of Mo and His People.* Indianapolis: Bobbs-Merrill.

BEALS, RALPH LEON, GEORGE WALTON BRAINERD, AND
WATSON SMITH

1945   Archaeological Studies in Northeastern Arizona: A Report on the Work of the Rainbow Bridge–Monument Valley Expedition. *University of California Publications in American Archaeology and Ethnology* 44(1). Berkeley and Los Angeles: University of California Press.

BINFORD, LEWIS ROBERTS

1978   *Nunamiut Ethnoarchaeology.* New York: Academic Press.

BLEGEN, CARL WILLIAM, AND MARION RAWSON

1966   *The Palace of Nestor at Pylos in Western Messenia, Volume I: The Buildings and Their Contents.* Princeton: Princeton University Press.

BOAS, FRANZ

1910   Symbolism. In "Handbook of American Indians," edited by Frederick Webb Hodge, pp. 662–664. *Bureau of American Ethnology, Bulletin* 30. Washington: Smithsonian Institution.

BOURKE, JOHN GREGORY

1884   *The Snake-Dance of the Moquis of Arizona: Being a Narrative of a Journey from Santa Fe, New Mexico, to the Villages of the Moqui Indians of Arizona.* New York: Scribner. [Reprinted University of Arizona Press, 1984.]

BRADY, IVAN, editor

1983   Speaking in the Name of the Real: Freeman and Mead on Samoa. *American Anthropologist* 85(4): 908–947.

BRAINERD, GEORGE WALTON

1942   Symmetry in Primitive Conventional Design. *American Antiquity* 8(2): 164–166.

BREW, JOHN OTIS

1946   Archaeology of Alkali Ridge, Southeastern Utah. *Papers of the*

Peabody Museum of American Archaeology and Ethnology 21. Cambridge: Harvard University.

1949a   The Excavation of Franciscan Awatovi. In "Franciscan Awatovi," by Ross Gordon Montgomery, Watson Smith, and John Otis Brew, pp. 45–108. *Papers of the Peabody Museum of American Archaeology and Ethnology* 36. Cambridge: Harvard University.

1949b   The History of Awatovi. In "Franciscan Awatovi," by Ross Gordon Montgomery, Watson Smith, and John Otis Brew, pp. 1–43. *Papers of the Peabody Museum of American Archaeology and Ethnology* 36. Cambridge: Harvard University.

1949c   Introduction. In "Franciscan Awatovi," by Ross Gordon Montgomery, Watson Smith, and John Otis Brew, pp. xix–xxi. *Papers of the Peabody Museum of American Archaeology and Ethnology* 36. Cambridge: Harvard University.

1952   Foreword. In "Kiva Mural Decorations at Awatovi and Kawaika-a," by Watson Smith, pp. vii–xii. *Papers of the Peabody Museum of American Archaeology and Ethnology* 37. Cambridge: Harvard University.

1968   Introduction. In *One Hundred Years of Anthropology*, edited by John Otis Brew, pp. 5–25. Cambridge: Harvard University Press.

1971   Foreword. In "Painted Ceramics of the Western Mound at Awatovi," by Watson Smith, pp. xvii–xviii. *Papers of the Peabody Museum of American Archaeology and Ethnology* 38. Cambridge: Harvard University.

1972   Foreword. In "Prehistoric Kivas of Antelope Mesa, Northwestern Arizona," by Watson Smith, pp. ix–x. *Papers of the Peabody Museum of American Archaeology and Ethnology* 39(1). Cambridge: Harvard University.

BREW, JOHN OTIS, AND EDWARD BRIDGE DANSON

1948   The 1947 Reconnaissance and the Proposed Upper Gila Expedition of the Peabody Museum of Harvard University. *El Palacio* 55(7): 211–222.

BREW, JOHN OTIS, AND WATSON SMITH

1954   Comments on "Southwestern Cultural Interrelationships and the Question of Area Co-tradition," by Joe Ben Wheat. *American Anthropologist* 56(4): 586–588.

BULLARD, WILLIAM ROTCH

1962   The Cerro Colorado Site and Pithouse Architecture in the

Southwestern United States prior to A.D. 900. *Papers of the Peabody Museum of American Archaeology and Ethnology* 44(2). Cambridge: Harvard University.

BUNZEL, RUTH LEAH

1932   Zuñi Katcinas. *Annual Report of the Bureau of American Ethnology* 47: 837–1086. Washington: Smithsonian Institution.

BURGH, ROBERT FREDERICK

1960   Ceramic Profiles in the Western Mound at Awatovi, Northeastern Arizona. *American Antiquity* 25(2): 184–202.

CASTANEDA, CARLOS

1968   *The Teachings on Don Juan: A Yaqui Way of Knowledge.* Berkeley and Los Angeles: University of California Press.

1984   *The Fire Within.* New York: Simon and Schuster.

CHAMBERLIN, THOMAS CROWDER

1890   The Method of Multiple Working Hypotheses. *Science* O.S., 25(366): 92–96. [Reprinted in *Science*, 148:754–759, 1965.]

CHAPMAN, KENNETH MILTON

1927   A Feather Symbol of the Ancient Pueblos. *El Palacio* 23(21): 525–540.

1938   Pajaritan Pictography: The Cave Pictographs of the Rito de Los Frijoles. In *Pajarito Plateau and Its Ancient People*, by Edgar Lee Hewett, pp. 139–148. Albuquerque: University of New Mexico Press.

CHRISTENSON, ANDREW LEWIS

1987   The Last of the Great Expeditions: The Rainbow Bridge–Monument Valley Expedition 1933–38. *Plateau* 58(4).

CLIFFORD, JAMES

1986   Introduction: Partial Truths. In *Writing Culture: The Poetics and Politics of Ethnography*, edited by James Clifford and George Marcus, pp. 1-26. Berkeley: University of California Press.

CLOUGH, BENJAMIN CROCKER

1954   The Life and Legends of Josiah Carberry. *Brown Alumni Monthly*, December 1954: 3–9. Providence: Brown University.

1963   Carberry. *Pembroke Alumna*, January 1963: 11–13. Providence: Brown University.

COE, MICHAEL DOUGLAS

1961   La Victoria, an Early Site on the Pacific Coast of Guatemala.

Papers of the Peabody Museum of American Archaeology and Ethnology 53. Cambridge: Harvard University.

COLTON, HAROLD SELLERS

1931   The Archaeological Survey of the Museum of Northern Arizona. *Museum Notes* 4(1). Flagstaff: Museum of Northern Arizona.

1932   A Survey of Prehistoric Sites in the Region of Flagstaff, Arizona. *Bureau of American Ethnology, Bulletin* 104. Washington: Smithsonian Institution.

1939   Prehistoric Culture Units and their Relationships in Northern Arizona. *Bulletin* 17. Flagstaff: Museum of Northern Arizona.

1946   The Sinagua. *Bulletin* 22. Flagstaff: Museum of Northern Arizona.

1947   What Is a Kachina? *Plateau* 19(3): 40–47.

1953   Potsherds. *Bulletin* 25. Flagstaff: Museum of Northern Arizona.

1955   Pottery Types of the Southwest. *Ceramic Series* 3a. Flagstaff: Museum of Northern Arizona.

COLTON, HAROLD SELLERS, AND LYNDON LANE HARGRAVE

1937   Handbook of Northern Arizona Pottery Wares. *Bulletin* 11. Flagstaff: Museum of Northern Arizona.

COSGROVE, HARRIET SILLIMAN, AND
CORNELIUS BURTON COSGROVE

1932   The Swarts Ruin: A Typical Mimbres Site in Southwestern New Mexico. *Papers of the Peabody Museum of American Archaeology and Ethnology* 15. Cambridge: Harvard University.

CRANE, LEO

1929   *Indians of the Enchanted Desert.* Boston: Little Brown.

CROTTY, HELEN

1983   Honoring the Dead: Anasazi Ceramics from the Rainbow Bridge–Monument Valley Expedition. *Monograph Series* 22. Los Angeles: Museum of Cultural History, University of California.

CUMMINGS, BYRON

1915   Kivas of the San Juan Drainage. *American Anthropologist* 17(2): 272–282.

CUSHING, FRANK HAMILTON

1890   Preliminary Notes on the Origin, Working Hypothesis and Primary Researches of the Hemenway Archaeological Expedition.

Compte-Rendu de la Septième Session, Congrès International de Américanistes [Berlin, 1888], pp. 151–194. Berlin: Librairie W. H. Kuhl.

DANIEL, GLYN EDMUND

1968   *The Origins and Growth of Archaeology.* New York: Thomas Y. Crowell.

DANSON, EDWARD BRIDGE

1957   An Archaeological Survey of West Central New Mexico and East Central Arizona. *Papers of the Peabody Museum of American Archaeology and Ethnology* 44(1). Cambridge: Harvard University.

DE LAET, SIGFRIED

1957   *Archaeology and Its Problems.* London: Phoenix House.

DICK, HERBERT WILLIAM

1965   Bat Cave. *Monographs* 27. Santa Fe: School of American Research.

DICKENSON, ERNEST

1960   The Life and Times of Professor Carberry. *Brown Alumni Monthly*, December 1960: 10–13, 15. Providence: Brown University.

DINCAUZE, DENA FERRAN

1968   Cremation Cemeteries in Eastern Massachusetts. *Papers of the Peabody Museum of American Archaeology and Ethnology* 59(1). Cambridge: Harvard University.

DORSEY, GEORGE AMOS, AND HENRY RICHERT VOTH

1901   The Oraibi Soyal Ceremony. *Anthropological Series* 3(1): 1–59. Chicago: Field Museum of Natural History.

DOUGLAS, FREDERIC HUNTINGTON

1934   Symbolism in Indian Art and the Difficulties of Its Interpretation. *Denver Art Museum Leaflets* 61: 41–44.

1935   Types of Indian Masks. *Denver Art Museum Leaflets* 21(65–66): 58–64.

DOZIER, EDWARD PASCUAL

1954   Review of "Kiva Mural Decorations at Awatovi and Kawaika-a with a Survey of Other Wall Paintings in the Pueblo Southwest," by Watson Smith. *American Anthropologist* 56(1): 141–142.

DRABBLE, MARGARET

1985   *The Oxford Companion to English Literature*, fifth edition. Oxford: Oxford University Press.

DUERR, HANS PETER, EDITOR

1987 *Authentizität und Betrug in der Ethnologie.* Frankfurt: Suhrkamp Verlag.

DUMAREST, NÖEL

1919 Notes on Cochiti, New Mexico, translated and edited by Elsie Clews Parsons. *American Anthropological Association, Memoirs* 6(3): 135–236.

DUTTON, BERTHA PAULINE

1963 *Sun Father's Way: The Kiva Murals of Kuaua, a Pueblo Ruin, Coronado State Monument, New Mexico.* Albuquerque: University of New Mexico Press.

EARLE, EDWIN, AND EDWARD ALLAN KENNARD

1938 *Hopi Kachinas.* New York: J. J. Augustin.

EVANS-PRITCHARD, EDWARD EVAN

1976 *Witchcraft, Oracles and Magic Among the Azande,* abridged with an Introduction by Eva Gillies. Oxford: Clarendon Press.

FEWKES, JESSE WALTER

1895 The Tusayan New Fire Ceremony. *Boston Society of Natural History, Proceedings* 26: 422–458.

1896 The Micoñinovi Flute Altars. *Journal of American Folklore* 9(35): 241–255.

1897a The Group of Tusayan Ceremonials Called Katchinas. *Annual Report of the Bureau of American Ethnology* 15: 245–313. Washington: Smithsonian Institution.

1897b Tusayan Snake Ceremonies. *Annual Report of the Bureau of American Ethnology* 16: 267–312. Washington: Smithsonian Institution.

1898a Archaeological Expedition to Arizona in 1895. *Annual Report of the Bureau of American Ethnology* 17(2): 519–742. Washington: Smithsonian Institution.

1898b The Feather Symbol in Ancient Hopi Designs. *American Anthropologist* 11(1): 1–14.

1899 The Winter Solstice Altars at Hano Pueblo. *American Anthropologist* 1(2): 251–276.

1900 Tusayan Migration Traditions. *Annual Report of the Bureau of American Ethnology* 19: 573–633. Washington: Smithsonian Institution.

1903 Hopi Katcinas Drawn by Native Artists. *Annual Report of the Bureau of American Ethnology* 21: 3–126. Washington: Smithsonian Institution.

1919   Designs on Prehistoric Hopi Pottery. *Annual Report of the Bureau of American Ethnology* 33: 207-284. Washington: Smithsonian Institution.

1922   Fire Worship of the Hopi Indians. *Annual Report for 1920*: 589–610. Washington: Smithsonian Institution.

1927   Archaeological Field-work in Arizona. *Smithsonian Miscellaneous Collections* 78(7): 207–232. Washington: Smithsonian Institution.

FORD, JAMES ALFRED

1954   The Type Concept Revisited. *American Anthropologist* 56(1): 42–54.

FREEMAN, DEREK

1983   *Margaret Mead and Samoa: The Making and Unmaking of an Anthropological Myth.* Cambridge: Harvard University Press.

GIFFORD, JAMES COLLIER

1960   The Type-variety Method of Ceramic Classification as an Indicator of Cultural Phenomena. *American Antiquity* 25(3): 341–347.

GIFFORD, JAMES COLLIER, AND WATSON SMITH

1978   Gray Corrugated Pottery from Awatovi and Other Jeddito Sites in Northeastern Arizona. *Papers of the Peabody Museum of American Archaeology and Ethnology* 69. Cambridge: Harvard University.

GOLDFRANK, ESTHER SCHIFF

1927   The Social and Ceremonial Organization of Cochiti. *American Anthropological Association, Memoirs* 33.

GOULD, RICHARD ALLAN

1974   Some Current Problems in Ethnoarchaeology. In "Ethnoarchaeology," edited by Christopher Bruce Donnan and William Clelow, pp. 29–48. *Archaeological Survey Monograph* 4. Los Angeles: Institute of Archaeology, University of California.

GOULD, RICHARD ALLAN, EDITOR

1978   *Explorations in Ethnoarchaeology.* Albuquerque: University of New Mexico Press.

GRANT, BLANCHE CHLOE

1925   *Taos Indians.* Taos: Privately printed.

GUERNSEY, SAMUEL JAMES

1931   Explorations in Northeastern Arizona: Report on the Archaeological Fieldwork of 1920–1923. *Papers of the Peabody*

Museum of American Archaeology and Ethnology 12(1). Cambridge: Harvard University.

GUERNSEY, SAMUEL JAMES, AND ALFRED VINCENT KIDDER

1921   Basket-Maker Caves of Northeastern Arizona: Report on the Explorations, 1916–17. *Papers of the Peabody Museum of American Archaeology and Ethnology* 8(2). Cambridge: Harvard University.

GUMERMAN, GEORGE JOHN

1973   Review of "Painted Ceramics of the Western Mound at Awatovi," by Watson Smith. *American Antiquity* 38(2): 248–249.

GUNNERSON, JAMES HOWARD

1969   The Fremont Culture: A Study in Culture Dynamics on the Northern Anasazi Frontier. *Papers of the Peabody Museum of American Archaeology and Ethnology* 59(2). Cambridge: Harvard University.

GUTHE, CARL EUGEN

1925   Pueblo Pottery Making: A Study at the Village of San Ildefonso. *Papers of the Phillips Academy Southwestern Expedition* 2. New Haven: Yale University Press.

HALL, EDWARD TWITCHELL

1944   Early Stockaded Settlements in the Governador, New Mexico: A Marginal Anasazi Development from Basket Maker II to Pueblo I Times. *Columbia Studies in Archeology and Ethnology* 2(1). New York: Columbia University Press.

HAMMOND, NICHOLAS GEOFFREY LEMPRIÈRE, AND
HOWARD HAYES SCULLARD

1970   *The Oxford Classical Dictionary*, second edition. Oxford: Oxford University Press.

HARGRAVE, LYNDON LANE

1933a Bird Life of the San Francisco Mountains, Arizona, Number One. *Museum Notes* 5(10): 57–60. Flagstaff: Museum of Northern Arizona.

1933b Pueblo II Houses of the San Francisco Mountains, Arizona. *Bulletin* 4: 15–75. Flagstaff: Museum of Northern Arizona.

1970   Mexican Macaws: Comparative Osteology and Survey of Remains from the Southwest. *Anthropological Papers of the University of Arizona* 20. Tucson: University of Arizona Press.

HARVEY, PAUL

1981   *The Oxford Companion to English Literature*, fourth edition, revised by Dorothy Eagle. Oxford: Oxford University Press.

HAURY, EMIL WALTER

1931   Kivas of the Tusayan Ruin, Grand Canyon, Arizona. *Medallion Papers* 9. Globe: Gila Pueblo.

HIBBEN, FRANK CUMMINGS

1960   Prehispanic Painting at Pottery Mound. *Archaeology* 13(4): 267– 274.

1975   *Kiva Art of the Anasazi at Pottery Mound*. Las Vegas: KC Publications.

HODGE, FREDERICK WEBB

1937   History of Hawikuh, New Mexico, One of the So-Called Cities of Cibola. *Publications of the Frederick Webb Hodge Anniversary Publication Fund* 1. Los Angeles: Southwest Museum.

1939   A Square Kiva at Hawikuh. In *So Live the Works of Men: Seventieth Anniversary Volume Honoring Edgar Lee Hewett*, edited by Donald Dilworth Brand and Fred Harvey, pp. 195–214. Albuquerque: University of New Mexico and School of American Research.

HOEBEL, EDWARD ADAMSON

1955   Review of "Zuñi Law: A Field of Values," by Watson Smith and John Milton Roberts. *American Anthropologist* 57(6): 1308–1309.

HOUGH, WALTER

1902   A Collection of Hopi Ceremonial Pigments. *United States National Museum, Annual Report for 1900*: 463–471. Washington: Smithsonian Institution.

HUBERT, VIRGIL

1937   An Introduction to Hopi Pottery Design. *Museum Notes* 10(1): 1–4. Flagstaff: Museum of Northern Arizona.

JUDD, NEIL MERTON

1930   The Excavation and Repair of Betatakin. *Proceedings of the United States National Museum* 77(5). Washington: Smithsonian Institution.

1940   Progress in the Southwest. In "Essays in Historical Anthropology of North America," pp. 417–444. *Smithsonian Miscellaneous Collections* 100. Washington: Smithsonian Institution.

KABOTIE, FRED

1949   *Designs from the Ancient Mimbreños with a Hopi Interpreta-*

tion. San Francisco: Grabhorn Press.

KIDDER, ALFRED VINCENT

1914   Southwestern Ceramics: Their Value in Reconstructing the History of the Ancient Cliff Dwelling and Pueblo Tribes: An Exposition from the Point of View of Type Distinctions. MS, doctoral dissertation, Harvard University.

1915   Pottery of Pajarito Plateau and of some Adjacent Regions in New Mexico. *American Anthropological Association, Memoirs* 2: 407–602.

1924   An Introduction to the Study of Southwestern Archaeology, with a Preliminary Account of the Excavations at Pecos. *Papers of the Phillips Academy Southwestern Expedition* 1. New Haven: Yale University Press. [Reprinted with "A Summary of Southwestern Archaeology Today," by Irving Rouse, Yale University Press, 1962.]

1927   Southwestern Archaeological Conference. *Science* 66: 489–491.

1931   The Pottery of Pecos, Volume I: The Dull Paint Wares. *Papers of the Phillips Academy Southwestern Expedition* 5. New Haven: Yale University Press.

1949   Introduction. In *Prehistoric Southwesterners from Basketmaker to Pueblo*, by Charles Avery Amsden, pp. xi–xiv. Los Angeles: Southwest Museum.

1958   Pecos, New Mexico: Archaeological Notes. *Papers of the R. S. Peabody Foundation for Archaeology* 5. Andover: Phillips Academy.

KIDDER, ALFRED VINCENT, AND SAMUEL JAMES GUERNSEY

1919   Archaeological Explorations in Northeastern Arizona. *Bureau of American Ethnology, Bulletin* 65. Washington: Smithsonian Institution.

KIDDER, ALFRED VINCENT, AND MADELEINE APPLETON KIDDER

1917   Notes on the Pottery of Pecos. *American Anthropologist* 19(3): 325–360.

KIDDER, ALFRED VINCENT, AND ANNA OSLER SHEPARD

1936   The Pottery of Pecos, Volume II: The Glaze-paint, Culinary and other Wares. *Papers of the Phillips Academy Southwestern Expedition* 7. New Haven: Yale University Press.

KIDDER AWARD

1984   Alfred Vincent Kidder Award for 1983 for Eminence in the Field of American Archaeology. *American Antiquity* 49(4): 677.

KING, DALE STUART
1949   Nalakihu: Excavations at a Pueblo III Site on Wupatki National Monument, Arizona. *Bulletin* 23. Flagstaff: Museum of Northern Arizona.

KIRK, RUTH FALKENBURG
1943   Introduction to Zuñi Fetishism. *Papers* 34. Santa Fe: School of American Research [Reprinted from *El Palacio* 50(6–10), 1943].

KLUCKHOHN, CLYDE KAY MABEN, AND
DOROTHEA CROSS LEIGHTON
1946   *The Navaho.* Cambridge: Harvard University Press.

KROEBER, ALFRED LOUIS
1916   Zuñi Potsherds. *Anthropological Papers* 18(1). New York: American Museum of Natural History.
1948   *Anthropology: Race, Language, Culture, Psychology, Prehistory.* New York: Harcourt, Brace.
1957   *Style and Civilizations.* Ithaca: Cornell University Press.

LAMBERG-KARLOVSKY, CLIFFORD CHARLES
1982   The Peabody Renovates: First Major Reconstruction in 117 Years Addresses Collection Needs. *Symbols*, Winter 1982: 1–12. Cambridge: Peabody Museum and Department of Anthropology, Harvard University.

LANG, MABEL
1969   *The Palace of Nestor at Pylos in Western Messenia, Volume II: The Frescoes.* Princeton: Princeton University Press.

LAWRENCE, BARBARA
1951   Part I: Mammals Found at the Awatovi Site; Part II: Post-Cranial Skeletal Characters of Deer, Pronghorn, and Sheep-Goat, with Notes on Bos and Bison. *Papers of the Peabody Museum of American Archaeology and Ethnology* 35(3). Cambridge: Harvard University.

LEKSON, STEPHEN HENRY
1988   The Idea of the Kiva in Anasazi Archaeology. *The Kiva* 53(3): 213–234.

LISTER, FLORENCE CLINE
1964   Kaiparowits Plateau and Glen Canyon Prehistory: An Interpretation Based on Ceramics. *Anthropological Papers* 71. Salt Lake City: University of Utah Press.

LONGACRE, WILLIAM ATLAS
1970   A Historical Review. In *Reconstructing Prehistoric Pueblo*

Societies, edited by William Atlas Longacre, pp. 1–10. Albuquerque: University of New Mexico Press.

1974   Kalinga Pottery-Making: The Evolution of a Research Design. In *Frontiers of Anthropology: An Introduction to Anthropological Thinking*, edited by Murray John Leaf, pp. 51–67. New York: Van Nostrand.

LOWENTHAL, DAVID

1985   *The Past is a Foreign Country*. Cambridge: Cambridge University Press.

LUOMALA, KATHARINE

1938   *Navaho Life of Yesterday and Today*. Berkeley: National Park Service.

MACAULAY, ROSE

1953   *Pleasure of Ruins*. London: Weidenfeld and Nicolson.

MCGIMSEY, CHARLES ROBERT

1980   Mariana Mesa: Seven Prehistoric Settlements in West-Central New Mexico. *Papers of the Peabody Museum of American Archaeology and Ethnology 72*. Cambridge: Harvard University.

MCKERN, WILL CARLETON

1939   The Midwestern Taxonomic Method as an Aid to Archaeological Culture Study. *American Antiquity* 4(4): 301–313.

MARTIN, PAUL SYDNEY

1936   Lowry Ruin in Southwestern Colorado. *Anthropological Series* 23(1). Chicago: Field Museum of Natural History.

MARTIN, PAUL SYDNEY, AND ELIZABETH WILLIS

1940   Anasazi Painted Pottery in Field Museum of Natural History. *Anthropology Memoirs 5*. Chicago: Field Museum of Natural History.

MATSON, FREDERICK ROGNALD, editor

1965   Ceramics and Man. *Viking Fund Publications in Anthropology* 41. New York: Wenner-Gren Foundation for Anthropological Research.

MATTHEWS, WASHINGTON

1897   Navajo Legends. *American Folklore Society, Memoirs* 5: 1–290.

1898   Ichthyophobia. *Journal of American Folklore* 11(40): 105–112.

MEAD, MARGARET

1928   *Coming of Age in Samoa: A Psychological Study of Primitive Youth for Western Civilization*. New York: William Morrow.

MERA, HARRY PERCIVAL

1937   The "Rain Bird": A Study in Pueblo Design. *Memoirs* 2. Santa Fe: Laboratory of Anthropology.

1939   Style Trends of Pueblo Pottery in the Rio Grande and Little Colorado Cultural Areas from the Sixteenth to the Nineteenth Century. *Memoirs* 3. Santa Fe: Laboratory of Anthropology.

MINDELEFF, VICTOR

1891   A Study of Pueblo Architecture in Tusayan and Cibola. *Annual Report of the Bureau of Ethnology* 8: 3–228. Washington: Smithsonian Institution.

MONTGOMERY, ROSS GORDON

1949   San Bernardo de Aquatubi: An Analytical Restoration. In "Franciscan Awatovi," by Ross Gordon Montgomery, Watson Smith, and John Otis Brew, pp. 109–288. *Papers of the Peabody Museum of American Archaeology and Ethnology* 36. Cambridge: Harvard University.

MONTGOMERY, ROSS GORDON, WATSON SMITH, AND
JOHN OTIS BREW

1949   Franciscan Awatovi: The Excavation and Conjectural Reconstruction of a 17th-Century Spanish Mission Establishment at a Hopi Indian Town in Northeastern Arizona. *Papers of the Peabody Museum of American Archaeology and Ethnology* 36. Cambridge: Harvard University.

MORRIS, EARL HALSTEAD

1939   Archaeological Studies in the La Plata District, Southwestern Colorado and Northwestern New Mexico. *Publication* 519. Washington: Carnegie Institution of Washington.

MORSS, NOEL

1931   Notes on the Archaeology of the Kaibito and Rainbow Plateaus in Arizona: Report on the Explorations, 1927. *Papers of the Peabody Museum of American Archaeology and Ethnology* 12(2). Cambridge: Harvard University.

NELSON, NELS CHRISTIAN

1914   Pueblo Ruins of the Galisteo Basin, New Mexico. *Anthropological Papers* 15(1). New York: American Museum of Natural History.

1916   Chronology of the Tano Ruins. *American Anthropologist* 18(2): 159–180.

NEQUATEWA, EDMUND

1946   The Place of Corn and Feathers in Hopi Ceremonies. *Plateau*

19(1): 15–16.

NEQUATEWA, EDMUND, AND MARY-RUSSELL FERRELL COLTON

1933 Hopi Courtship and Marriage. *Museum Notes* 5(9): 41–54. Flagstaff: Museum of Northern Arizona.

PARSONS, ELSIE WORTHINGTON CLEWS

1920a Notes on Ceremonialism at Laguna. *Anthropological Papers* 19(4): 85–131. New York: American Museum of Natural History.

1920b Notes on Isleta, Santa Ana, and Acoma. *American Anthropologist* 22(1): 56–69.

1921 Further Notes on Isleta. *American Anthropologist* 23(2): 149–169.

1925a A Pueblo Indian Journal, 1920–21. *American Anthropological Association, Memoirs* 32.

1925b The Pueblo of Jemez. *Papers of the Southwestern Expedition, Phillips Academy* 3. New Haven: Yale University Press.

1929 The Social Organization of the Tewa of New Mexico. *American Anthropological Association, Memoirs* 36.

1932 Isleta, New Mexico. *Annual Report of the Bureau of American Ethnology* 47: 193–466. Washington: Smithsonian Institution.

1936a Early Relations Between Hopi and Keres. *American Anthropologist* 38(4): 554–560.

1936b *Mitla, Town of the Souls, and Other Zapoteco-speaking Pueblos of Oaxaca, Mexico.* Chicago: University of Chicago Press.

1936c Taos Pueblo. *General Series in Anthropology* 2. Menasha: George Banta.

1939 *Pueblo Indian Religion*, two volumes. Chicago: University of Chicago Press.

1940 A Pre-Spanish Record of Hopi Ceremonies. *American Anthropologist* 42(3): 541–542.

PASSIN, HERBERT

1942 Tarahumara Prevarication: A Problem in Field Method. *American Anthropologist* 44(2): 235–247.

PECKHAM, STEWART

1979 When Is a Rio Grande Kiva? In "Collected Papers in Honor of Bertha Pauline Dutton," edited by Albert Henry Schroeder, pp. 55–86. *Papers of the Archaeological Society of New Mexico* 4. Albuquerque.

POWERS, ROBERT PORTER, WILLIAM BRUCE GILLESPIE, AND
STEPHEN HENRY LEKSON

1983   The Outlier Survey: A Regional View of Settlement in the San
Juan Basin. *Reports of the Chaco Center* 3. Albuquerque: National Park Service.

ROEDIGER, VIRGINIA MORE

1941   *Ceremonial Costume of the Pueblo Indians: Their Evolution,
Fabrication, and Significance in the Prayer Drama.* Berkeley:
University of California Press.

ROUSE, IRVING

1939   Prehistory in Haiti: A Study in Method. *Yale University Publications in Anthropology* 21. New Haven: Yale University Press.

1960   The Classification of Artifacts in Archaeology. *American Antiquity* 25(3): 313–323.

SCHIFFER, MICHAEL BRIAN

1978   Taking the Pulse of Method and Theory in American Archaeology. *American Antiquity* 43(2): 153–158.

SCHUYLER, ROBERT LEE

1971   The History of American Archaeology: An Examination of Procedure. *American Antiquity* 36(4): 383–409.

SEARS, WILLIAM HULSE

1960   Ceramic Systems and Eastern Archaeology. *American Antiquity* 25(3): 324–329.

SEBALD, HANS

1987   Die Märchenwelt des Carlos Castaneda. In *Authentizität und
Betrug in der Ethnologie*, edited by Hans Peter Duerr, pp.
280–289. Frankfurt: Suhrkamp Verlag.

SEKAQUAPTEWA, EMORY

1984   Foreword. In *The Snake-Dance of the Moquis of Arizona: Being a Narrative of a Journey from Santa Fe, New Mexico, to the
Villages of the Moqui Indians of Arizona*, by John Gregory
Bourke, pp. xiii–xvii. Tucson: University of Arizona Press.

SHEPARD, ANNA OSLER

1939   Technology of La Plata Pottery. In "Archaeological Studies in
the La Plata District, Southwestern Colorado and Northwestern New Mexico," by Earl Halstead Morris, pp. 249–287.
Publication 519. Washington: Carnegie Institution of Washington.

1956   Ceramics for the Archaeologist. *Publication* 609. Washington:
Carnegie Institution of Washington.

SMITH, WATSON

1945   RB 551. In "Archaeological Studies in Northeastern Arizona," by Ralph Leon Beals, George Walton Brainerd, and Watson Smith, pp. 42–62. *University of California Publications in American Archaeology and Ethnology* 44(1). Berkeley and Los Angeles: University of California Press.

1952a   Excavations in Big Hawk Valley, Wupatki National Monument, Arizona. *Bulletin* 24. Flagstaff: Museum of Northern Arizona.

1952b   Kiva Mural Decorations at Awatovi and Kawaika-a with a Survey of Other Wall Paintings in the Pueblo Southwest. *Papers of the Peabody Museum of American Archaeology and Ethnology* 37. Cambridge: Harvard University.

1960   Carberry. *Brown Alumni Monthly*, May 1960: 17–19. Providence: Brown University.

1962   Schools, Pots, and Potters. *American Anthropologist* 64(6): 1165–1178.

1966   Ceramic Studies and Ethnological Investigations. Review of "Ceramics and Man," edited by Frederick Rognald Matson. *Science* 152: 927–928.

1969   *The Story of the Museum of Northern Arizona.* Flagstaff: Museum of Northern Arizona.

1971   Painted Ceramics of the Western Mound at Awatovi. *Papers of the Peabody Museum of American Archaeology and Ethnology* 38. Cambridge: Harvard University.

1972   Prehistoric Kivas of Antelope Mesa, Northeastern Arizona. *Papers of the Peabody Museum of American Archaeology and Ethnology* 39(1). Cambridge: Harvard University.

1973   The Williams Site: A Frontier Mogollon Village in West-Central New Mexico. *Papers of the Peabody Museum of American Archaeology and Ethnology* 39(2). Cambridge: Harvard University.

1980a   The Excavation of Awatovi and Other Archaeology in the Hopi Country. Presented to The Hopi Tricentennial of the Pueblo Rebellion in Oraibi, 15 August 1980. MS, Arizona State Museum Archives, University of Arizona, Tucson.

1980b   Mural Decorations from Ancient Hopi Kivas. In *Hopi Kachina, Spirit of Life*, edited by Dorothy Koster Washburn, pp. 28–37. San Francisco and Seattle: California Academy of Sciences and University of Washington Press.

1984a   *One Man's Archaeology.* Tucson: Privately printed.

1984b   *Running, Jumping, and Standing Still.* Tucson: Privately printed.

1987   *Handy Guide for Doggerelists.* Tucson: Privately printed by the Morgue Publishing Company Resurrected.

1989   Report on the Results of an Etymological Research Project: "The Functions of Digraphs and Ligatures in the Effective Destruction of Mental Equilibrium in the Human Mind (if any). "*Archaeology in Tucson, Newsletter of the Center for Desert Archaeology* 3(4): 6–7.

SMITH, WATSON, AND JOHN MILTON ROBERTS

1954   Zuni Law: A Field of Values. *Papers of the Peabody Museum of American Archaeology and Ethnology* 43(1). Cambridge: Harvard University. [Reissued by Kraus Reprint, 1973.]

SMITH, WATSON, RICHARD BENJAMIN WOODBURY, AND
NATHALIE FERRIS SAMPSON WOODBURY

1966   The Excavation of Hawikuh by Frederick Webb Hodge: Report of the Hendricks-Hodge Expedition, 1917–1923. *Contributions from the Museum of the American Indian* 20. New York: Museum of the American Indian, Heye Foundation.

SPICER, EDWARD HOLLAND

1962   *Cycles of Conquest: The Impact of Spain, Mexico, and the United States on the Indians of the Southwest 1533–1960.* Tucson: University of Arizona Press.

1969   Review of "The Teachings of Don Juan" by Carlos Castaneda. *American Anthropologist* 71(2): 320–321.

SPIER, LESLIE

1917   An Outline for a Chronology of Zuñi Ruins. *Anthropological Papers* 18(3). New York: American Museum of Natural History.

SPINDEN, HERBERT JOSEPH

1931   Indian Symbolism. *Exposition of Indian Tribal Arts, Introduction to American Indian Art*, Part 2, Leaflet 2, pp. 3–18.

STEPHEN, ALEXANDER MACGREGOR

1936   Hopi Journal of Alexander M. Stephen, edited by Elsie Clews Parsons. *Columbia University Contributions to Anthropology* 23, Parts 1, 2. New York: Columbia University Press.

1940   Hopi Indians of Arizona. *Southwest Museum Leaflets* 14. Los Angeles: Southwest Museum [Reprinted from *Masterkey* 13(6), 14(1), 14 (3–6), 1939–40].

STEVENSON, MATILDA COXE

1894   The Sia. *Annual Report of the Bureau of American Ethnology* 11: 3–157. Washington: Smithsonian Institution.

1904   The Zuñi Indians. *Annual Report of the Bureau of American Ethnology* 23: 1–608. Washington: Smithsonian Institution.

STEWARD, JULIAN HAYNES

1942   The Direct Historical Approach to Archaeology. *American Antiquity* 7(4): 337–343.

STIRLING, MATTHEW WILLIAM

1942   Origin Myth of Acoma and Other Records. *Bureau of American Ethnology, Bulletin* 135. Washington: Smithsonian Institution.

STONEMAN, RICHARD

1987   *Land of Lost Gods: The Search for Classical Greece.* Norman: University of Oklahoma Press.

TAYLOR, WALTER WILLARD

1954   Southwestern Archeology: Its History and Theory. *American Anthropologist* 58(4): 561–570.

THOMPSON, RAYMOND HARRIS

1958   Yucatecan Maya Pottery Making. *Memoirs of the Society for American Archaeology* 15.

1989   Cliff Dwellings and the Park Service: Archeological Tourism in the Southwest. *International Perspectives on Cultural Parks: Proceedings of the First World Conference, Mesa Verde National Park, Colorado, 1984,* pp. 219–223. Denver: National Park Service and Colorado Historical Society.

THURBER, JAMES

1947   Here Come the Tigers. *New Yorker* 23(27): 23–26.

TITIEV, MISCHA

1944   Old Oraibi: A Study of the Hopi Indians of Third Mesa. *Papers of the Peabody Museum of American Archaeology and Ethnology* 22(1). Cambridge: Harvard University.

UPHAM, STEADMAN

1987   The Tyranny of Ethnographic Analogy in Southwestern Archaeology. In "Coasts, Plains and Deserts: Essays in Honor of Reynold J. Ruppé," edited by Sylvia Wright Gaines, pp. 265–279. *Anthropological Research Papers* 38. Tempe: Arizona State University.

VANDEN BERGHE, LOUIS

1965   Some Ceramic Contributions to a Knowledge of Culture in

Prehistoric Iran. In "Ceramics and Man," edited by Frederick Rognald Matson, pp. 248–253. *Viking Fund Publications in Anthropology* 41. New York: Wenner-Gren Foundation for Anthropological Research.

VOTH, HENRY RICHERT

1901   The Oraibi Powamu Ceremony. *Anthropological Series* 3(2). Chicago: Field Museum of Natural History.

1912a   Brief Miscellaneous Hopi Papers. *Anthropological Series* 11(2). Chicago: Field Museum of Natural History.

1912b   The Oraibi Marau Ceremony. *Anthropological Series* 11(1). Chicago: Field Museum of Natural History.

WASHBURN, DOROTHY KOSTER, editor

1980   *Hopi Kachina, Spirit of Life.* San Francisco and Seattle: California Academy of Sciences and the University of Washington Press.

WAUCHOPE, ROBERT

1938   Modern Maya Houses: A Study of their Archaeological Significance. *Publication* 502. Washington: Carnegie Institution of Washington.

1965   Alfred Vincent Kidder, 1885–1963. *American Antiquity* 31(2): 149–171.

WEST, GEORGE ARBOR

1927   Exploration in Navajo Canyon, Arizona. *Yearbook for 1925,* Vol. 5: 7–39. Milwaukee: Milwaukee Public Museum.

WHEAT, JOE BEN, JAMES COLLIER GIFFORD, AND WILLIAM WARWICK WASLEY

1958   Ceramic Variety, Type Cluster, and Ceramic System in Southwestern Pottery Analysis. *American Antiquity* 24(1): 34–47.

WHITE, LESLIE ALVIN

1932   The Acoma Indians. *Annual Report of the Bureau of American Ethnology* 47: 17–192. Washington: Smithsonian Institution.

1935   The Pueblo of Santo Domingo, New Mexico. *American Anthropological Association, Memoirs* 43.

1942   The Pueblo of Santa Ana, New Mexico. *American Anthropological Association, Memoirs* 60.

WHITMAN, WILLIAM

1947   The Pueblo Indians of San Ildefonso: A Changing Culture. *Columbia University Contributions to Anthropology* 34. New York: Columbia University Press.

WILK, STAN

1977   Castaneda: Coming of Age in Sonora. *American Anthropologist*
79(1): 84–91.

WILLEY, GORDON RANDOLPH

1988   *Portraits in American Archaeology: Remembrances of Some
Distinguished Americanists.* Albuquerque: University of New
Mexico Press.

WINSHIP, GEORGE PARKER

1896   The Coronado Expedition, 1540–42. *Annual Report of the Bureau of American Ethnology* 14, Part 1: 329–613. Washington:
Smithsonian Institution.

WISSLER, CLARK

1938   *The American Indian: An Introduction to the Anthropology of
the New World,* third edition. New York: Oxford University
Press.

WOODBURY, NATHALIE FERRIS SAMPSON

1984   Past Is Present: The Undying Digraph. *Anthropology Newsletter* 25(9): 3. Washington: American Anthropological Association.

WOODBURY, RICHARD BENJAMIN

1954   Prehistoric Stone Implements of Northeastern Arizona. *Papers
of the Peabody Museum of American Archaeology and Ethnology* 34. Cambridge: Harvard University Press.

1973   *Alfred V. Kidder.* New York: Columbia University Press.

1989   Foreword. In "Point of Pines, Arizona: A History of the University of Arizona Archaeological Field School," by Emil
Walter Haury, pp. xi–xiii. *Anthropological Papers of the University of Arizona* 50. Tucson: University of Arizona Press.

Index

About the Authors

WATSON SMITH, born in Cincinnati in 1897, was educated in the liberal arts at Brown University and in the law at Harvard University. He began his archaeological career in the early 1930s at the Lowry Ruin in southeastern Colorado and on the Rainbow Bridge-Monument Valley Expedition. He has excavated sites throughout the Western Pueblo region, especially the Hopi village of Awatovi. He has been associated with the Museum of Northern Arizona, the Arizona State Museum at the University of Arizona, and the Peabody Museum at Harvard University. He established a research branch of the latter, the Peabody Museum West of the Pecos, in Tucson from 1954 to 1975. He has received the Alfred Vincent Kidder Award of the American Anthropological Association, the Emil W. Haury Award of the Southwest Parks and Monuments Association, and the Byron S. Cummings Award of the Arizona Archaeological and Historical Society.

RICHARD B. WOODBURY, an archaeologist with special interests in the Southwest and in Mesoamerica, is emeritus professor of anthropology, University of Massachusetts, Amherst. From 1958 to 1963 he was on the faculty of the University of Arizona, researching prehistoric irrigation. He headed the Smithsonian Institution's Office of Anthropology in the 1960s. His first archaeological work was in northern Arizona, with Harvard's Awatovi Expedition, and in the 1950s he and his wife, Nathalie F. S. Woodbury, collaborated with Watson Smith in preparing "The Excavation of Hawikuh by Frederick Webb Hodge... 1916–1923." He has been active in the Society for American Archaeology, including terms as treasurer, editor, and president. He received the Alfred Vincent Kidder Award of the American Anthropological Association in 1989.

About the Editor

RAYMOND H. THOMPSON, former editor of American Antiquity and past president of the Society for American Archaeology, is Director of the Arizona State Museum and Fred A. Riecker Distinguished Professor of Anthropology at the University of Arizona, where he has also served as Head of the Department of Anthropology and Director of the Archaeological Field School. He first met Watson Smith in the late 1940s when he was a doctoral student at Harvard University.